No Time for Fear

My Path to Awakening

DIANNE SIEBENS

BALBOA.PRESS
A DIVISION OF HAY HOUSE

Balboa Press books may be ordered through booksellers or by contacting:

Balboa Press
A Division of Hay House
1663 Liberty Drive
Bloomington, IN 47403
www.balboapress.com
844-682-1282

Print information available on the last page.

ISBN: 978-1-5043-4794-5 (sc)
ISBN: 978-1-5043-4796-9 (hc)
ISBN: 978-1-5043-4795-2 (e)

Library of Congress Control Number: 2016900716

Balboa Press rev. date: 04/25/2022

Contents

This book is dedicated to my wonderful family. You have contributed to my "no time for fear" way of being, every day of my life.

To my husband, Stewart,

We were so young when we met. At that time, I never could have imagined all the fabulous adventures we would have together. If you had told me that one day, I would be helicopter skiing in the Canadian Rockies or fly-fishing in the wilderness of Alaska, surrounded by grizzly bears, I would have thought you were crazy! But so far, our life has been an incredible journey, and I still look forward to many more wonderful adventures with you. Thank you for our fabulous life, for loving me, and for letting me love you all of these years. You have always been and always will be my love.

To my daughter, Heidi,

I was so thrilled the moment I first laid eyes on you. I am so happy that you are my daughter. Since the day you were born, being with you has been an absolute delight. Thank you for being such a wonderful daughter. You have filled my heart with so much love, and I am so proud every time I look at you. I feel that you are my best friend, and I love each precious moment we can have together.

To Hailey, Ashley, and Lilly,

It is such a joy to have the three of you in my life. When you run into my arms, my heart just sings. All of your excitement, sparkle, and childlike wonder remind me to also look at the world in such a wonderful way. I wish you a lifetime of adventures, love, true happiness, and joy. This book was written especially for you!

A miracle is a shift from fear to love.
—Marianne Williamson

Air to breathe, light to see. A soul needs nourishment
all its own. Whoever you are, wherever you're from,
whatever tradition guides your way, there comes a time
when we all need to be touched through the heart.

—*Graceful Passages*

Introduction

By the time I realized that my life was different from lives of most people, I was a grown woman. As a child, I didn't know how to compare my life's experiences with anyone else's. In fact, I thought everyone was experiencing the same things that I was experiencing. As an adult, I realized that I had had an amazing life with tremendous opportunities as I was growing up. I think that this awareness is a wonderful opportunity to embrace the past for all of its lessons, even though some of those lessons were very hard at the time. Instead of dwelling on the problems of what happened in the past and getting stuck in unhappiness, I learned to move on and let those problems go.

We can choose to grow from those experiences. We have very little control over what happens to us; in fact, we honestly have no control over anything but our own responses to what happens to us. I believe that this kind of acceptance allows our hearts to fully open to the miracle of every moment, and in those precious moments, we will have happiness.

My entire life has been an amazing patchwork of interesting, highly unusual, and some very funny experiences, many of which I can't explain. I've shared them with friends, family, and people all over the world. For years and years, everyone has said, "Dianne, you have to write a book! No one would believe all the things you've done and all the things that have happened to you." It was one of my unusual stories that led to the book that is now in your hands.

In 2000, in Cape Town, South Africa, I attended the funeral service of my dear friend, Danielle Smith. She had been married to the South African author, Wilbur Smith. Danielle, also an author had found out that she had developed a cancerous brain tumor. She called me in Cayman and asked me to go to Barrow, Alaska with her to help her do research for a book she was writing. It was about a young girl who was engaged to nobility; her fiancé was whisking her away from all hectic and stressful planning of their wedding to have peaceful week at an Alaskan fly-fishing lodge. When Danielle invited me to go with her, I said yes immediately. We had an amazing adventure in Barrow.

We discovered that it is the northernmost human settlement in North America. People live 303 days of the year in weather that falls below freezing. There are no bugs or flies in Barrow, Alaska, because there are no trees, grass, or even hills. It is all frozen tundra. For a refrigerator, the people just dig a hole in the tundra behind their homes. There, they are able to store their game and perishables.

We stayed in a Quonset hut that had been converted into a hotel. Outside our hut, a group of the Inupiats demonstrated the "blanket toss" for us. A group held the edges of a blanket, and a tall teenager jumped in the middle of the blanket. They then tossed him high, and because the tundra is so flat, it enabled him to see if there were whales nearby. Whales are a staple in their society, and they often used this blanket toss to spot them.

Although Danielle's movements were very restricted, because her brain tumor affected her physical movement, we had an incredible time. I feel blessed and privileged to have shared that experience with her. She later finished her novel, and it is titled, *A Cry of Silence.*

At Danielle's funeral, Wilbur approached me with a gift. It was a beautiful box containing a half-gold, half-malachite Mont Blanc pen that he had purchased for her. He had intended it as a present for her when her book was finished, but she had passed away before her book was published. He gave this pen to me and said, "*Write!*" I was so moved in that moment. That also gave me the idea to finally get my stories down on paper, and this book was born.

Gold and Malachite Mont Blanc pen from Wilbur Smith

As I started writing, ladybugs kept showing up all around me. In fact, hundreds were inside my room at a Four Seasons Hotel one day! I started exploring their symbolism and was amazed at what I learned. Their presence in my life has been a metaphor for so many of my experiences. This was a wonderful surprise that inspired me to make ladybugs the theme of these memoirs. At the start of each chapter, there is a symbol of a ladybug.

Shamans believe that the ladybug is the animal symbol of past-lives enlightenment. I knew they were a symbol of good luck and wishes to be fulfilled, but I didn't know that their symbolism included rebirth, renewal, and fearlessness. I discovered that ladybugs are believed to be an embodiment of Lady Luck, bringing good fortune and prosperity with them. As this tiny insect leads such a vibrant and colorful life, it also influences one to experience the joys of living life to the fullest. Ladybugs symbolize the childlike nature in everyone. They are here to tell us to get out of our own way and let love and wonder be part of our everyday lives. We should experience life with the heart of a child and know that all of our dreams will come true. The biggest message that ladybugs bring is to release our fears and return to love. In the end, there isn't anything else. There is only love.

Part 1
ADVENTURES

Chapter 1

BIRTHDAY

Run towards fear. Be more afraid of
not living the life you want.

—KAH WALLA, ADVOCATE/LEADER

Thursday, February 10, 1994, 9:30 a.m.

We landed in our helicopter at the top of a ski run called Morning Glory in the Canadian Rockies. The weather was extremely cold, and it started snowing very hard. The conditions were almost a blizzard when we started down the run. As I was skiing and the helicopter was flying right over my head, the avalanche broke. Because the noise of the helicopter was so loud, I never heard the tremendous thud of the cornice breaking. Some of the other people who were skiing with me heard it and had skied out of the avalanche path, but I was right under the noisy helicopter.

Next, I fell over and thought it was surprising, because I wasn't doing anything unusual. I usually don't fall when I ski. I had just been enjoying the beautiful powder skiing, not realizing that the avalanche had actually pushed me over. Then, I started tumbling in the snow. At that point, I realized I was caught in an avalanche. It felt like I was in a washing machine. I didn't know which way was up or down. My hat, my goggles, my skis, and my poles were ripped away from me. I was just rolling in the avalanche. When I realized what was happening, I started praying to God and all of our guardian angels to save us all as we were being tumbled down the slope in this avalanche. I didn't realize that there were only three of us in the avalanche. I thought we were all caught in it.

I was in a white ball of swirling snow and couldn't see a thing. I was upside down, right side up, backward, and forward. It was just like being caught in a riptide in the ocean. When you are underwater and caught in a wave, you don't know which way is up. I used to surf in California, so I decided to try to body surf in the snow. But I didn't realize that I was completely upside down. I was actually "surfing" myself deeper into the snow instead of coming out of it. During the entire event, everything seemed to move in slow motion, and I continued to pray for everyone. Then, just like that, in a split second, the avalanche stopped. I was encased in solid snow.

I was buried alive.

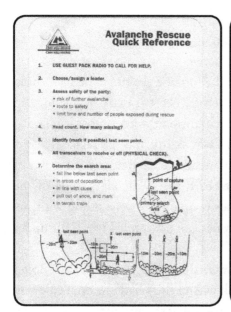
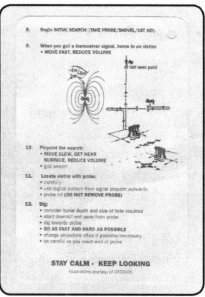

Avalanche Rescue Card

I knew from the avalanche safety drills that I was supposed to try to make an air pocket in the snow by moving my arm up and down in front of my face, but I couldn't even manage to move my little finger, much less move my arm to make an air pocket. When the avalanche suddenly stopped, it had packed me in the snow so tightly that it felt like I was in solid ice. My legs were wrapped around each other in the eagle position of yoga, and one arm was pinned across my body. My other arm was thrown up above my head. Then, I sensed that I was hyperventilating. I had been trying to body surf the avalanche, and that was a lot of exertion.

All of a sudden, something in my mind said to me, *"Slow down your breathing. You don't have a lot of oxygen now. Hyperventilating uses a lot of oxygen. Instead, take a long, deep yoga breath."* So, I slowed down my breathing and took a deep yoga breath. Then I thought, *All right, I've had as much fun as I can stand. I'm going to scream right now. It is time to scream!* But something or someone spoke to me again: *"Don't be an idiot. You can't hear them. How in the world do you think they will hear you? And remember, screaming uses oxygen. You don't have a lot of oxygen here right now."*

I didn't scream. I was wearing a transmitter under my ski clothes, and I thought that the others would pick up my signal and find me. That's what the skiing guides had always taught us in the avalanche safety drills, and I believed them. My last thought before I passed out was, *The guides are going to find us.* Not for one moment did I think I would die. There was no time for fear.

I completely blacked out. All of a sudden, I was surrounded by an incredibly beautiful and loving, white light. It was so peaceful and loving that I felt I could have stayed there forever. My mind said, *Wow, would you look at this? It is just so beautiful!* I also thought the sun must have come out because I was in an amazing sparkling white light. In bright sunlight, the white snow just sparkles. Sometimes you can see turquoise, pink, and gold glittering in the sun's reflection on the snow. And now, I was encased in the bright white light, and colorful, glittering sparkles were everywhere. Everything felt so warm and full of peace. I had the most overwhelming feeling of *love*.

You've probable heard the words, *unconditional love*, but this feeling was just so much more than that. I don't believe there are words for what I felt. It was beyond anything I've ever experienced. It was indescribably wonderful, and it felt so loving and safe. It was the most beautiful and peaceful experience I have ever had. I know it was absolutely *pure love*.

* * * *

My husband, Stewart and I had been going helicopter skiing for about seven years with a company called Canadian Mountain Holidays. We were excited to return to the Caribou Mountains, one of their beautiful destinations in British Columbia. It was the fifth day of our trip at the Caribou Lodge, which is a lovely wood-and-stone building. When you are a guest there, you feel like you are in a lodge in the mountains of Austria. Meals are all served family-style, with groups of ten at four or five big tables. You get to know everyone in the lodge really well because you spend an entire week not only eating and socializing as a group but also having exciting wilderness skiing adventures together.

Our group was made up of forty-four people from all around the world. We were all thrilled to experience skiing in the fresh-powder snow again. We would ski in groups of ten with two guides. One guide would ski down the run first to show us the best line to take. We would try to ski alongside his tracks. The other guide would ski behind us and would help us get up if we fell in the deep powder. On this particular week in the Caribous, we happened to meet some Germans who had come to Canada to try helicopter skiing for the first time. Ingeborg and Wolfgang were from Frankfurt. Horst was from Munster. Volker was from Bad Vibel, and Willy was from Oberusel. The whole helicopter-skiing experience is so unifying and fun. Even though I didn't speak German, I felt as if we could communicate. We used our hands a lot for extra explanations. During that week, we enjoyed being together so much that we became close friends. Over the years, we have continued to travel together on many lovely holidays.

This day had started out like any other. First, we got partially dressed for our stretch class, where we were guided through a series of stretches to loosen our muscles. We then enjoyed a beautiful large breakfast together. After breakfast, we got fully dressed for the day. At that time, everyone was required to wear a one-piece ski outfit. The transmitters were to be strapped around our shoulders, underneath our one-piece ski suits. If we wore only a ski jacket, the avalanche could rip it off. Then, the transmitter might come off as well. The transmitters needed to be in a secure place because without them, it would be impossible to find us quickly.

* * * *

Dianne on top of the world, helicopter-skiing

It was minus 26 degrees Celsius, which was very cold. The sky was steel gray, and it had been snowing heavily all morning. There were many different runs for the guides to choose for our skiing each day. During our breakfast, two guides would fly out to decide which runs would have the best powder snow for us to ski. After we had breakfast, we walked outside and up a hill to the helicopter pad. The guides were talking and laughing with us as we all waited for the helicopter. There were many great jokes told which had us all laughing. It was going to be a great day of powder skiing. When we took off, the scenery left me breathless. We flew through mountain passes and kept going up above the tree lines. At that level, the tips of the mountains looked like granite spears peeking up through the clouds and snow. The pilot found a tiny spot where the helicopter could land. When we finally reached the landing pad, the run which descended straight down, seemed as if it would be steep and rugged. Luckily, the other side had the gentler slopes that we decided to ski.

It was both beautiful and thrilling at the same time. As many times as Stewart and I had taken these trips, I still could hardly believe where the helicopter would fly and land. It was so amazing to land on a tiny spot on the very top of the mountain. We were above the clouds.

My heart was in my throat as we touched down at the top of a run called Morning Glory. By then, the snow had changed to blizzard conditions. It was snowing so heavily that the helicopter had landed with a tornado of snow swirling all around. It was snowing so hard that I could hardly see two feet in front of me. The guides told us to hold tightly to our hats and goggles because the wind could take them up into the engine. I climbed out of the helicopter and got down on my knees, holding my hat and goggles tightly with my hands while I bowed my head. I started praying, right then and there, for all of our guardian angels to help us down this run. Then, I stood up, walked over to my skis, and started putting them on. I thought, *I guess I'd better get these on quickly because I don't want to be left here by myself.* Everyone else was ready to go, and I got swept away in the anticipation and excitement of skiing the powder snow. I forgot about anything else except the skiing. There was no time for fear.

Even though it was snowing hard, I was laughing and talking with everyone. We started lining up at the top of the run. Stewart had decided to take the avalanche pack, which holds the extra radio, extra clothes, the shovel, and the probe. He liked to carry the pack on his back and ski last so he could help anyone who fell. Also, he could make his own tracks.

Most of the time, I would ski in the back of the group with Stewart, but that morning, I decided I would ski in the front with the ladies. I'd been skiing for a few days, so I felt confident. I thought, *Okay, I am going ski closely behind our guide. I will follow Ingeborg from Germany and Jacqueline from Switzerland. We will let the men ski behind us.* Our guide took off first. Ingeborg followed him, with Jacqueline following her. Jacqueline was combing Ingeborg's and our guide's S-turns, and I was combing her turns. Our S-tracks looked so nice in the powder snow.

I called out to Jacqueline, "I love following you!" She was making wide, easy turns, and I was skiing exactly alongside her turns. Horst was following me. I looked down at my skis and saw that the snow was breaking in perfect chevrons, which looked like big triangles. I thought that because of the heavy snow conditions, the snow was sloughing off down the mountain. But when an avalanche comes, it breaks up the snow pack in front of it. That's what was happening. It was an avalanche, although I didn't know it at that moment.

Then, I fell. The avalanche had pushed me over. When I started tumbling, I realized we were in an avalanche.

As the avalanche hit, Horst, Jacqueline, and I were all buried. Only Jacqueline's hand was sticking out, and the snow continued swirling around like a tornado. Horst's head and shoulders were the only parts of him above the ground. He was yelling in fear that the snow was still going to cover him before the group could dig him out.

After the avalanche, everything was dark and stormy. It looked like a dark tornado of snow. The guides had skied over me to dig Jacqueline out of the snow because they immediately saw her hand sticking out of the snow. Some other skiers in our group were digging Horst out of the snow. The group had split apart, and they couldn't see where everyone was, so the guides did a roll call. When they called my name, I didn't answer, and they then realized I was completely buried. Stewart told all the skiers to turn their transmitters from *transmit* to *receive*. One of the ladies, Maggie finally received a signal from my transmitter. She was close to where I was buried under the snow.

Everyone converged on my spot. They used the probe from the avalanche backpack to find me. It is a telescopic probe that folds up to fit in the backpack. When it opens, it's about ten feet long and has a point at the end that you can stick into the snow. When you probe through snow and hit a rock, you can feel it's a hard rock. It's a lot different feeling from hitting a body, which is softer. They probed right into me and found me. The probe scratched my arm. I was lucky, because they could have probed into my eye.

I was in a one-piece red ski suit. They dug deeper and discovered my belt buckle. They got so excited that they started digging really fast, using the shovel that was in the avalanche backpack. Some people even dug through the ice and snow with their hands. They dug the wrong way and uncovered my boots first. My head was still buried under the snow. Then, they all dug the other way until they uncovered my face.

When they finally uncovered me, I was frozen solid and hadn't been breathing for over ten minutes. It turned out that I had been buried three feet under, in packed snow and ice. When they uncovered me, my eyelashes were solid ice, my hair was solid ice, my skin was translucent, and my lips were black. I had lost all bodily fluid.

Wolfgang said, "It's too late. She looks like an angel." Later, when I heard he'd said that, I was so moved. I thought it was so perceptive of him. When I was in the white light, I felt as if I were with an angel, encased in his wings.

As I came back, they said that I spit snow in their faces. I really don't remember that. During the avalanche, when I was hyperventilating, I was breathing so quickly that I was breathing in snow, not air. My mouth and nose were packed with snow. My right lung was entirely filled with snow, and my left lung was three-quarters filled. As I came to, I couldn't breathe. I don't remember much. As I looked up, I saw everyone's faces staring at me through an oval opening in three feet of snow. It was surreal. I actually felt that I wanted to stay in the peace and love. It was just like an alarm clock waking you from a beautiful dream, and you just want to sleep a little longer because it's so enjoyable. But suddenly, I snapped back to reality. I realized what had happened.

The crew radioed for the emergency helicopter to take me to the hospital. Back at the lodge, the crew first thought it was just an avalanche drill. The chef had just put a cake in the oven. He actually asked if I they would be able to do this "drill" later, but the guides yelled back on the radio, "Negative, negative! This is real!" And the entire crew at the lodge went into avalanche mode.

I was wearing thick, expedition-weight long underwear under my one-piece ski suit. Because I had lost all of my bodily fluids, I thought the snow would be yellow beneath me. I kept thinking how embarrassing that would be when the guides picked me up. So I moved my hands madly in the snow to cover it up. They didn't know what I was doing.

They helped me sit up. But as I tried to sit up, the world spun around me. Because my lungs had only a tiny bit of space left, I could hardly breathe. In order to breathe, my feet had to be elevated over my head, the same way they had found me. They laid me that way in the helicopter. We took off for the hospital in Revelstoke, which was about twenty minutes away. Because my breathing was so shallow, the pilot flew me to the hospital heli-pad of the hospital. That was very unusual because they usually land at an airport and ambulance the patient to the hospital. But because I was having trouble breathing normally, the pilot landed right at the front door.

Once we got to the hospital, I began to thaw out. If I sat up, the world and everything in it still spun around. My eyelashes and hair were now dripping wet. All the doctors talked to me to see how I was. I thought I was okay. Even though they wanted to keep me in the hospital, I didn't want to stay. I didn't have a toothbrush. I didn't have any money or even a credit card. I didn't have a comb or any of my makeup. I asked the doctors what they were going to do with me.

One said, "We are keeping you for observation, and you will need oxygen. The snow is melting in your lungs and is turning to water. Your lungs will fill up with water. There is a possibility that you could get pneumonia. You will need oxygen to help your lungs to clear."

Luckily, we had been skiing with a group of doctors that week. I asked the guides if they had oxygen back at the lodge. They did, so I decided to go back to the lodge and let the doctors take care of me there.

When I arrived back at the lodge, the Germans were celebrating with champagne and toasting that I was alive. They cheered. "We're drinking to the first day of your new life! Happy birthday!" A group of men had to carry me up the stairs because I couldn't walk. I couldn't get one foot in front of the other. They carried me to my room, and Stewart brought me soup. When I tried to use a spoon, I couldn't get it to my mouth. The spoon would go from the soup to my ear. And the world around me was still spinning. I thought, *Oh, I'm going to need a lot of therapy to get back to normal again.* My brain had been oxygen-deprived for at least ten minutes, and nothing was working right at that point.

The doctors who had been skiing with us came in. One said, "Don't you know that oxygen prevents wrinkles?"

I smiled and said, "Well, then, give it to me!"

I just stayed in bed in my room with the oxygen on, nonstop. One of the doctors came in every hour on the hour, all night, to make sure I was still breathing. Before we went to sleep, Stewart poured soup in a mug and held it to my lips so I could drink.

When we were finally alone, Stewart broke down and cried. We had just purchased some land in Whistler, British Columbia, and we also had just purchased land in Cayman. Stewart said, "Dianne, it just wasn't your time. I guess it's time for us to build." After he said that, we cried together.

* * * *

From Stewart

It was our eighth or ninth time helicopter skiing. Dianne liked the first trip so much that I signed us up to go two or three times each year. The day of the avalanche, I was skiing at the back of the group with the backpack. I always enjoyed skiing back there. The ladies were in the front, following the guide. I heard what sounded like a crack of thunder, and then the sky became darker—very gray. It was almost like a cloud of snow rising into the air and blocking the sun. When the dark cloud cleared, I found myself looking at pure avalanche rubble the size of a football field. It took me a few seconds to realize what had happened. The fracture line was about forty inches deep, and all that surface had just moved down the mountain. I looked across from me and saw that Horst was about two-thirds buried. Only his head and shoulders were out of the snow, and he was yelling. I called for everyone who could hear me to take out their transmitters and set them to *receive*. I skied over to Horst and opened his jacket to get his transceiver. I changed it to *receive*. After I did that, I removed my skis.

The two guides had fallen down from the force of the avalanche. By then, they had gotten up and started taking roll call by yelling out people's names. Dianne didn't answer. It was at that point we realized Dianne was missing. I felt completely numb. Everything began to move in slow motion. Rather than become terrified, I started to recall what we had been trained to do in safety drills, if this should ever happen. At first, I realized I was trying to help, and I hadn't put my skis back on. There was already another emergency helicopter overhead with another guide as we dug out Horst and Jacqueline, whose hand was visible above the snow.

The guide from the other helicopter told us all to turn off our transmitters, at least while we were standing together. He did a quick search for the people who were down lower on the mountain. They were okay and had their transmitters on receive.

They started to get Dianne's signal. Then, Maggie and John got a stronger signal and realized it was Dianne's. They all traversed to where she was buried. A Scottish gentleman started digging with his hands, right on the spot where he got her signal. As he was digging down, he came across Dianne's gloved hand. He shouted out, "I've got a glove!"

Everybody started frantically digging with hands and shovels at the same time. We weren't sure where her head was and dug uphill first. We found her legs and boots. We realized that we had dug the wrong way, and then we started digging downhill. When her face was uncovered, her lips were completely purple, and the guide was yelling, "Come on—breathe! Come on, Dianne. Breathe for us!" The sensation of the air on her face caused her to spit snow out of her mouth, and she started to breathe. It was such a huge relief!

The rescue team wanted to take her in the toboggan over to the stretcher to get to the helicopter. She said no, thinking she could walk, but I had to help her walk over to the helicopter. Once we got there, she sat down and said she couldn't breathe very well. We got her to lie down, which helped. It turned out that there was so much snow accumulation in her lungs that sitting up made it impossible to take a breath. At that point, I was completely numb, not thinking, and just responding to what the guides were telling us to do. We'd practiced how to find someone for years, every time we went helicopter skiing. You recognize who is in charge, and you follow that person's direction.

Once I knew Dianne was going to be all right, the emotions of the experience began to sink in. We had been starting down the road of planning our Cayman house and moving there. I just said, "Dianne, we have a lot to do. It's not your time. It's time for us to build."

* * * *

Once we arrived back at the lodge, the doctors had said I would need a lot of therapy since my brain had been oxygen-deprived. But about two days later, in what seemed like an instant, everything came back. I could walk, talk, and eat, and I felt perfectly fine. I was laughing with everyone, and they were teasing me about the wrinkles and the oxygen. That Friday night, Horst and the Germans decided they would lead us in a champagne party around the lodge. It was going to be a big celebration, and our group would make a grand entrance to the party. Horst wanted us all to wear towels over our bathing suits instead of regular clothes. We would also wrap another towel around our heads and put our ski goggles on over our head towels. This was quite an outfit. Then, we would march in, holding the shoulder or waist of the person in front of us. We looked so funny wearing these outfits that we already were laughing hard. Horst commanded, "Left, right!" If we

14

weren't on our left or right foot exactly, he'd stop the group. We'd all fall into each other, laughing hysterically.

After a lot of champagne, even the helicopter pilots, who usually don't drink, were celebrating that I was alive. It was so much fun. They were all toasting me in German, saying, "Today is your birthday! Happy birthday! It's the first day of your new life!" We were starting to become great friends. Going through the experience of surviving the avalanche together created a lifelong bond that would never have happened without my near-death experience. Since then, Stewart and I have visited them in Frankfurt, and they have taken us to many places we would never have known. They came to the Cayman Islands for our daughter, Heidi's wedding. We were so honored that they were there.

Throughout the whole experience, I never once thought to be afraid. And my life was about to transform in ways I couldn't even imagine.

"Life is 10% of what happens to me and 90% of how I react to it."

– John Maxwell

Chapter 2

A NEW PATH

The real voyage of discovery consists not in
seeing new landscapes, but in having new eyes.

—MARCEL PROUST

We left the Caribous and landed back home in Dallas on a Sunday afternoon. That same afternoon, I got a phone call from a friend, who gave me some sad news. She told me one of our other friends was leaving her husband. The couple had built their beautiful dream home together, but the husband had had an affair with their interior decorator. Their marriage was over. It was my friend's last night in her home before her divorce. She decided she was having a girls' slumber party for her last night in that house, and she wanted me to come to the party.

I had not even been to the doctor yet to check my lungs, but I called all my friends and asked them to come to her party. I didn't tell anyone about the avalanche at that point. I said, "Get your pajamas. We're going to a pajama party!" I got so excited. I wore my pajamas and big fluffy slippers. I put the top down on the Mercedes and drove out of the garage to pick up my girlfriends.

The sun was still up, and I began having a unique experience. I actually stopped the convertible and got out to stare at the grass. I became so aware of just how amazing the green color of the grass appeared. I just stared at the grass for a few minutes in pure wonder of how beautiful it was. It took my breath away. I had never noticed grass to the point where I could just stand and stare at it, mesmerized. Afterward, if I really looked at a flower, I would have tears in my eyes. Flowers were so magnificently beautiful to me. I couldn't believe how fascinating it was to just admire a gorgeous flower.

When I got back into the car and turned on the radio, the music sounded so incredible that I thought angels had written those songs. Who else could write music like that or sing those beautiful words? It was as if the avalanche experience had awakened my awareness to see the beauty of nature and everything else in the world.

I picked up one of my girlfriends, who came out in her big hair rollers, bunny slippers, and baby-doll pajamas. We were singing and laughing the entire way to the party, just as we would have done if we had been in high school. When we got to the party, we decided we would call a radio deejay and ask him to play all our favorite songs that evening, just like we used to do at slumber parties when we were teenagers.

We had a big surprise when we arrived. We were the only ones in pajamas! All the other ladies were wearing suits and dresses. When my girlfriend had said "slumber party," I'd taken that literally. The other ladies wondered if we were high on something.

That evening, everything looked and tasted incredible to me. Someone had brought a Velveeta cheese dip, which I'd never tasted. When I did taste it, I was overwhelmed. All of my senses seemed heightened. I said, "Oh, my God, this is so delicious! What *is* it?"

Everyone thought I was acting differently. They kept asking, "What is Dianne on?" I didn't care. I just smiled at the ladies in their suits and dresses. Then, I called the deejay and requested "Johnny Angel" and other songs from way back when. I was dancing the night away with my other pajama-clad girlfriends. The other women in their suits sat there the entire time with their eyebrows arched up to the ceiling.

The slumber party was Sunday night. The next day on Monday morning was our book club, at which the guest speaker featured Betty

Eadie, author of *Embraced by the Light*, a best-selling story of her near-death experience. She told us she remembered many things about being in heaven. I had never read about near-death experiences before and couldn't believe what I was hearing. Her experience and the way she felt seemed so similar to my experience.

But I had brought my mother to this book club meeting with me, and I hadn't yet told her that I had been in an avalanche. I didn't want to worry her, especially because we were going helicopter skiing again in another month. So, I just listened to Betty Eadie. I was fascinated and wanted to ask her questions without letting my mother know that they were about me. I went up to Betty Eadie afterward and said, "My friend was in an avalanche. She didn't feel like she saw anyone she knew, but she felt an incredible peace and love. She was encased in the most beautiful, white sparkling light."

Betty Eadie looked at me and simply said, "She was with her angels."

She didn't know that I had prayed to all our guardian angels to help us down that run and that I had felt that I was enveloped in angel wings.

Later, I had a dream that my angel was my dad. He was holding and protecting me. When he died, a good friend had sent me a sympathy card on which she wrote, "You now have a new guardian angel, and his name is John. He will protect you always." That dream made me cry, thinking it could have been my father holding me in his wings.

The avalanche changed everything about my reality. Before the avalanche happened, I was very shy and taciturn. I lived my life in what I call the "Group Unconsciousness," doing exactly as I was told and doing what I thought I *should* do. I was an Air Force Colonel's daughter. I lived my life saying, "Yes, Sir" to everything.

After the avalanche, I woke up into what I now call "Conscious Awareness." I started noticing things that I'd never took the time to notice like the beautiful color of grass. I began to see people differently too. Everyone was so special. It didn't matter what they did, who they were, or where they'd come from. Everyone's eyes were full of beautiful light and love. Because of the experience of being in the white light, I now believe that this Life is simply a school where we learn how to remember what our souls already know. Perhaps it is simply unconditional *love*.

* * * *

When the date for our next helicopter-skiing trip approached, only a month after the avalanche, I told Stewart I didn't want to go. He smiled at me and said that we'd already paid, and he thought I needed to go. "You have to get back on a horse again after you've fallen off." He also said, "And really, Dianne, how many people do you know who have been in two avalanches?"

So, off we went.

When we arrived at the ski lodge, the first thing the guides told us to practice was the avalanche safety drill. That's when tears welled in my eyes. The guides were teaching us how to use the probe and the transceivers to find somebody buried in the snow. This had happened to me only one month previously. They also talked about how to react if we got caught in an avalanche. We were to make an air pocket in front of our faces in the snow with our arms, and we should take our poles and hit the bindings at the back to try to get our skis off.

When you are rolling in an avalanche, you could get injured if the skis didn't come off. I wanted to say, "You don't have to do that! The avalanche will do that for you. And, there is no possible way to make an air pocket when you are buried in solid ice or to get to your skis with your poles when you are rolling in a huge wave of snow."

That first evening at the lodge, as we all sat together at dinner, we talked about getting ready to go out the next morning for the first powder runs. I still felt some trepidation. Then, Mark Kingsbury sat down next to me.

"I'm having dinner with you tonight," he said. Mark was the President of Canadian Mountain Holidays. He's adorable and very good-looking. During our dinner, he said to me, "I'm skiing with you tomorrow."

I felt so happy then, because I knew Mark would find the safest and best runs.

When we woke up the next morning, it was one of those beautiful blue-sky days. The powder snow was so soft and exactly right. You could just pick it up and blow it from your hand. It was the perfect snow that draws people to helicopter skiing. Mark had the pilot take us to one of the back bowls. He started to ski down slowly, and then he stopped after four turns, looked back at me, and said, "C'mon. It's beautiful."

I started the first turns very slowly. The snow was perfect, and it was such a pretty day that the skiing was easy and fun. By the end of that run, I had a smile on my face from ear to ear. And I was laughing again, just laughing.

Stewart was skiing behind us all the way down. I enjoyed the feeling of being present in the moment, and I felt very safe being with Mark and Stewart. We had untouched powder and a wonderful blue-sky day. There was not one cloud in the sky. The sun was shining, and the snow was sparkling. It was just cold enough that the snow was really light, and it was the kind of snow to fly though. I just felt like we were flying while we skied down the mountain. Each turn was so easy, and there was no fear, just pure enjoyment. After that first run, I was ready for the next, ready to get back in the helicopter, and ready to go to another run to ski. From that moment, the fear vanished entirely.

The avalanche helped me really understand that the present moment is so important. We never know what the future has in store for us. A few years later, we lost two of our good helicopter-skiing friends.

Mark Kingsbury, the President of CMH was killed in a motorcycle accident. He had wanted a Harley-Davidson, so his wife gave him one for his fiftieth birthday. During that summer, he was riding his Harley through the mountains when a truck hit him from behind. He was killed instantly.

And Maggie, the lady who first found my signal after the avalanche stopped, developed breast cancer, and she later died of that cancer. You never know when that final moment is going to be. Being fully present every moment is a reminder to let stress go and to experience all the joy you can. A wonderful saying by Carl Sandburg sums it up. "Let joy keep you. Reach out your hands and take it when it runs by."

That is also where letting go of fear applies. There is no time for fear. I believe that we have angels and guides all around us who are guiding and supporting us all the time. Both Mark and Maggie were angels in my life. Spending time stressing and worrying about things you have no control over is a waste of your precious time and the precious moments in your life. Someone once described fear this way: *f* stands for false, *e* for expectations, *a* for appearing, and *r* for real. So *fear* is *f*alse *e*xpectations *a*ppearing *r*eal. You make it up in your mind. It hasn't even happened. You just imagine it will happen sometime in the future. Fear is nothing at all. *All that is real is love!*

I began to see this almost immediately after my near-death experience. It seemed to me that angels guide people to write songs. The words in some songs were so beautiful that they would touch my heart. The beauty of nature was just unbelievable. I had new eyes that saw the beauty in the world and the beauty in the eyes of people, animals, and all living things.

After surviving the avalanche, I was on an entirely new path. After I met Betty Eadie, I started reading everything I could find about near-death experiences. I realized that during my time in the white light, I had been in an angel's arms and in the unconditional love that exists where we're all going. I understand that there is more to come. Dying is not the end. It is actually another new beginning. Our souls *do* go on.

During this lifetime, we all have our own lessons to learn. Those lessons are our greatest challenges. We are all on different paths to the same place. Each path is individual. This life is about being on that path, and we learn our own lessons along the way.

I also began listening to tapes by a spiritual teacher Dr. Wayne Dyer. Everything started to come together for me because what he said made so much sense. I bought more of his tapes and listened carefully to what he was saying. *When you hear the truth, you know it!*

I had been raised as a Baptist. My parents weren't that strict, but I always thought, *I like wearing makeup and dancing, but I've been told that is a sin.* Even though my parents hadn't made me feel the least bit guilty about those things, I had made myself feel guilty by my own thinking. Wayne Dyer's words made so much more sense than some of the restrictions from the Baptist religion. I stopped feeling guilty and began living differently. I also started listening to Deepak Chopra and C. W. Metcalf's *Lighten Up! The Amazing Power of Grace Under Pressure*. I also read books by past-life specialist, Dr. Brian Weiss and anything else that I could get my hands on about near-death experiences. These teachers opened up a whole new way of thinking for me.

> *Death is just another beginning – and the most beautiful one you can ever imagine!*

Chapter 3

THE UNIVERSE STEPS IN

We do not heal the past by dwelling there; we
heal the past by living fully in the present.

—MARIANNE WILLIAMSON

Looking back, I am amazed at how the years after my near-death experience unfolded. Now, it is so clear it is to me that the universe knows exactly what it is doing. We might not know why we are doing things or why things happen to us, but the universe does.

When Stewart said, "It's time to build," he meant our home in the Cayman Islands, where we live now. In 1993, we had acquired land on what was called Britannia Estates. Over the next few years, we were busy with the planning and construction. To oversee everything, we decided to live in a condo at the Hyatt Regency in Grand Cayman. At that time, Britannia Estates was partnered with the Hyatt Regency. That is where I first met Dr. Choe, a renowned healer who has come to play a major role in my life and well-being. He also has helped in the health and well- being of many people in my world.

A special neighbor lived on the floor below us at our condo, and we could see his balcony from our balcony. He was Werner Erhard, the famous founder of Erhard Seminars Training (EST) and one of the early leaders of the human potential movement. We became friends with Werner and his companion, Gonneke Spits. We didn't know that Werner Erhard was so famous; we just knew him as our friend, Werner. The four of us would walk together on the beach in the mornings, taking backpacks with our breakfasts in them. After our morning beach walk, we would sit under the palm trees, talking and eating. We also went out to dinner together or joined Werner and Gonneke at dinner parties.

Because they knew that I had bad knees and a few surgeries from my helicopter-skiing falls, they had talked to me about Dr. Choe and his healing abilities. They said he was incredible. When I asked what he did, Werner said, "Well, we can't really explain exactly what he does. He works on us, and we feel so much better. You will too!" That was all the explanation I received.

One day, Werner called and said, "Dianne, Dr. Choe is here. Could you come over from two and three to see him?"

Of course I said yes. As I hung up the phone, I thought, *Well, that seems unusual. Did he say two to three? Did he give me a time when I'm supposed to leave? Usually people don't do that when they ask you to come over.* At that point, I didn't know that Werner had paid Dr. Choe to treat me for that hour. It was his gift to me, one that I would pass along to many others.

As I was getting ready, I thought we were going to sit around their condo and talk. I thought, *What am I going to talk to a Korean doctor about for an hour?* I put on a pair of slacks, a gold belt, and my high-heeled sandals and walked down to their condo. Werner, Gonneke, and Dr. Choe were at the front door to greet me. Dr. Choe had the most beautiful smile on his face. He is a handsome man, about five feet eight or nine inches tall. When I first saw him, it was clear that his soul was working at a very deep level. When we met, he appeared to be in his forties or fifties, and he doesn't seem to age. After 19 years of knowing him, he still looks the same, and I still have no idea how old he is.

Werner and Gonneke immediately opened the bedroom door, urging me to go in. They had taken the bedspread off the bed and laid it out on the floor. There was a pillow at one end of the bedspread and a paper towel at the other.

Dr. Choe said, "Take your shoes off, take your belt off, and lie down here."

I didn't know I was having a treatment, so I had no idea what was going on. I looked at all of them and said, "Excuse me?"

Gonneke and Werner then smiled and said, "He's just going to work on you. That's how he will treat you."

I took off my belt and shoes and lay facedown on the bedspread, having no idea what to expect. I wasn't afraid. I wasn't thinking anything except, *Wow, I'm going to get a treatment.* I put my head on the pillow, but Dr. Choe said, "No, no, no, put your head on the paper towel and your feet on the pillow." I followed his instructions. To my surprise, Dr. Choe started standing on my ankles. I said, "Dr. Choe, I've had several knee surgeries. I have really bad knees from so much skiing." I tried to tuck my head sideways to talk to him. He kept smiling but didn't answer. He started walking up my calves to my knees. Then I said, "Dr. Choe, I have a pin and bolt in my knee and have had a ligament removed. I lost my PCL [posterior cruciate ligament] from the last surgery." I kept trying to talk, but he still didn't say anything. He just continued smiling and walking on me. He started walking up the back of my thighs. Then, he put one foot on my lower back and another foot on my neck. He was balancing back and forth while walking all over my back.

He jumped off and said, "Now, turn over." He was very limber, and he sat up with a straight back while bending his knees right up under him. He picked up my leg, and to me, it seemed as if he was going to try to bend my knee.

I said, "Oh, I can't bend that knee very much, Dr. Choe." He looked at me, smiled, and cracked my knee. I could hear it crack! The pain was tremendous; it shot right through the top of my head. I thought, *Oh my gosh, he just broke my knee. Now I definitely will have to get a knee replacement.* I didn't say anything; I just screamed because it hurt.

Then, still smiling, he put his hands on my knee and said, "Five seconds, five seconds, five seconds." Miraculously, the pain disappeared in five seconds! The energy from his hands felt very warm. He stood up, smiled, and then he said, "Stand up."

I think I said to him that I couldn't stand up because he had just broken my knee, but when I stood up there was *no pain*. I felt as if I were ten feet tall because he had opened up spaces in my vertebrae by walking on my back. I felt so light because he had opened circulation passages and had cleared blockages. I also realized he hadn't broken my knee like I'd thought. He had broken up scar tissue, and my knee felt better than it had for years.

Then he asked me to bend down. I said, "Dr. Choe, my knees won't bend. I haven't been able to bend down since my last surgery."

He kept smiling and repeating, "Bend down."

I thought I would show him that I couldn't bend down, but I bent down farther than I had been able to bend in years, and I could actually reach for things under tables. I was flabbergasted and walked all the way home with my mouth wide open.

That week, Stewart happened to be in Cuba, fly-fishing with David, a friend of ours from Northern Ireland. David's wife, Rosie was staying with me, and we decided to go to the beach right after my treatment. We were sitting there on the beautiful beach, and out of nowhere, I started crying. I didn't know why. I was just sobbing. Rosie looked at me and asked, "What in the world happened?"

I told her all about Dr. Choe's walking on me and breaking the scar tissue in my knee and how I couldn't wait to see him again. I went back to Werner's the very next day and told Dr. Choe about my crying.

He simply said, "Good. I felt a lot of sadness in you. It was time to release that."

I later learned that Dr. Choe was from a village in the mountains in South Korea. It was so small that all the people had to be completely self-sufficient. They didn't have big hospitals. Dr. Choe was the one who would provide alternative health care for the people. Dr. Choe's practice is called *Sugi*. He has done it for many years. He once had an office in the Prince Building in Hong Kong, where up twenty or thirty people a day would line up to see him. He would see one person after another at forty-minute intervals. So many people came to see him for treatments that he didn't have time to take off for lunch, so sometimes during treatments, he would eat his meals while standing on top of someone.

Dr. Choe has treated world-famous people such as the British royal family, one or two of the popes, world leaders, top businessmen, and movie stars. He also has worked on men who were dying of AIDS. At that time of their disease, all they could swallow were drips of water into their mouths. Dr. Choe's treatments brought these men back to perfect health.

Dr. Choe also has a son, Injae Choe, who was educated at many of the Ivy League and top universities. He has studied and completed many different courses. Injae is a genius and worked in business development for GTC Semiconductor in Silicon Valley. He gave up his business career to be a Sugi practitioner like his father. Injae is now practicing Sugi in New York. Dr. Choe's brother is also a Sugi practitioner, who practices in Wisconsin.

A few years after my first treatment with Dr. Choe, he called me out of the blue. When my phone rang, I had just flown in from the Cayman Islands to Dallas to see my mother.

Dr. Choe was calling from Korea. He asked, "Where are you? Can you come to Korea right away to see the grandmother?"

"I just arrived in Dallas and am on my way to see my mom," I told him. "She's not doing very well. Who else is going to Korea to see the grandmother?"

He answered, "Werner Erhard, Gonneke, myself, and another friend of mine from Korea who brought tae kwon do to America."

I asked, "Who is the grandmother, and what does she do?"

"She is a special healer who lives in the mountains. The only way we can get to her is by climbing the mountain. There are no roads. She lives in a cabin high on the mountain. When she opens her door in the morning, there might be twenty people standing outside. If she looks at you, you're healed."

"Dr. Choe, I don't think I can go with you right now. I wouldn't be able to climb the mountain. I've had several knee surgeries. But one day, I would love to go with you to see the grandmother."

I later learned that Werner, Gonneke, Dr. Choe, and their other companion found the grandmother. They were invited to spend the night with her. They slept in her cabin on the floor on reed mats. I had asked Dr. Choe to ask the grandmother why I was saved in the avalanche. He did. She told him it was because I would help a lot of people, but she didn't say how I would do that. Dr. Choe said it is by performing one act of kindness at a time. (Maybe it will help people by giving them hope and inspiration through this book as well.)

After that, I wanted to visit the grandmother and to see her with Dr. Choe. A few months later, I was at Dr. Choe's home in Dallas for a treatment. He told me that the grandmother had died.

I said, "Oh, my gosh. You know, I should have gone, but I couldn't have walked up the mountain."

Dr. Choe simply said, "I would have carried you. We all would have carried you." And to prove it, he picked me up, piggyback-style, and ran in his house, carrying me on his back.

* * * *

A few years later, I went to the Omega Institute in Miami, Florida, for one of Brian Weiss's past-life regression therapy workshops and a workshop with James Van Praagh. James is a spiritual medium who is able to communicate with people who have already passed. He also helps uncover past-life experiences. During his session, I was sitting in a group of over a hundred people.

James said, "I'm lowering the lights, and whoever is sitting beside you is your partner." As the room grew dark, the lady sitting next to me became my partner. We just looked at each other. We weren't allowed to talk. We were told, "Just stare at each other and see if you notice anything."

I stared at my partner for what seemed like a long time. After several minutes, I started noticing things. We were not allowed to say anything about what we saw until James directed us through this process. Finally, we were allowed to speak. I told my partner, "This is going to sound really strange, but your hair was moving up and down. I also saw an oval shape behind your right shoulder."

Suddenly, she burst into tears and told me that her father had just passed away. When he was alive, he would put his hand on the top of her head and stroke her hair as a gesture of love. During those moments in the dim light, she felt like he was there with us. And to both of our surprise, I'd seen that

Her description of what she saw when staring at me was very strange. "I saw something dark and heavy, moving down from your chin to your chest. It was like a beard, growing quickly."

For as long as I could remember, I'd had a nightmare where I would try over and over again to scream but couldn't. Then, I would scream at the moment I woke up. In my dreams, it felt as if my throat was being cut. Stewart used to sleep with earplugs because I would wake him up when I screamed after waking from that nightmare. I never thought that the nightmare was about me in another life I might have had, but at this conference, when my partner saw something moving down from my chin to my chest, I thought, *Ever since I was a teenager, I've had the dream about my throat being cut. She saw blood gushing down.* Right then, it flashed in front of me like a movie. I knew that this nightmare had been from a past life, where I must have passed away while my throat was being cut. I must have died screaming. Once I put that together, I never had that nightmare again.

The same week at Omega, a renowned Buddhist teacher was there. He was one of the most famous monks in the world, but I had no idea who he was. There were always people around him, asking for his autograph, so he carried paper. One afternoon, Brian Weiss was walking with him. By chance, I was walking behind them. The monk stopped, turned around, and looked at me. He drew a water lily on a tiny piece of paper and just handed it to me without saying anything.

I looked at it and thought, *Oh, my gosh! This is unbelievable.* Years earlier, when my daughter, Heidi, was born, I designed her birth announcements. On the back of those birth announcements, I drew a water lily at the bottom of the page because I loved drawing water lilies. Underneath the water lily, Stewart wrote in beautiful capital letters, "Designed by Dianne Siebens."

And here was this famous monk, drawing a water lily for me and handing it to me without saying a word.

Brian Weiss turned around and looked at me curiously. He said, "Who *are* you? He has never done that for anybody!"

To this day, I have no idea why the monk did that or how he knew about water lilies and me.

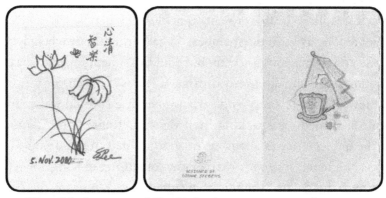

Water lily drawing and Heidi's birth announcement; the writing means, "A good, clean heart will know much happiness."

A few years later, I had a session with an astrologer who told me that right before this present incarnation, I was almost *there*, wherever "there" is. I was just starting to go "in," but I "heard the cry of humanity." She said that I turned my head, listened to that cry, and decided to come back. I think this means that I have had many past lives.

I started dividing my life into two time frames—before the avalanche and after the avalanche.

* * * *

From Stewart

It was clear that Dianne had a new outlook on life after the avalanche. I think she realized that, as our Irish friends say, "You're a long time dead." She was more loving, in general, and had much more sensitivity to other people, nature, and her overall environment. She developed an interest in spiritual things, which hadn't been there before. She also had more self-confidence, and her approach to life in general, with regard to what was really important, began to change.

"For truly we are all angels temporarily hiding as humans."

– Brian Weiss

Chapter 4

BEGINNINGS

> What lies before us and what lies behind
> us are small matters compared to what lies
> within us. And when we bring what is within
> out into the world, miracles happen.
>
> **—HENRY DAVID THOREAU**

My mother, Wilhelmina Cornelia Fazekas was a beautiful woman with wavy brown hair and golden-hazel eyes. She was five foot six and always curvy, which my father really liked.

Her mother and father were born in Hungary, but both left the country as young adults to escape the wars and unrest there. Each came to America by ship. Once in America, my grandmother became a young nanny to a wealthy Hungarian family. My grandfather became a Baptist minister. They met, fell in love, and got married in Philadelphia.

My mother was born and grew up in Philadelphia. She wanted to be more American, and she convinced her parents to change their surname from Fazekas to Faze. (I always thought *Wilhelmina Fazekas* was such a beautiful name.) My mother was now Wilma Cornelia Faze.

My father, Colonel John Robinson Hood Jr. was from North Carolina, where his family had lived for many generations. He was extremely intelligent and very good-looking. He was tall, blond, blue-eyed, and looked so handsome in his air force officer's uniform. When they were in their late twenties, my mother and father met one evening in Philadelphia on a moonlight cruise. The Glenn Miller band happened to be playing that evening on the cruise.

My father walked over to her in his officer's uniform and gently tapped her on the shoulder. He asked her if she would give him the honor of a dance, and the rest is history.

For her entire working life, my mother was a high school teacher. She taught general business, typing, and shorthand. She had double-majored in English and psychology at Temple University. This was very unusual at the time because most young women did not go to university. While she attended Temple, she was voted to be on the court of the May Day queen. This was quite an honor—only six women were chosen from the entire student body.

My mother continued teaching high school until she retired in California. Some of her famous students were the members of the Beach Boys, Tracy Austin, and Kurt Russell.

On December 23, 1946, I was born, limp and lifeless at Walter Reed Army Medical Hospital in Washington, DC. I was a "blue baby"; I was not breathing at all. They thought I was dead. Nobody knew that my parents both had a genetic condition that included the Rh-negative blood factor. This usually meant that those babies often didn't survive. In those days when women gave birth, they were strapped down and/or unconscious. When my mother woke up from the anesthesia, the doctors were trying to revive me any way they could. My mother began crying uncontrollably. She had already miscarried a baby before me, and there I was—born dead! As a last effort to revive me, the doctors hung me upside down by my heels, but I still refused to breathe. Finally, they gave me a total blood transfusion through my heel. As the new blood flowed through my tiny body, I took a breath, kept going, and came fully to life. My parents were ecstatic. We all went home, happily to their tiny one-bedroom apartment.

Their joy was short-lived. A few days later, my mother started hemorrhaging so badly that she nearly died. The bleeding just would not stop. She was rushed back to the hospital and stayed there for a few weeks. She was given blood transfusions. I was only four days old. Because I had been exposed to the outside world, I wasn't able to go back to the hospital nursery with the other newborn babies, but I was much too young to be left with a babysitter.

At that time, my dad was a command pilot in the air force. His job was to teach squadrons of men how to fly the new jet planes. He needed to teach them many maneuvers, including flying upside down. But he now had to care for a newborn. Since they didn't have a babysitter, he had no choice but to take me flying with him. He always said that he could do 360-degree turns in the plane while holding a cup of coffee, and the coffee wouldn't spill because of the centrifugal force. So when I was less than a week old, my father put me on a pillow on his lap and held me down with one hand while he flew in front of the squadron. There I was in my father's lap, flying in a new jet plane, doing all kinds of maneuvers with an entire squadron of men behind us. Those were the first weeks of my life, which certainly was not like most newborn babies.

When my mother came home from the hospital, she was so happy, and she decided she wanted to continue to learn how to fly. My next weeks of life included flying in their tiny plane.

My entry into this world, limp and lifeless and then, as an adult, almost losing my life in an avalanche wasn't so unusual when you consider the rest of my family's history. My father became a major in the US Air Force after the Second World War. When people asked him how he had become a major at such a young age, his answer was, "I survived."

During World War II, he was the commander of a squadron of bomber pilots. The commanders were always the first ones shot down because they were at the head of the V-formation. When he went into the war as an air force pilot, my parents decided not to have any children because they knew there was a good chance he might be killed during the war.

My mother went home to Philadelphia to live with her parents. She became a high school teacher. Since she had no rent to pay, she saved every penny she earned. She kept praying that my father would survive the war. One day, he was flying in the China/Burma/India front. His best friend, Edward from North Carolina, who was also his wingman, heard the radio report that there was heavy enemy fire ahead. At that point, Edward immediately flew his plane under my father's bomber to protect my dad. It worked, but his plane was blown up. Edward saved my father's life by sacrificing his own. My father came home from the war with shrapnel in the back of his legs from his best friend's plane. My father never talked about this incident. I didn't know this story until I was an adult and asked him what he'd done in the war.

When my father returned from the war, my mother was so happy he'd come back alive. She gathered all the money she'd saved and said that they could buy a house. My father looked at the money and said excitedly, "We can buy our own airplane!" So, they stayed in their tiny apartment in Washington, DC, and bought a plane. Since the war was over, and my father had survived, they decided to have children. My mother became pregnant with me. She then started learning how to fly when I was in her womb. My father kept a pilot's logbook, in which he would write one or two words. The day my parents married, he wrote, "married." On the day I came into this world, he wrote, "Dianne born."

My dad's log entry, the day I was born

I was named Dianne McNeil Hood. My middle name was in honor of my paternal great-great-grandfather, Colonel Archibald McNeil. Col. McNeil was in the Battle of Culloden in Scotland. After the battle, soldiers were granted land in North Carolina. Sometime prior to 1736, Colonel McNeil came from Scotland to North Carolina to start a huge cotton and cattle plantation on the Cape Fear River. In that region of North Carolina, a lot of Scottish people already were living there, so they felt right at home. Sadly, after traveling across the ocean, Colonel McNeil's wife died on the crossing of the Cape Fear River in North Carolina. He was devastated.

Their daughter, Jennie Bahn McNeil, became the brains in the family. In Scottish, *Jennie Bahn* means "Jennie the Fair." She was very beautiful, with reddish-blonde hair, blue eyes, and pale skin. Jennie became the businesswoman of the plantation, and she made it very successful. Legend says that Jennie and her father, Archibald McNeil, were the largest cattle ranchers in America before the Revolutionary War. Jennie helped to amass large portions of land, up to twenty thousand acres. She would sell cattle and buy more land. She is said to have driven cattle all the way to Philadelphia for a cattle sale. There, she met Benjamin Franklin. She was so taken with him that she named one of her nine children after him.

During the war, Jennie Bahn tried to protect her cattle and the plantation from the soldiers while her sons were away fighting. The cattle were in the field, and she knew the soldiers were coming, so she borrowed a red petticoat, which were worn only by "women of the night." She went out to the field, raised her skirts, swished her red petticoat, and scared the cattle into the forest. This saved the cattle from the soldiers, but because she'd worn that red petticoat, she became a shamed woman to the other Southern plantation wives—just for protecting her own land and cattle. After she died, the plantation was handed down to her firstborn son, my great-grandfather, who handed it down to his son, and so on. It was a Scottish tradition to give the land to the firstborn son in the family. Since my father was the only son, the plantation eventually went to him. I inherited it when he died because I am his only child.

When I was growing up, we didn't spend a great deal of time in North Carolina, mainly because my parents were both working. Also, my mother was not only a Hungarian, but she was a Yankee from Philadelphia. My father's mother was still reliving the Civil War. Because of that, my mother never felt at ease with her mother-in-law, my grandmother.

I felt adored by everyone, and the time we spent in North Carolina was always wonderful for me. I loved the farm, the animals, and the fresh vegetables and fruits. My father's family was always so hospitable and loving. Their Southern cooking was delicious, and I loved playing with the animals on the farm, especially the baby chicks and kittens.

* * * *

My coming into this world as a blue baby, my father's nearly being shot down before I was even conceived, and my nearly dying in an avalanche might be looked at as coincidence, but it seems like these near-death experiences in my family began at least a full generation earlier.

My mother's father, John Fazekas, was born in Hungary. He was one of eleven brothers. Sometime before 1917, he was riding in an elevator in Budapest when the elevator broke. It plummeted sixteen floors. My grandfather was thrown up to the ceiling and then crashed to the floor. When people found him unconscious, they thought he was dead because he wasn't breathing. They couldn't get him to breathe again, so they put him on the morgue train, where dead bodies were piled up on top of each other in one car. Because dinner was served back in the caboose, the soldiers had to walk through those cars of dead bodies to get to their dinner. As they passed the pile of dead bodies, they held handkerchiefs and towels over their noses and mouths. It must have been difficult to get through the smell. By some twist of fate, one of the soldiers saw my grandfather blink just as he was walking by. He stopped and yelled, "This one is alive!" No one knew how long my grandfather had been in that pile of dead bodies, but they pulled him out and saved him.

My grandfather, John Fazekas

My grandfather had traveled by boat to America, seeking a better life, but he never saw his family in Hungary again. In Pennsylvania, he became a Hungarian Baptist minister. His church was in Philadelphia, which is where he met my grandmother. She had come to America as a governess for a very wealthy family. My grandfather was a very tall and handsome man with big hands. In those days, the fashion was for women to wear tight corsets. My grandmother's waist was cinched so tightly that my grandfather could put his hands completely around her waist, with his middle fingers and thumbs of each hand touching.

Soon after they met, they fell in love and married. My mother was their first child; she was born in Philadelphia. Years later, my grandfather was walking through town in the evening, and he passed out on the street. People from his church saw him and thought he had passed out from too much drinking, but actually, he was starving. He didn't make much money as a minister, but he gave all that he earned to my grandmother. She used it to buy food for their children. When the people in his parish discovered he was starving, they increased his salary.

My mother was one of three sisters, and they would argue, as sisters do. But somehow, my grandfather always stayed calm and peaceful. As the girls would carry on, he would just sit there, turning the pages of his newspaper, ignoring everything and reading calmly. I think his near-death experience helped keep him calm. It took a lot to upset him. One incident was when my mother bought herself a beautiful blouse to wear out on dates. Her younger sister, Helen found it and wore it before my mother did. My mother was so furious that she threw her hairbrush at Helen. The brush missed Helen and flew into the window, which broke into a million pieces. My grandfather was very upset that my mother broke the window. That was one time he didn't stay peaceful.

As a little girl, my mother was teased about being Hungarian. Since she was the oldest child, she was always trying to be the boss. By the time she grew up, she decided that her family would only speak English in their home and when they were out in public. I don't know how she convinced them to do that, but it meant that I never had the chance to learn the Hungarian language from my family. They would speak Hungarian only when they didn't want me to know what they were saying.

My grandparents moved from Philadelphia, Pennsylvania, to Gary, Indiana. Later on, they moved to Glenview, Illinois, where they lived the rest of their lives and where I remember spending many happy days.

My mother, newly married

One of my earliest memories of my grandfather is when I would come down to the kitchen for breakfast when we were visiting them. My grandparents always had delicious, homemade, heavy brown bread, which they toasted in one of those old-fashioned toasters. They would be percolating the coffee and making toast when I came downstairs. It all smelled so wonderful. My grandfather liked his coffee with lots of sugar and cream in it. He would pick me up, sit me on his knee, take a piece of toast, dip it in the coffee, and feed it to me with a spoon. It was like a coffee milkshake with delicious bread, and I just loved it.

He also had a beautiful garden in their backyard, and he grew fruits and vegetables. He would can all the fruits that he grew. His peonies, lilies of the valley, snapdragons, and purple iris were always gorgeous. He loved his garden.

My grandparents eventually moved to Glenview, Illinois, which is near Chicago. My grandfather kept a beautiful garden there as well. My parents would take me to see them for a week or two every summer. My grandmother and grandfather were very kind to me throughout my childhood, and we always stayed close. In fact, when they were in a nursing home at the end of their lives, Stewart and I took our baby daughter, Heidi there to meet them. My grandfather was a very sweet and quiet man, and I still can picture him holding our baby so gently in his arms. I think his near-death experience helped keep him calm. He did not to dwell on things that bothered him.

* * * *

I believe that all of us are here to help each other. That is what makes our own lives so meaningful. Maybe my grandfather's and my near-death experiences awakened that in both of us. He did it by becoming a Baptist minister and helping a lot of people. I have received joy from helping people as well. I do that by connecting people who need each other. Somehow, it all works out perfectly. I also have learned that giving—in any way I can—is very rewarding. I think that is why we survived our near-death experiences and to let people know that this life isn't all there is. There is so much more to come, and it is so beautiful!

Chapter 5

A MOVING CHILDHOOD

All seasons are beautiful for the person
who carries happiness within.

—HORACE FRIESS

Because my father was in the air force, our family moved every two to four years. Usually, our transfers would take us between Washington, DC and Wright-Patterson Air Force Base (WPAFB), which is east of Dayton, Ohio. WPAFB was the largest air force base in the United States. My father was the deputy base commander of WPAFB. He had graduated from North Carolina State University as an aeronautical engineer and went on to receive his master's degree in nuclear physics at Ohio State University. With that training, he worked with teams of scientists and engineers who designed nuclear-powered aircraft and nuclear-powered automobiles.

After World War II, nuclear energy was thought to be the energy of the future. My father's jobs were so top secret that I never had a clue about what he actually did. He was not allowed to talk about his work. I only knew about his flying and where he would be going but never what he would be doing there. At this time, it was the height of the Cold War, and my father was involved in a lot of things that had top security clearance, which I recently found out because of the internet.

Me, age three *Fun in my Red Wagon*

* * * *

When I was about four years old, we moved to Oak Ridge, Tennessee for about three years. At that time, Oak Ridge was the known as "the Atomic City." Scientists gathered there from all over the world. It was also where the government was developing plutonium from uranium to use for atomic energy and the atomic bombs. In the early 1950s, they thought atomic energy would be the new fuel of the future. While we were there, my father worked with Edward Teller, the Hungarian physicist who developed the first atomic bomb. He liked to come for dinner because my mother would speak Hungarian with him. She loved to cook Hungarian dishes for him—he loved her stuffed cabbage. I remember lots of laughter and enjoyable evenings.

Because the work that these scientists did was so top secret, I didn't know any more about Edward Teller or what he did than I knew about my father and what he did. Plus, I was only four years old. Many years later, after my father had passed away, I found out that they had designed nuclear-powered aircraft. Apparently, my father was upset that the US Navy received money for the nuclear-powered submarines, but the air force didn't receive money for the nuclear-powered aircraft.

These groups of scientists and engineers also had plans to develop nuclear-powered automobiles. Every home would have a small nuclear reactor in the garage. The nuclear-powered car would be plugged into the small nuclear reactor, just like electric golf carts. That would give the cars enough of a charge to make it to the main highway, where there would be small nuclear reactors in the center of the highways for the cars to use.

In 1958, when we were stationed at Wright Patterson Air Force Base, my father worked with a team designing the Stealth Bomber. America was in the middle of the Cold War with Russia, and the concept of the Stealth Bomber was to operate, or "hide" without giving the Soviets any indication that it was there. Since my father was an aeronautical engineer, he worked on developing the material that covered the Stealth Bomber, which made the Stealth Bomber radar-proof. This honeycomb covering reduced radar detection by redirecting the electromagnetic waves from radar.

In the late 1950s, my father worked on Project Bambi, which was the forerunner to our current Star Wars Anti-Missile Program. During the Cold War, there was always a fear of a nuclear attack from Russia. Project Bambi was based on the idea of keeping many low-flying satellites, containing multiple nuclear arms, circling the globe in order to either destroy nuclear weapons released by Russia or to be ready for an attack to strike back, if a nuclear weapon was detonated first on America.

I wonder how many other secret projects my father was involved in. It must have been both an exciting and stressful time for him.

Oak Ridge Tennessee, the Atomic City

I had no brothers or sisters, but I always had a lot of animals—Siamese cats, parakeets, and ducks. From a very early age, all kinds of animals were drawn to me, and I was drawn to them—a mutual attraction that has continued throughout my entire life.

One Easter, when I was five years old, my parents gave me two yellow ducklings in my Easter basket. I was so thrilled with them and named them Quacky and Lucky. My parents kept them in a large bowl filled with water on top of the refrigerator, where they loved to swim. These little ducklings would follow me around the whole house, as if I were their mother. I would laugh so much as they chased me around the yard. They loved to be hugged and carried, and they would actually sleep with me at night. I remember falling asleep with them cuddled against my neck at night. My mother sewed little diapers for them because they lived inside our home. They grew up and became beautiful, fluffy white ducks, and I just loved them.

At the time, we were living in Washington, DC, and we were about to be transferred again. My father said we couldn't take the ducks with us on that move, so he suggested we let them go free. He thought the reflecting pool at the Washington Monument would be a wonderful place for them. There would be hundreds of other ducks there for them to play with. He said we could visit them whenever we came back to DC. We went to the Washington Monument to release them into the reflecting pool, and they took off and seemed to enjoy being with the other ducks.

The very next weekend, we went back to see them. It was cherry blossom time, and there happened to be a lot of Japanese tourists admiring the cherry blossoms. I was standing by the reflecting pool, looking at all the ducks gathered on the other side from where I was standing with my father. I called out, "Quacky! Lucky!" Out of at least one hundred ducks, two of them made a beeline over to me. They made a wake through the water because they swam and flew so quickly to see me. They flew right into my arms, and I just started kissing them. A Japanese man looked over at my father with such curiosity and said, "How did she do that?" He must have thought I was magical. To this day, I won't eat duck.

I loved all my pets so much. The cats slept with me, and they would wrap themselves around my neck when we went to bed. The parakeets would sit on my shoulders or my head and drink water from my glass. I liked to dress up the kittens like babies, putting my doll clothes and doll bonnets on them. I'm sure they didn't like it as much as I did.

I had one male Siamese cat named Lun Tha. I named him after the character who was the king's son, Prince Lun Tha in the musical *The King and I.* Everyone in the entire neighborhood loved him, and he stuck by my side no matter what, even when I was playing outside with other children. He ran with me when we played baseball. The other children thought he was great.

One day a gang of dogs surrounded him, and he was scared to death. So was I! His tail was up and all his fur stood on end. I was probably eight or nine years old, and I immediately ran into the center of all the dogs to save him. He was so petrified that he thought I was another dog. He bit me and scratched until my arms were bleeding, but I wouldn't let go. I had to rescue him from those dogs, which I did.

My parents let Lun Tha go outside all the time, and one day he disappeared. I think somebody stole him because he was such a great cat. I remember crying so hard. I tried to find him for weeks. I went to everyone's house and knocked on their doors to see if they had seen him. Losing him was one of my first heartbreaks.

* * * *

My dad, Col. John R. Hood, Jr.

The main memories I have of my father are about his time in the air force, which was his life's work. He absolutely loved flying, and he would take me to the air force base to show me the latest models of airplanes in those enormous hangars where they were stored. We stand on the tarmac at Wright-Patterson, go through different hangars, and look at and examine all the newest jet airplanes. He always tried to explain to me how jet engines worked. To him, it was so simple, but all I remember is thinking how those jet engines could lift such a massive airplane.

My father also was a command pilot and loved flying supersonic jets. He was so excited the first time he had to opportunity to refuel in the air while flying. This takes extreme precision flying techniques from both pilots.

Instead of my going to driver's training school, my father decided he would teach me how to drive, and he also would teach me how to fly. When he took me for my driving lessons, he taught me as if the car were an airplane. He would tell me to look all around, not just in one spot and not just straight ahead. I was taught to notice how the car sat in a certain position on the road and to make sure that I was centered in the driving lane. He taught me navigation skills that helped later in life.

Because he was so brilliant, he was great with helping me with my homework, especially math. He was also very spiritual and belonged to the fraternal order of Freemasons. At his funeral, a group of men put his Masonic apron on him. They offered their sympathy and, at the same time, handed my mother and me a sprig of evergreen. They told us the evergreen signified eternal life, and they offered us support, if we ever needed it.

When my father wasn't away on flying missions, he liked to take us to church on Sundays. On certain holidays, like Easter, he would give my mother and me gardenia corsages, which would make us feel special. Gardenia corsages always remind me of our Easter holidays with my father.

My father also loved animals. He bought me two parakeets and trained them to do many things. When he came home from work at night, they would fly to him and sit on his shoulders. He would make himself a martini, and they would watch him make it. Then, when he sat down to enjoy his martini, one parakeet would climb down his arm to the martini glass and sit on the rim. My dad would let the parakeet "sip" his martini.

Most of the time, my father was very quiet and private about his life and what he did. Although I knew he was a command pilot in the air force, I didn't know anything else about all the things he did. When I was in high school, he made special arrangements to take me into the underground city at the Pentagon, which was quite exciting. We were granted admission to the offices beneath the main Pentagon building. Before we entered, we were photographed and given security badges to wear. He introduced me to some scientists who were working with NASA, the astronaut program, and they took me into one of their private laboratory rooms. That day, they showed me how they were going to make furniture for space stations. This "furniture" design was just a pink tablet, the same color as Pepto Bismol. It was smaller than the palm of your hand. The astronauts would be able to zip this tablet into one of the pockets in their space suits.

They showed me this pink tablet and let me hold it. Then, they put a glass one third filed with water on the desk in front of me. They dropped the tablet into the water, and it immediately started foaming. Now, the water looked like a strawberry milkshake. Then the foam continued up and over the edge of the glass, covering the top of the desk and going over the edge of the desk. I sat there watching this pink foam cover the desk. The scientists didn't say anything; they just watched me to see what I would say.

Finally, when the foam reached a certain level of reaction with the air, it got to a point where they could shape it—they could shape it into a chair or a bed or even a sofa or a coffee table. In outer space, there is no gravity. The piece of furniture would have to be anchored or glued to the floor. This was the technique they would use to furnish space stations.

It was 1962, and I was fifteen years old when they showed me this. I was so amazed, and my imagination took off. I imagined all kinds of wonderful furniture.

The North American B25 – The plane my father was flying the day I was born. (Photo obtained from the GNU Free Documentation License.)

* * * *

I had a best girlfriend during junior high named Donna Fausak. We were typical junior high school girls, always dreaming about boys, talking about what kind of car we might like to have, and what it would be like to go steady and then be married. Back in those days, our favorite things to do were to play records, dance, talk on the phone, and experiment with makeup.

Donna's grandmother lived in a basement apartment in their home. If I slept over at Donna's home, in the morning her grandmother would make us thin egg pancakes, or crepes. I would eat a dozen of them because I thought they were so delicious.

Her father worked for Mrs. Smith's Pie Company and would come home with pies every night, which was just wonderful. To me, it seemed that they had such a happy family, and I loved spending as much time there as I could. It was always fun.

When my father attended North Carolina State, he played the trumpet in their military band, and he loved Dixieland music. After graduating, he continued playing the trumpet, and he always played music in the evenings after work. On weekends, he would sometimes have jam sessions with drummers and piano players in our basement. Those nights turned into great parties, and Donna and I loved the music and would dance.

My father was also a Civil War historian with a full library of the Civil War records and collectibles. He had a copy of an original Civil War officer's uniform made for himself, complete with the officer's hat with the flowing feather on it. He joined a group of men who were Civil War buffs, and they liked to participate in reenactments of the battles in the Civil War. It was a very large group of men; my father's group was called Jeb's Rangers. These reenactments were very realistic. They used actual Civil War muskets, revolvers, and cannons.

In the ninth grade, my girlfriend Donna and I were invited to go to a Civil War ball after one of the weekend reenactments. We were so excited. We copied pictures of ball gowns from a Civil War book and had them made to look exactly like ball gowns from 1865, complete with hoop skirts. My dress was yellow and trimmed with white lace, and Donna's was pink and trimmed with white lace. We were so excited about this ball because young "soldiers" would ask us to dance. We had the best time dancing with all the young men, but it was difficult to sit down in those hoop skirts. At first, our skirts would go up over our faces until we learned how to sit properly in them.

My father read everything he could get his hands on about the Civil War. During school holidays, he would take us to Civil War battlefields. Gettysburg was so interesting. At first, it is just like looking at a field of grass—until you realize what actually happened there. My father would describe the battle to us, and it became a sacred place to me after realizing all the sacrifices that were made on both sides.

Once my father took his metal detector to the battlefield. He found a lot of items from the Civil War that were still on the battlefield but had been covered by grass. He found a lot of bullets and was most excited when he found a powder horn, which was used to hold gunpowder. These items had been on that battlefield for over one hundred years. One bullet that he found looked like a piece of chewed gum. When men had their legs or arms amputated, the doctors would give them a bullet to bite on. This was all they had to help them get through their amputations. It was a hard realization of what the soldiers went through. Incredibly, we did end up with a collection of chewed-up bullets that my dad found.

During the Civil War reenactments, they didn't use real bullets in the muskets, but they did use gunpowder. One summer, we were driving to one of those reenactments in two separate Cadillac cars. My mom and I were in one Cadillac, following my father, who had the gunpowder in the trunk of his car. Suddenly, there was an accident in front of my dad. A car had run through the red light and slammed into the car ahead of my father's. My father slammed on the brakes so quickly that the tires burned tracks on the road. My mother was driving right behind him and knew there was gunpowder in the trunk of his car. She braked hard and quickly, and luckily, our car came to a stop. Thank goodness my mother had a quick reaction and didn't hit his car, or we all would have blown up that day.

* * * *

As I mentioned, we moved a lot, as my father was transferred every two to four years. I kept changing schools, meeting new people and making new friends. Other air force families moved around too. To me, this was normal.

In high school, I started to notice that some families were transferred to Europe, but my family was not allowed to travel overseas. It was the height of the Cold War, and my father was involved in top-secret work. If we had been transferred overseas, it would have been too dangerous for him. He could have been kidnapped and brainwashed. I didn't know that at the time, and I remember being jealous of friends who said, "We're going to Paris, France," or "We're going to Ankara, Turkey." There we were, going to Washington, DC, then Dayton, Ohio and back to Washington, DC again.

Through most of my high school years, we lived at Wright-Patterson Air Force Base in Dayton, Ohio. We were there during the Cuban Missile Crisis. My father was involved with that. Of course, I had no idea in what way. He might have been the one to release the planes carrying the atomic bombs. The Strategic Air Command (SAC) was located at Wright-Patterson. Because my dad was the deputy base commander, a lot of guards were sent to our home during that crisis. We had at least twenty enlisted men camped out all over our front lawn, with their rifles stacked on the ground in formation, like tepees. Men even camped out in our basement. When my mother and I went out, we were escorted by armed guards. I had to be escorted to school every day in a car by two armed enlisted men. I was never told why. I felt very special, but I had no idea how dangerous it might have been. In fact, when I saw a really cute enlisted young man on our lawn, I smiled at him. My father got really upset with me and said, "Don't smile at him." I was the base commander's and the colonel's daughter, but in the hierarchy of the military in those days, officers and their families weren't supposed to engage with the enlisted men.

I don't think any of us knew how close we came to bombing Cuba. As deputy base commander, my father was in charge of keeping two atomic bombs in the air twenty-four hours a day. One nuclear-armed supersonic plane would fly in the Northern Hemisphere and another nuclear-armed plane would be in the Southern Hemisphere. This was just in case they needed a quick response to Russia or Cuba—the supersonic planes with the bombs already were airborne. Every day, twice a day—exactly every twelve hours—a supersonic jet took off with an atom bomb and broke the sound barrier. Because it was a huge sonic boom, everything in our house would rattle. When we would have guests, and the sonic boom would occur, they would be startled and say, "What was that?" But, we didn't even notice since we were so use to it.

* * * *

In high school, I kept as busy as I could. I studied very hard and tried to get good grades. I became a member of my high school's drill team, marching up and down the field twirling my baton during band practice every evening until five thirty. It was a lot of fun.

In Ohio, the high school bands and drill teams were amazing. We practiced hard to learn a new routine every week for our football games. Every year, our school also produced a musical. The drill team became the dancers in the plays. We were in *The King and I, Annie Get Your Gun*, and *Kiss Me, Kate*. I was thrilled to have the solo dance, "Too Darn Hot" in the musical *Kiss Me, Kate*. Those musicals were so much fun. I loved being on stage and dancing. All of my girlfriends were on the drill team, and we are still friends to this day.

I continued to try to do everything I could to be "perfect." I liked to concentrate on the good times. This was a theme that would carry over into much of my adulthood.

My mom and me in maxi-skirts, circa 1970

We did have wonderful family times. Every summer, we'd go away for a month to the Castaway Hotel in Miami Beach or to North Carolina or Chicago to visit my grandparents and other relatives. Since my mother was a teacher and my father had a month off every year, we had lovely, long summer holidays. One of my favorites was the month we spent in Hawaii. I took up surfing then and continued surfing when we moved to California, after I graduated from high school. Overall, I think I had a very good upbringing.

Looking back, I understand the value in everything that was challenging about my childhood. I learned to accept that bad things happen every day—that's life. If you only pay attention to what's difficult, that is what you will remember—and guess what your life will be like? You have to try to let go of what is hard and focus on the positive moments. While I didn't realize it at the time, I am grateful that these seeds were planted in my childhood.

Chapter 6

TEEN ANGEL

What you need to know about the past is that no matter what has happened, it has all worked together to bring you to this very moment. And this is the moment you can choose to make everything new.

—AUTHOR UNKNOWN

Living at Wright-Patterson Air Force Base when I was a teenager was a lot of fun. Every summer, the Air Force Academy sent their cadets to Wright-Patterson for two weeks to tour and study on an air force base. When these cadets showed up in their uniforms, most of the girls would drop their local boyfriends and date the cadets. It was so exciting to have these university cadets at Wright-Patterson. When the cadets were finished with their two-week tour, the base would host an Air Force Academy Ball at the Officers' Club. My girlfriends and I would be so happy because we would have fun shopping for formal dresses to wear to the ball. When all the cadets showed up for the ball in their formal white uniforms, we thought they were very handsome.

When I was in the tenth grade, I started dating Raleigh, an older boy who lived down the street from me. He was a senior at my high school, and it was exciting to be dating a senior when I was only a sophomore. I thought he was my first love. His father was a colonel in the air force.

I was so proud to have him drive me to school in the mornings, because most of the other girls in my grade were taking the bus. Raleigh was tall and always tanned, with a gorgeous, sparkling smile. He was a great swimmer, and we went on dates to the Officers' Club pool at Wright-Patterson. I loved watching him swim.

When he left for college, I was heartbroken. We didn't stay in touch very well, and after two years, he found another girlfriend. At that age—I'd just graduated from high school—I felt like my life was over. Then I went to the University of Miami, and my dating life really developed.

* * * *

For my sixteenth birthday in 1962, my father surprised me a turquoise-and-white 1953 Chevy in mint condition. It had beautifully polished chrome and whitewall tires. I was thrilled with that present, but I wasn't allowed to drive it off the base. That might give you an idea of how big this air force base was.

In 1962, it was unusual for a girl to have a nice car like that, so I felt lucky. And I was happy to have that car when I started university. I drove it all the way from Dayton, Ohio to the University of Miami in Florida. My cousin from North Carolina helped me drive it down. When we stopped in Georgia for the night, a hurricane came through that area where we were staying. My cousin and I were young and didn't know anything about hurricanes. We thought it would be fun to go for a swim in the eye of the hurricane, so when the winds settled down, we ran outside and jumped in the pool. We were lucky that we had enough time to swim in the eye of the hurricane and then run back in. My father was horrified. But, my cousin and I were laughing and said we would never forget that moment.

I always listened to my parents and did everything they told me to do, but one night during my senior year of high school, I decided to go on a joy ride in the restricted Strategic Air Command (SAC) area around the base with my best girlfriend, Deanna Kocher. I was curious about what was behind those guarded gates of the SAC. I would drive by during the daytime and see the armed guards standing on each side of the gates. (Wright-Patterson also has an underground area that people do not know about. It might even be bigger than the underground area at the Pentagon.) I was always very curious about the restricted areas.

Back when I was in high school, I thought that the armed guards who stood at the gates to the SAC Division wouldn't be there at night. There were huge DO NOT ENTER signs on big fences around that area. One day, while I was exploring the base, I found a way to enter the restricted area. I saw an opening in the fence, but to get through that opening, I would have to drive over the curb and then over the grass. One evening after dark, I called my girlfriend Dea. We talked about it and decided to take a ride into the restricted area. She came over to my house, and we took my car. I drove us over the grass and through that opening that I had found. We were now in a very restricted area, and it was pitch-black outside. There I was, the deputy base commander's daughter, driving in a secret area where we had never been and where we *definitely* didn't belong. I didn't get far.

It was now 1963, and we were in the middle of the Cold War. All of a sudden, it looked like a scene from the alien movie *ET.* Men in white hazard, protective-breathing suits with tanks on their backs came out and surrounded my car. They were transporting something, but we couldn't tell what it was.

Other armed men surrounded my car and detained both of us. Truthfully, I was more terrified of getting caught by my father than by anything they were doing. At the time, I didn't piece together why they were dressed in hazard suits with protective gas masks and guns. I just knew we'd been caught. I told them who I was, and they called my father. I had never been screamed at so much! I think I was grounded for the rest of my life.

After thinking about it, I concluded that those men might have been transporting something top secret. Dea and I had witnessed it. It wasn't until I saw *ET* years later that I thought, *Oh, my God, they were transporting aliens!* Decades later, I saw a video on YouTube that disclosed many of the secrets about the government's hiding and experimenting on extraterrestrials at Wright-Patterson. I also watched the documentary

Unacknowledged on Netflix. That documentary highlights all the places where my father flew on missions. It's a wonder to think that Dea and I might have witnessed such an event when we were in high school in 1963.

* * * *

It was during my senior year in high school that I went skiing for the first time. I met an air force cadet named Roger Williams, who was at Wright-Patterson for his two weeks tour of duty that summer. We met at the Cadet Ball when he asked me to dance. We had a lovely evening with his fellow cadets and my girlfriends. After that night at the ball, he asked me out again; I was thrilled.

When he went back to the academy, he wrote to me. The Air Force Academy is in Colorado near the Arapahoe Basin ski area. That winter, Roger invited me to go skiing there with him. Arapahoe Basin was great for people our age because it had dormitory-style lodging. All the girls were on one floor of the lodge and the boys on another. In those days, nothing was co-ed.

My mother took me shopping for ski clothes, and I flew out to Colorado for my first ski trip in the Rockies. But tragically, the airlines lost my suitcase with all my new ski clothes. All I had when I arrived were the clothes that I was wearing and my makeup case, which I had carried on the airplane. I was devastated. I went to the dormitory with the other girls, and luckily, they lent me everything, including their hair rollers. In those days, when the airlines lost your luggage, they gave you money to buy new clothes. Suddenly, I had new ski clothes. The airline replaced everything, and I had a wonderful time skiing at Arapahoe Basin with Roger. It was fun and thrilling to be a high school girl, dating an air force cadet.

Roger had given me a lavaliere, which was an air force insignia necklace with a beautiful blue topaz in the middle of the medallion. I didn't know that it meant we were practically engaged. I just thought, *Oh, this is a pretty necklace.* Later, when I was at the University of Miami, I wore it on one of my first dates with a young fraternity man.

My date said, "The next time we go out, would you mind, please, leaving it at home?"

My girlfriends later told me that wearing the lavaliere meant that Roger and I were going steady, but I didn't even think of that. I still have that lavaliere in my sorority jewelry box, but I never wore it again.

Roger was studying at the Air Force Academy in Colorado, and I was studying at the University of Miami. We hardly saw each other. We stayed in touch by writing letters. His home was Monterey, California, and I lived in Los Angeles. We were so far apart from each other that our relationship just drifted apart. I have often wondered whatever happened to Roger. It was the start of the Vietnam War, and he was a fighter pilot.

During those teenage years, I did my best to enjoy all the experiences that were typical for a girl my age: dating, friendships, sorority, and university. I loved UM and decided to join a sorority. It was such fun being in college. Most of the coed girls went through Rush Week. All the sororities had Rush parties for us and would sing the praises of their sororities. We spent time with each sorority and then decided which parties we to go to the next day. UM didn't have sorority houses, but they did have a Pan-Hellenic building. Each sorority had a beautiful living room, dining room, and a kitchen in this building.

I thought the Delta Gammas were so much fun that I pledged and became a Delta Gamma. Later, I became the treasurer for our sorority. We had two formals every year. On campus on Sundays, we had to wear skirts—no slacks or jeans were allowed. Our big formal at the end of the year was at the Fontainebleau Hotel in Miami Beach. It was one of the best hotels at that time. Our dates wore black tie, and we wore lovely formals. It was glamorous, exciting and so much fun!

When it was time for me to enter university, I was only seventeen. My choices were either Duke University in North Carolina or the University of Miami in Florida. Somehow, I managed to be accepted at both. All my father's relatives lived in North Carolina, so my parents thought I should go to Duke University. My father said, "Go to Duke and become a medical doctor." Of course, I listened and said okay, and I actually got into pre-med at Duke. I never followed through to go to medical school, though because I would faint at the sight of blood. In those days, most girls became secretaries, nurses, or teachers. I enrolled at the University of Miami and double-majored in elementary education and early childhood education.

At the time, my father, being an aeronautical engineer, was involved in designing the space shuttle. He thought he would be stationed at Cape Canaveral in Florida, which is now Cape Kennedy. I decided to go to the University of Miami, thinking he would be transferred to Florida, but he ended up being transferred to the Air Force Space Division in El Segundo, California. There I was at the University of Miami, and my parents were now living in Los Angeles.

My parents told me, "Finish studying at the University of Miami in four years. We can't afford to send you for any more." There was no question; I would stay in Miami and study hard. I very much enjoyed living in Los Angeles and surfing at Redondo Beach every summer. Then, in the fall, I would go across the country, back to the University of Miami. I ended up loving Miami and my Delta Gamma sorority. Before long, I had lots of good friends and lovely sorority sisters.

That is when I met Stewart.

*My Dad and I during Christmas Break
from the University of Miami*

Chapter 7

FREE TO BE ME

This world is nothing but a school of love; our
relationships with our husband or wife, with
our children and parents, with our friends and
relatives are the university in which we are meant
to learn what love and devotion truly are.

—SWAMI MUKTANANDA

University and Sorority Days

University was a new and exciting world for me. The University of Miami is a private university, located in Coral Gables, Florida. There were two girls' dorms, built right next to each other. One was air conditioned, and the other, for some reason, was not. I lived in the air-conditioned dorm, and I was happy about that fact. I had a private room with my own bathroom, complete with a bathtub and maid service. My linens and towels were replaced with clean linens and towels every Friday. It was great.

It was an all-girls dorm, and each floor had a floor mother who would watch over us and keep track of us. Every night, she would come to our rooms to do what was called "bed check," making sure we were in our rooms. As freshmen, we had to be in bed in our rooms at nine o'clock at night, with all our lights out by ten. My room was at the end of the hall. If I needed to study late for a test the next day, I used to sit in the bathtub and pad it with towels and blankets to make it comfortable. Then I would fix the pillows in my bed so it looked like I was sleeping in the bed. I would put a towel under the bathroom door so the floor mother couldn't see that I had the light on in the bathroom. When she looked in my room for bed check, it looked as if I were asleep in my bed. That's how I was able to stay up late and study.

There was quite an incentive to make good grades. If we made good grades, we were given the opportunity to stay out on our dates until ten o'clock on Friday and Saturday nights, instead of having to be in the dorms at nine. Bed check would then be at eleven o'clock on Fridays and Saturdays. I really wanted to do that, so I studied hard to make good grades. I achieved mostly A's and some B's, so I was able to have those later hours. Most of the girls made their grades because they also wanted to stay out later on their dates. There would always be a huge traffic jam outside the dorm at ten o'clock on Friday and Saturday nights, when our dates would bring us back. All the girls seemed to come back at once—and not one minute before ten. We sat in the cars with our boyfriends so we could talk and kiss good night.

During my first semester, I was on the university's swim team. Practice was in the morning from six thirty to seven thirty. My first class was at eight o'clock, so I would arrive there with dripping-wet hair. All the other girls in class would be fixed up and looked beautiful. The classes were filled with handsome young men and beautiful young women.

This was the time when girls wore hairpieces, such as falls and ponytails. I wanted to fix my hair and be dressed like my classmates. I decided to quit the swim team after that first semester so I wouldn't have wet hair when I went to class. At that time, I wore my hair in a platinum-blonde flip. I also wore false eyelashes, and I tried to stay very tanned. It was the style at the time. I finally realized I didn't have to take classes at eight in the morning. The following semester, I arranged my schedule so I would go to class from nine to eleven o'clock in the morning. Then, I would go to the beach for some sun from eleven in the morning until two in the afternoon, and I would start classes again at three o'clock. It was wonderful.

After my first year at the University of Miami, I had a remarkable animal experience on my summer holiday in California. I got a summer job working for Marineland in Palos Verdes, California—a working marine laboratory. They would rescue orphaned or injured ocean animals, bring them back to health, and then release them back into the ocean. It was before Hanna-Barbara took over Marineland and turned it into a theme park, but they did have a dolphin show. My job was working as a waitress in an elegant restaurant called the Galley West at Marineland. I would look out the windows of that restaurant and see all the dolphins.

One day, one of the young men who trained the dolphins invited me to go out on the boat, which would gather dolphins to bring back to Marineland to train for the dolphin shows. The idea was to capture the dolphins that seemed to want to interact with us. I stood on the bow of the boat, and all of a sudden, a school of hundreds of dolphins was all around our boat. They started jumping alongside our boat while I was standing there at the front. The captain would accelerate, and they would accelerate. They swam up to the bow of the boat, and I sat down with my legs over the bow, trying to reach over to touch one of the dolphins. The dolphins actually came up on their tails and played with me. The trainers and handlers put the soft shammy around the bodies of some of those, kept them in the water, and slowly brought them back to the Dolphin College to train for the shows. Now, I realize that we took them from their families, but I didn't know any better then. I was seventeen years old and playing with hundreds of dolphins. I loved them.

* * * *

My social and sorority life at university was a wonderful experience. Delta Gamma was one of the top sororities, and I loved my sorority sisters. We all became very close friends. Each year, we would participate in Songfest, which was a singing competition between the sororities and fraternities. This fierce competition was held at the Fontainebleau Hotel in Miami Beach. The winner received a beautiful trophy, and we displayed it in our sorority suite in the Pan-Hellenic building. All the girls in the sororities made time in their school schedules for singing practice.

The song that my sorority chose to sing was "It Might as Well Be Spring," from the musical, *State Fair* on Broadway. Half of our sorority dressed in pink gingham dresses and the other half wore pale-blue ones. We practiced and practiced that song. For our stage decorations, we each had to make forty flowers out of pale pink and blue tissues. Then, we found a tall fake tree to decorate with all the Kleenex flowers we had made. In our sorority room at the Pan-Hellenic building, we thought that our springtime tree was beautiful, blooming with flowers. And our dresses were the same colors—pink and blue. Not one of us thought about how we were going to get this tree on the stage at the Fontainebleau.

I volunteered to find some male friends to help me get that tree in the back seat of my car. The stand stuck out on door on one side of my car, and the branches stuck out the other door. The trunk of the tree was across the back seat. I drove my car, carrying that tree, with my car doors open from the university to the hotel. I pulled up to the grand entrance of Fontainebleau Hotel and asked their valet parkers to help me take the tree out of my car. Somehow, we got that tree on the stage. We redecorated it with all those pale pink and blue flowers. We had painted a background mural of a springtime theme. Our song was great, and we looked pretty on stage in our pink and blue dresses with the springtime tree. We really thought we would win the competition. But our rivals were the Tri Deltas, and they sang the Beatles songs. The songs by the Beatles were new and very popular then. The judges loved the Beatles songs, so the Tri Deltas won the competition. We were so disappointed. I don't remember if we removed that huge tree from the stage; I think we just left it there.

Fabulous shows were also available to us in Miami Beach at places like the Eden Roc Hotel and the Fontainebleau Hotel. The hotels had shows starring Diana Ross and the Supremes, the Lettermen, and many more famous groups. One fraternity hired Diana Ross and the Supremes to perform their songs at their fraternity party.

Our sorority was invited to host the Lettermen when they came to perform at our campus. We had a lot of fun showing them our beautiful campus. Of course, some of my sorority sisters ended up dating them. We didn't go very often to see the shows in Miami Beach, but sometimes we were able to have incredible parties at the hotels in Miami Beach. Miami was a great place to be enrolled in university because of all the exciting things offered there. We had a beautiful beach and all the water sports and boating too.

* * * *

The fraternities were lucky to have fraternity houses on Fraternity Row. Once a month, they would invite the sororities for brunch. We were always excited about that because we would meet some really nice young men. I think the fraternities liked it too because they would meet all the new freshman girls that way. Some fraternities would elect "Little Sisters" to their fraternity and induct the Little Sisters into their fraternities in a lovely ceremony. This was quite an honor. The Little Sisters were then invited to their fraternity parties every weekend. I was a Little Sister to Alpha Tau Omega (ATO). It was exciting to be a Little Sister. The boys really did serenade us, as in the song, "The Sweetheart of Sigma Chi." As Little Sisters to Alpha Tau Omega, we were given Big Brothers and ATO Little Sister pins, which we wore proudly next to our sorority pins.

My Big Brother in Alpha Tau Omega was Atlee, and he happened to be Stewart's roommate. Atlee and I became such good friends, and we still are today. Atlee's Big Brother was Richard, whom we called Doc. Doc was in pre-med and was the president of Alpha Tau Omega.

He was also my first date at university. When we went out, Doc was between girlfriends.

Before we went on our date, he needed to stop by his IFC (Intra-Fraternity Council) office. He asked me to get something out of a drawer. When I opened the drawer, I discovered a cat he was dissecting for one of his pre-med courses. It scared me half to death. We kissed in his office, but there was no chemistry. I think I was still in shock about the cat. Also, I was young, just seventeen years old, with "Mr. University of Miami." From then on, we became like brother and sister. We double-dated most of the time in university. To this day, I still have a wonderful friendship with both Doc and his wife, Leslie. We became the best of friends and have since traveled together all over the world.

Doc was an only child, and that's probably why we became such good friends. He was a medical student when I met him and also the right-hand man to the president of the University of Miami. Doc eventually became a naval two-star admiral who was in charge of the Bethesda Naval Hospital. When Princess Di came to the States in 1997 for her campaign against the dangers of land mines, Doc was her escort. He said she was so charismatic and had the most beautiful eyes, but she was more beautiful inside. He said it was easy to fall in love with her immediately.

It's so interesting how you never know what people will end up doing with their lives. Back in university, Doc was the "Big Man on Campus." Later in life, he became an esteemed leader in his career.

Doc was also the president of the Intra-Fraternity Council, which oversees and keeps track of all the fraternities. They picked girls from the sororities to be Intra-Fraternity Council hostesses. I was lucky enough to be picked. I eventually became president of the IFC hostesses. We had gold-colored uniforms and wore them on campus on Fridays. We would automatically be invited to every fraternity party each weekend and had our choice of which one we would attend. Every weekend there would be huge fraternity parties, with very famous singers and musicians. Sometimes after the shows, the entertainers came to the fraternity parties too. The sororities would host the entertainers on campus. It was so exciting.

In ATO fraternity, Doc was Atlee's Big Brother. Stewart pledged ATO as well, but when they asked him to participate in the pledge activities, like fund-raising car washes on weekends, he declined and told the fraternity that he was going fishing. He had already participated in fund-raising activities throughout prep school. Besides, he would rather spend his time fishing. I should have seen this as a sign of things to come. It was through Atlee, my Big Brother that Stewart came into my life.

After meeting me, Atlee went home and told his roommate, "Stewart, I've just met the girl you're going to marry." I don't think Stewart paid attention to that. It wasn't until almost forty years later that Stewart told me what Atlee had said. Stewart is such a quiet man. Somehow, Atlee knew that Stewart and I would be perfect together, so he fixed us up for a blind date. Stewart and I wanted to meet before we went out for our first date, so we made a plan to meet on campus.

If we needed to stay up all night to study for a big exam, my friends and I would go to the campus doctor and say we needed diet pills. He'd give us an amphetamine, which we used to take to stay awake so we could study. We didn't remember very much of what we studied in the long run, but somehow, we got straight A's on the exams. After being up the entire night by taking an amphetamine and then taking my exam early in the morning, I met Stewart.

When I first saw him, he was walking up a hill to meet me, wearing the gray lederhosen he had purchased in Austria. His hair was bleached blond from the sun. He was very tall, athletic-looking, tanned, and so handsome. He looked just like the actor John Davidson. With no sleep and diet pills, I went up to him and said, *"Hi-i-i!"*—just like that. I was looking at this gorgeous young man wearing lederhosen and sandals. He looked like such a nice person, and he was so handsome that I decided to go out with him.

We had our first date that night, and it was lovely. Most of the boys I dated would take me to McDonald's or Burger King and then a movie.

But, Stewart picked me up in his little blue Volkswagen and took me to a lovely restaurant for dinner. He looked much nicer than he had looked just a few hours earlier, because he changed from his lederhosen into a white shirt with pink slacks. He stood out from all the other boys; he had a very Palm Beach–look. He looked gorgeous to me.

Stewart and his parents originally had lived in Canada, but when Stewart was thirteen, they had moved to Lyford Cay in the Bahamas. His mother was excited that he was going to university. She dressed him over-the-top stylishly, and he was so handsome, with sparkling blue eyes. She once sent him a velvet smoking jacket and blue velvet dinner slippers, as if he were a prince. He wore the blue velvet slippers to classes on campus one rainy day, and his feet turned blue. Those slippers didn't survive the wet campus walks.

We had a wonderful time on our first date and made plans to see each other again the very next Saturday. I could hardly wait.

In those days, if you didn't have a date by Monday night for both Friday and Saturday nights, it was a big disaster. I was president of the Inter-Fraternity Council hostesses, so I was invited to all the fraternity parties every weekend. Stewart didn't join a fraternity, but as president of the IFC hostesses, I had the fortunate opportunity to choose which fraternity parties to go to each weekend. Stewart didn't have to be in a fraternity because I was invited to all the parties. If we decided to go to a fraternity party, Stewart could be my date. For our second date, I had decided which party was the best and planned to go there with Stewart. Because I was so excited to see him again, I wore a new outfit. I waited and waited for him, but he stood me up. He didn't come; he didn't even call. I didn't know what happened, but I was so disappointed.

The next day, Stewart showed up at my door, completely sunburned and smelling like raw fish. I should have known this was an omen, because Stewart loves to fish and has continued fly-fishing all over the world. I told him I never wanted to see him again, but he had a long story about how he and his friend went fishing on a little rented boat. They ran out of gas while out on the ocean. They could still see the shore, but the small boat had no oars for them to get back to shore.

They had tied up to a lobster trap for the night before being given gas by a Cuban refugee boat. This refugee boat was asking for directions back to Cuba.

I never would have believed a story like that, except that he was sunburned—the color of a tomato—and smelled like fish. He had come to my dormitory straight from being rescued by the refugee boat after stopping for a sandwich. He and his friend had gone to the grocery store to get sandwiches. Everyone let them ahead of them in line because they were so smelly.

I forgave him. He went home and showered, and we went out that night.

That was it for me. I dated a little bit more, but no one came close to Stewart. He was everything I'd ever imagined I wanted. He was handsome, with an incredible demeanor. He was always so considerate and empathetic and had an gentle, soft voice. He loved animals, and they loved him, just like they loved me.

* * * *

From Stewart

When I first met Dianne, neither of us was dressed for a date. Along with the lederhosen, I was wearing leather moccasins that were worn out, exposing my toes. But Saturday evening, when I picked her up, I was all cleaned up in "date mode." It was a very pleasing moment, knowing that I was going out with a very attractive lady. I hadn't dated all that much, and dating Dianne was very nice. When Atlee told me that he had met the woman I was going to marry, I had no concept of what that meant. There was just something very comfortable in being together with Dianne. Our relationship developed naturally, and before long, we started to date each other and no one else.

* * * *

Many years later, I learned that during his first semester, Stewart had to take a bus to campus because he didn't have a car. His parents didn't give him enough money for food or transportation, and he had symptoms of malnutrition. He was living on oranges from an orange tree in the yard and had to walk far to classes. He finally went to the university infirmary because he was so sick.

When he went home for a school break, he went to his family's doctor in Lyford Cay in the Bahamas. The doctor took one look at him and called his father. "Harold, you cheap son of a bitch," he said. "Buy your son a car, and for God's sake give him money for food!"

His parents felt bad, bought him a little blue Volkswagen, and finally gave him more money for food.

On Saturday nights on campus in Miami, the dress code for young men was suits or jackets and ties. The women wore cocktail dresses. It was so fun to get dressed up. We'd go out to dinner at places like the Doral Hotel, which had the Starlight Room, with the stars on the ceiling. The band played all evening, and between dinner courses, we would dance. It was very romantic. I thought I was in heaven with this handsome young man next to me.

The summer after we met, I went home to California. Stewart's parents took him to Europe, and while they were there, his mother bought him custom-made suits and jackets. We didn't see each other for two and a half months, but we wrote letters every day. If he called me in California, he would say, "I love you" over the phone. We had fallen in love and couldn't wait to see each other again.

In September, I flew back to Miami for Rush School. Our Delta Gamma sorority would meet a week before classes started and work on our skits for Sorority Rush Week. I met Stewart to drive me to the dorm. When we saw each other for the first time after that kind of wait, sparks flew!

He had hand-carried the new clothes his mother had bought him in Europe in a suit bag. He threw the suit bag on top of my car, grabbed me, and kissed me. We got in the car to drive back to school. He drove off, completely forgetting that his new clothes were on top of the car. He lost all of them! He had to tell his mother, and she was so angry that she never replaced them. It was funny and sad at the same time.

71

When the time came for me to meet Stewart's parents, we flew to Lyford Cay. He had previously told me that his parents had the only home there with a swimming pool. When we flew over the island, I could see the Lyford Cay Country Club with its swimming pool from the air, but I didn't know it was the country club; I thought it was Stewart's house because of the pool.

I became really nervous, but his parents and his little sister, Mary Jane, were so nice to me. Walking into their large, lovely home was just like walking onto a movie set. They took me out to dinner to the Lyford Cay Country Club, which was very elegant. At any time, the Fisher family of Detroit would be there or the royal children from Monaco and England. Lee Radziwill, Sean Connery, and many people that I'd only heard about were there. It was such a fabulous private club in the 1960s.

I will never forget one New Year's Eve when we were there. My future mother-in-law said, "See that lady over there? Look at the two huge emeralds in her hair. She used to be Mussolini's mistress, and he gave her those emeralds!" It was such a different world for me after being raised on air force bases. I felt so lucky to be there. It seemed fabulous to me.

Later in our relationship, Stewart and I started participating in lots of outdoor sports. That's how Stewart was raised, and I always enjoyed being outdoors in the sun. It was in Lyford Cay that I first learned to go deep-sea fishing. I loved going out on his father's boat because it was such fun to fish, and it was a great way to get a tan.

* * * *

From Stewart

Dianne was raised to be a lady. She would never go out without wearing the right attire and wouldn't be seen without looking glamorous. That's just the way it was. From the beginning, my parents were very fond of her.

I had been raised to enjoy all kinds of outdoor activities. Being in nature was a huge part of my life. In fact, in my last year of high school, students would take what-should-I-do career questionnaires. Mine always indicated that I should be a cowboy or a forest ranger because of my responses. I always wanted to be outside. So when Dianne and I got together, I carried on with what was natural to me, doing things outside. After participating in sports that are in remote areas of the world, such as fly-fishing, I come back mentally cleansed and physically exhausted.

My dad had a sports fishing boat in the Bahamas, which my mother didn't enjoy because she never learned to swim. He loved it when we were there because it meant he had someone to go out fishing with him. He also enjoyed having Dianne on the boat because she always wore a bikini. She genuinely enjoyed fishing with both of us. She never complained or got seasick, even when the weather made the fishing rough. This type of deep-sea fishing used spinning rods, not fly-fishing rods. She would cast in the lines with the bait, sit in the main fishing chair, and wait for a bite. When the fish took the line, it was always amazing to see Dianne reel in the fish. She pulled back on the line gently and hardly ever lost a fish. And she seemed to enjoy it so much. In fact, she out-fished both of us, which made my dad laugh. Even after fishing all day, she still managed to look glamorous with her false eyelashes and bikini.

* * * *

Eventually, I learned all about Stewart's family. His mother's name was Jessie Estelle Donaldson, but she preferred to use Estelle as her first name. Stewart was born in Calgary, Alberta, Canada. At birth, Stewart was named Stewart Dinsmore Clouston, which is the name listed on his birth certificate. Stewart never knew his birth father because his father left Estelle right after Stewart was born. The only thing she gave Stewart from this man was a crystal mug from King George the 6th's coronation. (It must be special because it is the only thing Estelle saved from him.)

Stewart grew up in Calgary with his mother and his grandmother. When Stewart was seven, his mother met and married Harold Siebens, who then legally adopted Stewart. They changed his middle name to his mother's maiden name, which was Donaldson. Stewart became Stewart Donald Siebens.

Harold was an entrepreneur who had grown up in Storm Lake, Iowa, and later moved to Saint Louis, Missouri. Harold's father owned the American Sporting Goods Company. By the time World War II ended, when all the men came home from the war, the store had accumulated a lot of surplus of sporting goods. Harold came up with the idea of catalog sales, which was a huge success.

In 1948, due to health problems, Harold sold the company. Then, with the money from the sale, he outfitted two airstream trailers to take his family to visit Alaska. He took his mother; his two daughters, Gloria and Nancy; and his son, Bill, along.

While traveling through Calgary and Edmonton on his way to Alaska, he filmed a blown-out well and saw the Leduc oil fields. He had an idea! He returned to Canada and opened an office in the Palliser Hotel in Calgary. He started to acquire petroleum and natural gas leases. Eventually, he started drilling for oil. That's how he and his son, Bill built Siebens Oil and Gas, which later became the basis for the Siebens Foundation.

Harold had three children from his first marriage: Bill, Gloria, and Nancy. After Estelle and Harold married, they had a daughter together. They named her Mary Jane. She was born when Stewart was ten years old. So, Stewart gained a father, two older sisters, a brother, and a younger sister. This totaled five children for the new Siebens family; that was the family Stewart grew up with.

Harold was very strict with all of them, just as his parents must have raised him. But Harold loved outdoor sports, such as ice boating, pheasant shooting, skeet shooting, and deep-sea fishing. All the older children became fond of those sports. Even today, Nancy Siebens is a great fisherwoman. And every year, they meet in Canada for a family shoot for pheasants. Now, the nephews have joined in. They all love being together, sharing those sports to which Harold had introduced his children. In fact, Stewart continues to hunt and fish all over the world, just like his father did.

In grade nine, Stewart was sent away to Ridley, a private boarding school. There, he was interested in both football and hockey. He became the goalie on the hockey team because he had been ice-skating all his life. His grandfather Donaldson would use the garden hose to freeze the backyard into an ice rink. He continued playing hockey, even after we were married. In Toronto, he played hockey on a team for National Trust, the second company he worked for.

Stewart's parents traveled during the winter months when they lived in Calgary. When he was on vacation from school, his grandmother Donaldson would stay with him to take care of him. He became very close to his grandmother Donaldson. In fact, one of his fondest memories of being with her was when she baked him homemade bread and served it with her homemade strawberry jam. As he got older, he also stayed with his uncle and aunt, who lived in Calgary. He had many happy memories there too. In fact, after we were married, he took me to Vancouver to meet his aunt and uncle and then to Calgary to meet his grandmother. Of course, she made homemade bread and strawberry jam for us.

* * * *

We dated from my sophomore year in college through graduation. Because Stewart is Canadian, we decided to move to Canada after we graduated. He went to Canada first and got a job in Toronto as a computer programmer with Shell Oil. Stewart found a one-bedroom apartment in Toronto. He is color-blind in the two colors brown and green, but he can see the color blue. Blue is his favorite color.

His apartment had blue walls, a dark blue carpet, a turquoise-blue phone, a blue sofa, and a blue bedspread. Everything in his entire place was blue. Stewart called me and said, "I just bought a blue rug from a bank branch that was closing. And from them, I bought a mahogany desk for fifty dollars, which I just have to refinish. I also bought a new blue phone and a blue bedspread." He had every shade of blue in his apartment. When I first saw it, I thought it was the most beautiful place I had ever seen—because it was his!

I started teaching fifth grade, then fourth grade, and then third over the next few years. Although it was challenging, I loved being a teacher. Because I had a double major in education and early childhood education and a university degree, they put me in a portable classroom with thirty-eight students in grades four and five. This was my first real job. There was no art teacher, no music teacher, and no physical education teacher. I also had to do lunchroom and recess duty because I was new. For music lessons, I would put albums such as *Sing Along with Mitch* on the record player, and we would sing along. The children enjoyed this. For physical education, I asked the janitor to freeze two areas of the playground. I made sure each child had ice skates, even if I had to buy them myself. The boys played hockey on one side, and I skated with the girls on the other side.

In the springtime, I decided the children needed to be outside. We would sit under a tree for their reading lessons. Because I hardly had a minute off each day, I was exhausted all the time. I would come home and collapse. I told Stewart that I must be ill, so he took me to the doctor to have some tests. After a lot of blood tests, the doctor said, "Welcome to the working world!"

In the evening, I would walk over to the subway station to meet Stewart after work and walk home with him. One night, I was walking over there and strolled into a pet shop. I saw a tiny Siamese kitten hanging onto the cage with his claws. This poor little kitten was screaming. I had grown up with Siamese cats and loved them. I was so horrified that I opened the cage, picked him up, paid the cashier, and walked out with this little kitten in my arms, which is how I showed up at the station to meet Stewart.

Stewart took one look at us—he'd never had cats—and said, "What is that—fish bait?" Soon, Stewart loved him. We named him Lun Tha, after my first cat. Looney, as we called him, fell in love with Stewart. The kitten loved to sit on top of our refrigerator. When Stewart walked into the apartment, Looney would take one look at Stewart and jump off and go straight around Stewart's neck. Stewart would wear Looney like a fur collar every night.

We loved Looney, and he loved us, but nobody else could touch him. When company came over, Looney would jump right into their laps. At first, they thought that was sweet, but we always had to say, "Don't touch our cat." When they tried to pet him, he'd go crazy, clawing and biting them. That's another reason we called him Looney.

* * * *

In Toronto, my first year's teacher's salary was only about four hundred dollars a month. I couldn't afford my own apartment. In those days, though, couples would not dare to live together. Our parents would have killed us if we had.

One day, I looked at Stewart and said, "You know, I can't afford to rent my own apartment. We should just get married." That's all I said.

And, Stewart said, "Okay"—just like that. As he always says, it simply made sense.

I was thrilled that I didn't have to search for an apartment. We looked at his turquoise blue telephone and kept pushing it back and forth toward each other. I kept saying, "You call your mother first," and he would say, "No, you call yours first!"

He was twenty-two years old, and I was twenty-one. We were so young, but we thought we were mature. Finally, we called our mothers. We each said, "We're getting married next week at city hall. Would you like to come?"

Once they got involved, they decided we would have a beautiful little wedding in a church. They didn't want us to be married at city hall.

My mother was teaching, so Stewart's mother flew to Toronto to help me with the wedding plans. It took a month to arrange a wedding. Each day, we did something new. First, we needed to pick out invitations, then find the dress, then pick out the cake, and finally ask our friends to be bridesmaids and groomsmen. I asked my best friend Pam from Chicago, to be my maid of honor. I called Stewart's little sister, Mary Jane, and said, "Would you be my bridesmaid?" They both said yes, and I was happy to have my best friend and Stewart's beautiful little sister in my wedding.

For their dresses, I only told them to pick out something blue. Pam's dress was a light-blue silk, and Mary Jane's dress was dark-blue velvet. Because we loved blue, even our wedding cake had white and pale-blue flowers. It all worked out nicely. We did something every day for an entire month until it was all done. I still have Mary Jane's dress in my closet in the Cayman Islands.

We invited our family and close friends to the wedding, so there were only about twenty-five people. It was a very small affair but really beautiful. The night before the wedding, Stewart's parents hosted a wonderful cocktail party for us at the Royal York Hotel, where the reception would be held the next day. They invited their friends, family, and business acquaintances. It was magical; that evening at the Royal York was wonderful. Nancy, Stewart's sister was our official photographer, but she forgot to put film in her camera. It was so funny.

The next day, the ceremony was in Saint Thomas's Anglican church at the University of Toronto. That day was an Indian summer day, when the leaves were golden. It was a pretty little church, and after our wedding ceremony, the church bells rang and rang. It was just glorious.

The ceremony went smoothly. During the reception at the Royal York, Stewart's grandmother caught the bouquet and chased all the young men around the room. Then, while we were cutting our gorgeous wedding cake with the blue flowers on top, my veil caught on fire from the candles in the candelabras! Stewart yanked it off of my head and threw it in a corner. The guests stomped on it to put out the flames.

I caught on fire at my wedding celebration. Stewart said I was "really hot!"

Cutting the cake, right before I caught on fire

Because we hadn't discussed it, I wasn't expecting to go home to our blue apartment. I assumed we would stay at the Royal York Hotel, but that wasn't in the budget. Stewart took me back to his apartment after our wedding. When we walked into the bedroom, I saw his laundry all over the bed. He must not have had time to put it away, so I started putting away laundry in my wedding dress—not what was I expecting for a wedding night.

The next morning, we went back to the Royal York Hotel to say goodbye to everyone. I put Looney inside my coat and smuggled him in to show everyone our new "baby." Our married life had begun, and I was filled with joy and happiness.

* * * *

From Stewart

My parents gave us a budget of five hundred dollars for our wedding. With that money, we rented a suite at the Royal York Hotel, one of the big hotels in Toronto, where we decided to hold the reception. We picked out some Canadian wine, one from the Niagara region, at $1.99 a bottle. Our friend, Frank Crothers helped us pick out the wine. We had purchased three bottles of wine to taste to decide which wine to serve at our wedding. One was expensive, the next was moderately expensive, and the last was the least expensive. The problem was that we drank the entire bottle of the expensive wine. Then, we drank the entire bottle of the moderately expensive wine, and when we got to the least-expensive wine, we thought that was the greatest wine we'd ever tasted! That was three bottles of wine later, so we chose the least-expensive wine to serve at our wedding! It had a screw-on top, no cork.

The only food choice we had was Chicken a la King, which my mother actually loved. So that was our wedding meal—plus, it was my mother's favorite dish. She did have a big influence on this wedding.

We had a wedding cake with blue flowers because we both loved blue. My mother helped organize everything. I couldn't afford an engagement ring, so she gave me one of her diamond rings with a black pearl to give to Dianne.

Since I had spent the entire five hundred dollars on the wedding, I couldn't afford a wedding night at the hotel, so I just took Dianne back to my apartment. Unfortunately, I had done laundry earlier that day and was running late for all the wedding things, so I didn't have a chance to put away the clean laundry. It was scattered all over the apartment. I don't think that untidy apartment fit Dianne's image of what her wedding night was going to be. It was more like "Welcome to Marriage." We got up the next morning and went back to the Royal York to see family and say goodbye to them. Of course our cat, Looney came with us.

* * * *

I love the way Stew is looking at me with rice in his hair.

"Thousands of candles can be lighted from a single candle, and the life of the candle will not be shortened. Happiness never decreases by being shared."

– Buddha

Chapter 8

WELCOME TO
MARRIED LIFE

Do all things with love.

—OG MANDINO

Just married, New Year's Eve, Lyford Cay

From Stewart

It was apparent from the start that Dianne didn't know how to cook and didn't know anything about housekeeping. We'd never discussed it, but it was understood right away that she had been raised to be a perfect lady. Even in her college dorm, she'd had a maid. During our very first week of marriage, Dianne said, "We need more dishes because we've used them all."

We figured out that we needed to wash the dishes if we wanted to have some for the next meal, so we took turns washing dishes. I had some experience with chores growing up, so I could do laundry and vacuum. When I lived at home, my dad would have a yellow pad, where he'd write out all the chores for me to do. I wasn't allowed to go out and play until all the chores were done. But, Dianne had never been taught to do any household tasks.

At dinnertime, we would just look at one another and say, "What are we going to do?" Then, we'd say, "OK, let's see. There's sandwich meat. We can make sandwiches!"

From there, how and what we were going to eat began to evolve. Dianne called her grandmother for advice.

She got a recipe for a bean dish and cooked that a lot. The bean dish would get us through the week. Then, on the weekend, I'd barbecue hamburgers or steak. We ate that bean dish for a long time.

Dianne eventually got a recipe for pork chops, tomatoes, and pears from her Hungarian grandmother. The way to cook it was to season halved tomatoes, pears, and pork chops and put them on the broiler pan. She did the preparation, opened the bottom drawer of the oven, and put the pork chops in. She was going to use the timer, but we really didn't know how to set it. We both played with it and assumed it was not working.

After about an hour, I opened the oven, and all that food was still at room temperature. We both stuck our fingers on the meat, and it still felt cool. We thought the oven wasn't working, so we called the superintendent. When he arrived, I said, "There is something wrong with the oven. We set the broiler, but nothing is cooking."

He looked at where we had put the meal and said, "You didn't put it in the broiler. You put it in the storage drawer. Meat has to go in the oven to broil."

There was an instruction book for the oven in the apartment. He handed it over to us and walked out the door.

And, here I thought my bride knew how to use an oven. She said her mother had always put the meat in the "bottom drawer" of the oven. I'm guessing that was a different style oven, and the broiler was underneath. After reading the instructions, we then learned how to turn the oven on and off, which led to a late dinner that evening. Once we got it cooked, it was fine. Then we had two dishes: the bean dish and pork chops. We lived on those, plus sandwiches, for quite some time.

We also didn't know that there was such a thing as Tupperware for storing leftovers. Dianne would cook four or five pork chops, and we would eat them all. We never thought of saving them. We also discovered how to cook escargot in garlic butter, which we loved. Basically, we ate just a few things—the bean dish, the pork chops, sometimes steaks, and the escargot. With all that and the very addictive Canadian date bars and butter and raisin tarts, which we bought by the dozen, we both started gaining weight.

Over time, Dianne became an excellent cook, once she started collecting recipe books.

* * * *

After our October wedding in Toronto, it wasn't long before winter set in. I looked at the snow and thought it would be fun to go skiing. Stewart had been a hockey player when he lived in Calgary many years earlier, but he had never been snow skiing. I started skiing in high school, but it was just for fun. None of us took any lessons. With only a little bit of ski experience, I had no idea what I was doing, taking Stewart skiing. It just seemed like it would be fun. We decided to go to Collingwood, outside of Toronto, for a weekend. We drove up there and rented some wooden skis with cable bindings. We also had to rent leather ski boots that had to be laced up like tennis shoes.

I told Stewart I would teach him to ski, but I hadn't thought it through. We put the skis on and got in line. I wanted to go to the top of the mountain, so we tried going up the T-bar lift. As it got steeper, I got scared and started snow plowing by putting the tips of my skis together and pushing the heels out with Stewart standing next to me. I pushed him over, and we both fell off the T-bar. When we got up, I said, "Let's go up the chairlift. It's much easier."

The moment the chair was coming around, I told Stew to put his poles in one hand and grab on to the chair with the other hand. He tried but dropped his ski poles just as the chair scooped him up.

I looked at him and said, "Don't worry. I don't use my ski poles anyway. You can use my ski poles when we get to the top."

As we got to the top of the chairlift, a sign said, "Raise Safety Bar." Stewart asked, "What's that?"

I had no idea. We hadn't even put the safety bar down because I didn't know we were supposed to. At that point, I couldn't imagine how we were going to get off that chair.

I saw a ramp at the top, all covered with snow. As we approached the top, I told Stewart, "Just jump off!" When I jumped off, I did a ninety-degree right-hand turn and skied down the stairs of the ski operator's booth! Stewart looked at me, fell off, and started rolling. The chairlift operator couldn't believe what he was seeing! He pushed the emergency button and stopped the entire chairlift while we tried to get out of the way.

By then, Stewart was getting the idea that I didn't know what I was doing. We were finally at the top. I handed him my poles and said, "Follow me." I didn't know how to teach him to turn because I didn't know how. I just kept saying to him, "Turn!"

We both were falling and getting up, all the way down to the bottom. As we neared the end of the run, he started picking up speed because he's heavier than I am. He was going fast but couldn't control what he was doing. He skied down the hill, through the ski lift line, across somebody's skis, into the parking lot, over the gravel, and finally stopped by putting his hands on a car. I didn't know how to teach him to stop on skis. I just kept yelling, "Stop! Stop!"

When he put his hands on the car, he turned around, looked at me, and said, "We're taking lessons!"

* * * *

From Stewart

I should have known that Dianne's knowledge of skiing meant that she had participated in that sport. When we were first married, I realized that she had never even gone downhill on a toboggan.

Our first winter in Toronto, there was a big snowfall. I surprised her and bought a toboggan. We went to an outdoor park to try it. Of course, Dianne's hair was all done. I told her she would want to wear a hat. She had one made of fur that sat quite far back on her forehead. I said, "When we get up to the top of the hill, why don't you sit in the front of the toboggan?"

We climbed up the hill with our new toboggan. She sat down in the front, looking very glamorous. I got behind her and pushed off. Of course, the toboggan picked up speed, and all the snow blew over the top of toboggan. Normally, you take your ski hat and pull it over your face—I forgot to tell Dianne that. When we got to the bottom, Dianne's hat, face, forehead, and false eyelashes were totally caked in snow! Obviously, she didn't want a second ride.

* * * *

Our official honeymoon wasn't until the Christmas holidays because neither of us had time off from our jobs until then. Stewart signed us up for ski lessons in Mont-Tremblant in Quebec. We packed up the car and drove there. Of course, Looney came with us. We brought our own wooden skis, and I think Stewart broke one pair each day. That entire week had blizzard conditions, with temperatures down to twenty-nine degrees below zero. It was absolutely frigid. On the third day, Stewart came down with the Hong Kong flu. It was a very bad flu, and many people died from it. There we were—Looney, Stewart, with this horrible Hong Kong flu, and me—on our honeymoon at a small ski lodge in Mont-Tremblant. We had to call a doctor because Stewart was so sick, and the doctor came to our place in snowshoes. Stewart decided that since we had paid for ski lessons, I should continue taking them. It was so cold that I didn't want to go out there. But, he repeated, we'd paid for a ski instructor, and I needed the instructions, so off I went.

On the last morning, the instructor and I were on the T-bar, going up the hill, when the spring mechanism on our T-bar froze. The ski instructor weighed more than I did. When the spring on the top of the T-bar froze, he twisted the bar back, and I fell off in front. As he let go of the T-bar, it came straight for me. He screamed, "Duck!"

The T-bar came straight toward my shoulders, and as I ducked, the bar hit me smack in the face and drove a front tooth up into my jawbone. I was bleeding everywhere. I came back inside, completely frozen, with a bloody mouth. Stewart was so sick that he couldn't even sit up. It was our last day, and I said, "Okay, this is enough of a honeymoon. We're going home!"

We were driving home to Toronto on the Laurentian Autoroute in our brand-new Mustang. The road was solid ice. We had to go through tollbooths on this highway. The lady in the car in front of me stopped suddenly, as she was trying to get the change out of her purse for the tollbooth. Stewart was lying down in the back with Looney, and I was driving with a swollen mouth. We skidded right into her stopped car and had a front-end collision. Our brand-new Mustang now couldn't be driven. We ended up in the middle of nowhere in a French-speaking town at a bed-and-breakfast until Allstate could come and take care of us.

Stewart was so sick, and we had no money or car. We were forced to stay there. We called Stewart's parents to ask for help, and his father said, "Serves you right. We told you to come to Nassau to stay with us."

But, staying with his parents had not been our idea of a perfect honeymoon. After our experience, we called our honeymoon the "honeymoon from hell."

* * * *

From Stewart

Mont-Tremblant in the Laurentian Mountains is very French. There were ski lodges with attached cabins that all had the same roofline. When we arrived, there was a tremendous amount of snow and very cold weather. We had our new wooden skis and didn't know we were supposed to put wax on the bottom of them. We brought them into our room at the ski lodge; that decision was not very good.

The first day, we told the attendant that we'd like to buy a lift ticket to go up the mountain. She said she could sell us two single-ride lift tickets. We said no because we wanted to ski a lot. We thought that the entire mountain was only the first ridge that we could see. We didn't understand that the mountain had ski areas that went over other ridges. We finally bought a half-day lift ticket.

On our first run, we got off the chairlift with no wax on our skis. We had no idea how to ski, and the snow was incredibly deep. We would ski only ten to twenty feet, fall, and then get up and start again. It took us two hours to get down. It turned out that we didn't need to buy a half-day lift ticket. It took us all that time to make it down one run! We were covered in snow and were soaking wet, like snowmen.

The next morning, the instructors were going to allocate everyone to their classes. They had a little run where they could assess people. Of course, the snow was really sticking to our skies because we hadn't waxed them. I didn't know about waxing skis.

I could make it down the hill because of my weight, but Dianne fell every ten feet because the snow was sticking to the bottom of her skis. She was sent to a beginner class, and I was sent to one class higher. It was funny because I had not skied much before this trip, and Dianne had skied since high school.

After three days of skiing, I came down with the horrible Hong Kong flu, although we didn't know that's what it was. At that point, I couldn't stand the smell of food. I had to stay in our ski cabin with Looney. Dianne didn't want to go out in that frigid cold to ski, but I said that we had paid for the lessons, so she should go. Pretty soon, I was surviving only on water. For the last couple of days, all I could do was sleep.

On the last morning, I told Dianne to go out with her instructor. When the T-bar froze and split her lips, she looked like she'd been hit with a hockey puck.

Finally, we piled everything in the car to leave. I certainly wasn't well enough to drive. We were heading to a tollbooth to pay the toll when the car twenty yards in front of us suddenly stopped. Dianne braked but skidded right into it. The road was solid ice. A tow truck came and took us to a nearby town, where we went to a hotel and waited for Allstate to show up.

Dianne had brought along a portable six-inch Sony TV with a handle and an aerial, but all the shows were in French. The neighbors could hear everything through the bathroom wall, so I am sure they couldn't figure out who was next door, watching French cartoons.

It took another three days for Allstate to come. I was still so sick. When they showed up, we finally had the car fixed. We were able to drive home to Toronto, where I spent another five days in bed at home. That was our romantic honeymoon!

* * * *

We wanted to wait to have a baby because we were both working so hard. I was teaching for very little pay. But after about a year, I accidentally became pregnant; we really hadn't planned it. When I told Stewart, he made the decision that we should have an abortion. He explained to me that we couldn't afford a baby. I just went along with him and didn't think about it one way or another. We were both so young that we didn't think of the consequences. We just knew we couldn't afford a baby at that time.

Normally, I weighed about 117 pounds, and I had already gained about four more pounds. I didn't realize I was pregnant, so I started drinking some kind of weight-loss liquid that they sell in the drugstores. I thought I was just gaining weight. I didn't even think I could be pregnant. I realized that this weight-loss liquid probably wasn't good for the pregnancy. Maybe the baby would not be healthy.

It was hard to get an abortion in Toronto at the time. Stewart asked one of his prep school friends, whose father was a doctor, to do the operation. We had to drive to Hamilton, Ontario, which was a steel mill town. I felt like I was in a movie. The town was all gray and smoky. The doctor didn't want to do the procedure. It wasn't something they would do in a hospital in those days. He only did it because he knew Stewart. Afterward, he told me it had been a healthy pregnancy, but he didn't tell me anything else.

After I recovered, the doctor decided to teach me about contraceptives. I was so young. About a month later, I went to his office for a checkup. He brought out a box of different sizes of diaphragms. He didn't have time to explain those to me. As he was putting the box on his desk, he dropped it. All the different-sized diaphragms had rolled around his office. I picked them up and handed them to him. It was actually funny.

Through working and saving, things got better financially. Stewart's parents also began to help us financially. They had no idea what we had gone through. Finally, I could afford to stop teaching and start our family. We managed to get a three-bedroom apartment. I had always wanted to be an interior designer, so I was busy decorating and making our new apartment beautiful. We also started going on a lot of ski holidays. We both wanted to ski as much as we could before I got pregnant. About seven years later, we decided it was time to try to have a baby. We tried, and I became pregnant right away.

My pregnancy was easy. I gained thirty pounds at most. Heidi was due on my birthday, December 23. We loved to have Christmas parties, and we would invite our friends over for ham, turkey, eggnog, and Christmas cakes and cookies. I had gone for my pregnancy checkup a few weeks before our Christmas party. The doctor told me to call if I felt anything. I was still doing my water exercises in the pool at the Fitness Institute. On December 15, I woke up and felt very slight Braxton-Hicks contractions. I called the doctor. He told me to go to the hospital right away. I hadn't even packed my suitcase yet. It never occurred to me to be worried or afraid. I wasn't in any pain. I was busy cleaning up after our Christmas party, and I was sure this was just going to be a checkup.

Stewart packed a suitcase for me. I asked him why he hadn't taken one of my new white Samsonite suitcases. Stewart told me, "This suitcase was Grandmother Donaldson's suitcase. She meant a lot to me, and I want her to be here with us when our baby is born." She was the one who had helped raise him and showed him so much love. His parents would leave him with her every summer when they were traveling, and he loved being with her. In the end, I was glad that Grandmother Donaldson was "there." He loved her so much.

On the way to the hospital, it seemed to take forever. I told Stewart, "We can't come this way when I'm really having the baby because it will take too long. You are hitting every red light, and I will probably be in a lot of pain."

By the time we got to the hospital, I was already seven centimeters dilated. My water hadn't broken, so the doctor said, "I'm breaking your water; you're having the baby now."

I said, "You can't. I have my water exercises today."

He ignored me, broke the membrane for the water, and put me in a labor room. Stewart, thinking this would take a long time, went downstairs and got a package of Juicy Fruit gum. I knew the doctor had broken my membrane to release the water, but I still had not had one labor pain. We thought we were in for a long day. Stewart came back to the labor room and gave me a piece of gum. I was connected to an IV, and we just sat and waited.

All of a sudden, I had to go to the washroom, but there were no nurses around. I stood up, walked across the hall, rolling the IV with me, and went to the washroom. The nurse came to give me the epidural and had no idea where I'd gone.

After the epidural, which was done by another doctor, I never felt one contraction. When the nurse came back in to examine me, she said to another nurse, "You'd better get the doctor because I can already see the baby's hair." Heidi was crowning and already coming, and I had no idea.

Later, they told me I could have had her when I went to the washroom. Quickly, they rolled me into delivery, and the birth was so fast that Stewart barely had time to change clothes and get into the delivery room with me. In those days, the father would put on scrubs to be with the mother in the delivery room. Stewart is tall, but he was in such a hurry that he didn't realize there were different sizes of scrubs. He picked out some from the first box he saw. They were the small size. The pants were too tight, and the jacket wouldn't close. The hat sat on top of his head. He came waddling in like a penguin, and I started laughing so hard.

This was 1975, and my doctor looked a bit like Woody Allen with frizzy red hair. There I was, having a baby, with Woody Allen on one end of the table and a penguin on the other. I was in hysterics.

There was a mirror near me so I could see the birth, but I told them I didn't want to watch. I was laughing out loud and had absolutely no pain. The nurses had to hold my stomach, and when they felt it get really hard, they told me to push. I didn't know I was having a contraction. Heidi was born at seven pounds, eleven ounces. The nurses put her right on my breast, and she started nursing immediately. It was such an extremely easy and funny delivery.

Heidi was beautiful and sweet, and I was happy. At that time, Pierre Trudeau was prime minister of Canada, and socialized medicine had just been implemented. There was something new called "rooming in," which meant that Heidi could stay in my hospital room with me all day. At night, the nurses would look after her in the newborn nursery, so I could have a great night's sleep.

At that time, Stewart and I were alone in Toronto. My mother was still teaching in California. Stewart's mother was in the Bahamas, taking care of Stewart's father. There was no way we could afford a nanny. In this Toronto hospital, I was in a private room with rooming in. Every evening, they gave us different menus to order dinner from nearby restaurants. We were in heaven. I didn't want to go home. I was afraid to take care of our precious bundle. I thought I might hurt her if I bathed her. At the hospital, the nice nurses bathed her for me and taught me how to do everything. Finally, they came to us and said we might want to go home, since we had been there for ten days.

When we finally went home, we had a little white rocking cradle for her, where she would sleep when she was so tiny. We'd bring her out to the dinner table and wheel her around the apartment in that cradle. She was such a darling baby. My granddaughters use that cradle now for their dolls and stuffed animals. I also had a little Moses basket, which was lined with blue gingham and white lace. That's where she slept whenever we took her out. When we flew, we would take that Moses basket on the airplane so she could sleep at our feet. The airlines were so accommodating at that time, and Heidi loved it.

Stewart was adorable with her. He would come home from work, lie down on the sofa in his office, and hold her on his chest until she fell asleep. Eventually, we could afford someone to come in about three times a week to help me with Heidi. Her name was Xenia, and I think she was from Iran. She absolutely adored Heidi and was with us for about a year. For Heidi's first birthday, Xenia gave Heidi a silver lavaliere matchstick. She said Heidi would "light up the world" wherever she went.

* * * *

From Stewart

When Heidi was due to be born, it was a matter of our preparing to leave for the hospital. We'd had a Christmas party the night before, which was a Sunday. I had made eggnog for this Christmas party. I spiked it with scotch or rum, which gave it a nice taste. I think that is what caused Dianne to go into labor early. The doctor had examined Dianne the day before, and he told us to come to the hospital if she felt anything. On Monday morning, when Dianne was experiencing those Braxton-Hicks feelings of tightening in her abdomen, we decided to pack a bag to go to the hospital. At the time, I thought Grandmother Donaldson's suitcase was the most precious one of the group. It was a blue-gray knitted material. The inside was a light-blue, silvery-colored fabric with pockets and ties. You could tie your clothes into it. Grandmother Donaldson had had it for years. It still had the odor of her perfume in it. It was a wonderful memory of her for me, and I wanted to take that one with us.

Once we arrived at the hospital, I checked Dianne in. We just sat around in the room for a while. Finally, they took Dianne to the delivery room. Then, they took me into a large closet. The nurse pointed to a chest that held delivery room clothing for the husbands. She never said anything about the sizes. I grabbed the first thing I saw because I was so excited. I put everything on as directed, and I hurried into the delivery room. I had chosen from the size-small box, and I should have had a size large! I could hardly walk, so I waddled into the delivery room.

When Heidi was born, I was caught up in the excitement of the moment. When a baby comes out, she is all covered in the afterbirth. I only thought, *Oh!* At that moment, you wouldn't have thought of her as a beautiful child. Then, as they went through the procedures, it got worse. Her head was misshapen because they had to use forceps to pull her out. Dianne didn't feel the contractions. Now I thought, *Oh this is how it all works.* I was so pleased to be there, just observing the team at work. I had no thoughts or worries. And, Heidi started nursing right away. It was beautiful.

When we first came home, of course there was the thrill of fatherhood, of having something so small to care for. But then, we had to start the process of learning what to do. Heidi didn't come with a manual. Learning how to change diapers and all that was part of our learning experience. The nurses in the hospital had been looking after her so well that it had been nice to be there. I eventually became an expert at changing diapers, bathing Heidi, and all the other Mr. Mom things. If I would lie down and put her on my chest next to my heart, she would just cuddle. I realized that she became calm and would fall asleep on my chest. My heartbeat had a soothing influence on her.

Of course, I had learned to cook when Dianne and I got married. When Heidi was born, Dianne and I traded off each evening on who would cook. In those days, food was never that important. We might just have scrambled eggs and toast for dinner.

At that time in 1975, we were living in a three-bedroom apartment on the thirty-sixth floor of a building called Leeside Towers. It was located over the Don Valley Parkway in Toronto. We would take Heidi outside in her stroller. When she got older, we took her on out on our bicycles. We would ride through the park with Heidi on a seat behind us. She loved that.

* * * *

After Heidi was born, and I saw how beautiful she was, it really bothered me that I'd had an earlier abortion. At that point, I thought the reason for our abortion was wrong—Stewart had told me we couldn't afford a baby at that time. But, Stewart's parents were very wealthy; they would have easily helped. So, that reason did not make sense to me. We were so young that we weren't thinking straight. At the time, we thought we were doing the right thing. We made the decision not to ask them for help. The sad thing was that I wanted to have more children but never got pregnant again. To this day, I can't believe I had an abortion. I started having a lot of guilt and sadness that I lived with for a very long time. Even now, it tugs on my heart.

I started to cry every time I thought about it. I kept it all to myself for many years, never even telling Stewart. I would make myself stop crying before it might have been noticed. Throughout my life, that's what Mother had told me to do. If I was really sad, I was able to stop crying and walk through the door as if nothing had happened; I would turn it all off. I learned to block out all sadness, which must have been how I got through the difficult times growing up. I also learned to concentrate on the positive things instead.

Years later, I was listening to a woman speaker on a tape, who shared what she did when she felt sad. She would put on her oldest bathrobe, go into her bedroom, close the door, and start crying. She said she cried and cried until she got it all out. She even slumped to the floor and cried some more. She stayed in the bedroom until she was ready to open her eyes and say, "I'm going to stand up." Then, she would get up, take off her old bathrobe, and get on with her life. I can't remember ever crying like that, but I think people should let it all out. I believe holding in emotions can make you very sick. Emotional hurt leads to physical hurt. And once you cry as much as you need to, there comes a point where there are no more tears. At that point, you can stand up, like Scarlett O'Hara, and say, "Tomorrow is another day."

Looking back, I can see how Stewart's parents were trying to use good judgment by not helping us financially; we probably wouldn't have appreciated it enough. They had a lot of wealthy friends in Lyford Cay who had out-of-control children. Many of those kids had incredible trust funds, didn't have to work, and got involved in drugs and other bad things. In the long run, not having the financial help gave us great appreciation for everything we were able to acquire.

Everybody has challenges. Sometimes, I think maybe I've had other lives that were even more difficult than this one. And maybe those challenges helped me handle the ones I was given this time around. Love is the answer and the antidote, and forgiveness is the answer too. As Wayne Dyer says, "I recommend being gentle with yourself and loving yourself unconditionally, regardless of what comes your way." Forgive everyone, including yourself.

Chapter 9

A NEW LANDSCAPE

You will enrich your life immeasurably, if you
approach it with a sense of wonder and discovery,
and always challenge yourself to try new things.

—NATE BERKUS

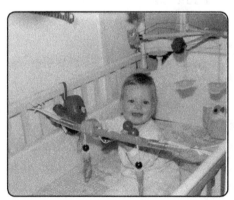

Heidi, as a baby

My early years with Heidi
were such fun and very happy. I
was enthralled with her. We had
Looney, and I wasn't working.
We had worked and saved for
seven years after we were married
so things would be better for
us financially. Stewart wanted
to feel we could afford a baby
so we could enjoy her without
worrying about money.

Stewart's parents began helping us financially. I was able stop
teaching about three years before Heidi was born. Stewart was working,
and his parents gave us a Christmas check every year that was ten
thousand dollars. We would live on it if we had to. Most of the time,
we would put it away and save it.

In 1972, before Heidi was born, Stewart's mom took me on my first visit to Paris and London. I hadn't been able to travel to Europe before that time. As I mentioned, my father was so involved in the Cold War situation that we weren't allowed to travel to Europe. Now that I was married, however, I could travel there with my new family. My mother-in-law and I had a wonderful time.

Before that trip, I was always designing rooms on paper. I had taken a lot of art classes in university. I really enjoyed the process of decorating our new apartment. In my heart, I always wanted to be an interior designer, but I didn't know it then. In those early years, I was busy taking care of Heidi, buying furniture, and trying to make everything in our life beautiful.

Our life with Heidi was easygoing and fun. Both of us were crazy about her. I had time for myself, since we had a nanny come to help us three or four times a week. We took pictures of every little thing Heidi did. I didn't have to worry about working anymore, so we could concentrate on Heidi.

At first, we were worried about Looney because he had a habit of scratching new people if they touched him. Somehow, though, he knew that Heidi was our baby and part of our new family. He never got into her cradle or crib. In fact, he would sleep under her cradle and seemed to want to protect her. He was very sweet with her. He knew she was our little angel from God.

When we traveled, we took Heidi along with us, and she slept peacefully in her basket at our feet. As she grew, we continued traveling because she was such an easy baby. We took her to Lyford Cay every Christmas to visit Stewart's family and to California in the summer to visit my family. At Lyford Cay, my mother-in-law's maid, Mirthlene, helped take care of Heidi.

Mirthlene had started to work for my mother-in-law when she was only thirteen. She had lied when she applied for the job and said she was sixteen. She was just a little girl too. Mirthlene loved Heidi, and they played together. She was supposed to put Heidi to sleep at a certain time, but when we'd come home from our night out, they would both be wide awake and giggling. Mirthlene spent her entire life taking care of my mother-in-law. Many years later, when Heidi had her first child, Hailey, Mirthlene babysat for us on New Year's Eve. Mirthlene and Hailey were still up giggling and laughing when we got home. It was wonderful to have Mirthlene still in our lives.

When Heidi's second baby, Ashley, was born, Mirthlene took care of both Ashley and Hailey for New Year's Eve. We were always amazed to come home to all the happiness and excitement, even after midnight. We thought the girls would be sleeping by then; we were so wrong! They loved Mirthlene, and she loved them. New Year's Eve became a celebration for all of them. They all had such a good time, watching the fireworks and Junkanoo, which is a street parade of costumed drummers dancing and singing around the island. They were always excited to tell us about the fireworks they saw and the music they heard.

* * * *

Overall, Heidi's growing-up years were very happy and fulfilling times for us. When Heidi was in elementary school, we left Toronto and moved to Chicago. Atlee, Stewart's college roommate and my Big Brother in ATO fraternity, was living there. You might remember that Atlee had told Stewart that I was the girl that Stewart was going to marry, which neither Stewart nor I knew at that moment. But, Atlee had a feeling about us.

Atlee had since married Nicole. When Atlee was drafted into the navy, he somehow met the admiral's daughter, Nicole. They fell madly in love and later were married.

Atlee and Nicole had purchased a beautiful condo on Lake Shore Drive in Chicago. We went there on a visit, and that is when Atlee asked Stewart to join the investment company he had started. That's how the investment firm of Kohl, Lane, Siebens began. John Lane, another great friend of ours from the University of Miami, and Stewart went into business with Atlee. It became a wonderful time with these fabulous friends from the University of Miami.

When we first moved to Chicago, we rented a home. After a while, we bought our very first house. I had so much fun fixing up that house and got seriously involved in decorating. Years later, when we moved to Dallas, Kohl, Lane, Siebens bought a decorating company. I enjoyed that very much. It was exciting to see all the new things that were available to us at the Dallas Mart.

We were doing well in Chicago, but decided we wanted to move to a nicer climate. Atlee, Nicole, Stewart, and I took a trip to San Diego. We thought we would love to live in La Jolla right on the ocean. But the lots sold for at least a million dollars each, even back then. The homes would be expensive. Another consideration for their investment company was the time difference for their work. Atlee and Stewart were doing a lot of work with the London Stock Exchange. There was a three-hour time difference between the East and West Coasts. Living on the West Coast would mean that Atlee and Stewart would have to get up awfully early for work. So, we all decided to look for property in Dallas, Texas, which was in the middle of the US. The property there was a lot less expensive. We could spend a million dollars and have a beautiful home. In La Jolla, that same money would only buy a lot.

Kohl, Lane, Siebens moved to Texas. Our new homes would be in a suburb of Dallas. We were such good friends that Atlee and Stewart decided to build our custom homes next door to each other. Our homes were designed by the same architect to be built on two adjoining lots. It was complicated, but they made it work. We loved our houses. We had a private walkway, where we just had to open the fence to walk back and forth between our homes. Heidi went through junior high and high school in Texas. When it came time for her to go to university, she chose Baylor University in Waco, Texas. All three of Atlee and Nicole's children also went to Baylor.

It was during those Dallas years that I began to join Stewart on his helicopter-skiing trips. He had discovered helicopter skiing, or heli-skiing, with some of his male friends and had heard about the attraction and fun of this extreme sport. Helicopters could take skiers to remote mountain locations where the terrain and snow conditions were perfect. He discovered untouched powder snow. All that made traditional ski resorts much less appealing.

At first, when Stewart wanted me to go, I refused. "You and all your brain-damaged friends can do that!" I told him. "I will never go heli-skiing!" I thought you had to be out of your mind to ski in such steep, untouched, wilderness terrain.

But, my attitude began to soften after he came home from his trip and told me he had skied with Nancy Green, the Canadian Olympic gold medalist in the women's downhill. He showed me photos of beautiful blue skies and perfect powder with no moguls. He said, "Dianne, look—you can do this." Then, he showed me pictures of crazy costume parties at the lodge. It looked like so much fun. I finally agreed to go but only if we brought Rob, my ski instructor from Aspen, with us; he would help me ski in that terrain. Stewart agreed to bring Rob along on my first trip.

We flew to Calgary and spent the night in the hotel at the airport. The next morning, we boarded a bus for a five-hour drive through the beautiful Canadian Rockies. We drove through Banff and Lake Louise, admiring the beautiful snowy scenery. During that trip, we met other people on our bus who would also be skiing with us all week. One lady was a countess. Another single lady on the bus had met a handsome young man, who was going to be Rob's roommate at the lodge.

We got to the landing area where we would meet the helicopter and waited for it. The helicopter came down, blowing snow all over us. The helicopter pilot, Captain Mac got out of the helicopter in shocking-pink bicycle shorts and a T-shirt, wearing a hangman's noose around his neck! He was a hysterical character who always had a trick up his sleeve. He asked me if I wanted to sit next to him in the front seat of the helicopter. I said yes and got in next to him. He put the headphones with the speaker attachment on my head so we could talk. He lifted the helicopter off the landing pad, and away we went. He flew us to the edge of the mountain, and then let the helicopter drop quickly over the edge. I screamed so loudly into my speaker attachment that I'm sure it hurt his eardrums.

The first night, we enjoyed being in the lodge for dinner. We discovered we were supposed to sign up in groups for skiing the next day. There would be four groups. Rob, our ski instructor looked around the room. Based on the ages of everyone else, he said, "Dianne, you can out-ski anyone in this room." He signed me up in the top group, not knowing we were sitting there with the former Norwegian gold medal ski team! And, I was now in this top group!

Stewart and I went to bed early to get ready for the big day. We had unpacked and were just getting into our bed when we heard screaming and then tremendous laughing. We went out into the hall to see what had happened. Rob told us that Captain Mac had come into the bar area, where Rob and the countess were talking. Captain Mac asked if anyone wanted to see the perfect body. He then stood up quickly, lifted up his shirt, and pulled down his pants! Everyone was in hysterics. Stewart and I missed that show.

My first time helicopter skiing in this top group was with Ernst, the head guide from Austria. He was also the head manager of the lodge. I was petrified in the helicopter from the views of the top of the world and nothing but the tops of the mountains. Stewart kept telling me to look out the window because he thought it was so beautiful. But from my side, the mountain dropped off into a total cliff. I said to him, "Don't you dare make me look out the window! I am so scared."

The helicopter landed on the top of this mountain, and everyone got out. We waited until the helicopter lifted off before we put our skis on. Ernst and the Norwegian group were so excited to ski that they quickly skied right off the top. I watched as the tops of their ski hats disappeared over the ledge right in front of me. I couldn't move!

The wind was howling all around us. I looked at Rob and said, "I can't do this." He was trying to get me to bend my knees, but I was scared stiff and couldn't do it. On my first turns away from the landing pad, I was leaning backward so much that I fell. I tried to grab a huge chunk of ice as I went down. Instead, I ended up ripping the ligaments in my thumb. It was painful, but somehow, I managed to ski down that first run to meet the group at the helicopter pickup. I got back into the helicopter and asked them to take me back to the lodge. I told the crew I never wanted to helicopter ski again.

When I got back to the lodge, I was so upset that I grabbed a huge chocolate bar and went to our room. I locked Stewart out and told myself, "I'm never skiing again." Then, I ate the whole chocolate bar and sat alone in my room for the afternoon.

Stewart convinced me to go back out. He said we could duct tape my thumb and hand so I could ski again. But, this time I would go out with the intro group, which was for first-time helicopter skiers. The first day, when I hurt my thumb, a father in the intro group had a terrible accident, trying to keep up with his son. His arm went through the crust of the snow. It was a compound fracture, and the bone was exposed. He had to be airlifted to the hospital. If I had seen that in the intro group, I'm not sure I would have tried to go out again. But, I was lucky I just had a broken thumb. I started out petrified, but by the end of

the trip, I had grown to love all of the exciting experiences. It was so much fun, and we met fascinating people from all over the world.

When we returned to Dallas, I went to the doctor. I ended up in a big cast, with my arm in a sling. The doctor couldn't believe I'd skied all week with a broken thumb. I told him duct tape was great!

We brought Rob again the second time we took a heli-ski trip together. I walked into the lodge holding on Rob's and Stewart's arms. A lady came up to me and asked, "Which one is your husband?"

I pointed to Stew and said, "This is my husband." Then I pointed to Rob and said, "This is my holiday husband!"

Stewart and I in our million foot suits. Every million vertical feet you ski with Canadian Mountain Holidays, you are presented with a special colored blue and yellow ski suit. The suits have to be earned and can not be bought.

We all laughed so much. I began to like going. Stewart loved it, and it made him happy that I was there too. It was always an exciting and exhilarating trip. We started going heli-skiing several times a year.

There was another incident during one of our later heli-skiing trips with CMH when I am sure my guardian angel was holding me. The weather was nice, but the guides had decided that it would be safer and that we would have better conditions if we skied in the trees. The directions they gave us were these: "Don't look at the trees, only look at the spaces between the trees. If you look at the tree, you will ski right into it! And, you will need to pair up with a partner. If one of you falls into a tree well, the other one will be able to dig you out."

The tree runs are usually steep, but having deep-powder snow slows you down a little. I was a bit nervous after those instructions. Our guide took off first and made nice turns between trees that were close together. I jumped immediately into his tracks to follow his line through the trees—but it was like being on a luge run. I was skiing faster and faster down the slope between those trees. Since I was in his tracks, I didn't have the powder snow to slow me down. Stewart was behind me and finally said, "Stop! You are going too fast."

He stopped me and told me to come over to the left of where our guide had skied. There, the trees were spread apart more, and we were able to make wider turns through these trees. We enjoyed ourselves skiing there. I thought *Why did the guide take our group down that side of the run when the trees are easier to ski on the left side?* Then, I saw Stewart had completely stopped in front of me. He was looking ahead down the mountain. When I skied up next to him, I saw why he had stopped.

He was standing on a cliff, looking down at the trees below us! I stopped right next to him, now realizing why the guide had gone the other way. We could hear the helicopter below us, but we couldn't see it. I started to panic because there was no way the helicopter could land to rescue us. There were too many trees around us. And, it would be impossible to go back up the steep slopes because this was now at the end of a tree run.

The next thing Stewart said to me was, "See that pine tree right below us? Jump on top of it, and ski down the branches. There is a lot of snow on the branches, and then you can ski to the right and follow the rest of the group's tracks to the helicopter."

I thought he was crazy! He could tell that I was panicking. I was at the edge of the cliff, looking at that pine tree, when he put his hand on my back and pushed me off that ledge! I landed right on top of the pine tree, tucked into a racing position, and skied down the branches. Snow and pine needles were flying in my face, but I somehow managed to land on the snow without falling. I was furious that Stewart pushed me! I skied fast to get away from him and ended up following the group's tracks all the way to the helicopter.

When I got there, they didn't have any idea what had just happened. But when they asked where Stewart was, I realized I'd left him on top of that cliff, and all he had to land on was a de-snowed and de-needled pine tree. It took a long time for him to get to us, and I was relieved to finally see him ski to the helicopter. It turned out that he'd fallen, and his skis had come off. He had to dig them out of the tree well and then get them on again. There was not enough snow left on that pine tree for him.

Stewart was my guardian angel that day and saved my life. If he hadn't pushed me off that ledge, I would still be there, frozen, today. Thank goodness he had no fear and had such faith that I would be able to ski down that tree!

Ladybugs remind us to let go of our fears and get back in touch with the joys of living. If I had allowed fear to rule my life, I would have missed the most transformative experience of my entire existence.

Chapter 10

TRANSITIONS

Light precedes every transition. Whether at the end of
a tunnel, through a crack in the door, or the flash of
an idea, it is always there, heralding a new beginning.

—TERESA TSALAKY

Life is filled with change, and all of us face challenges over time. My father had gall bladder cancer, which had gone undiagnosed for quite some time. He always complained of stomachaches, but the doctors thought it was an ulcer and were treating him for that. By the time he was diagnosed, the cancer had spread to his liver, and eventually, it spread throughout his body.

During the 1982 Summer Olympics, I flew from Dallas to California to be with my mother. At that point, my father was not doing well; he couldn't even eat. My mother needed to take care of him twenty-four hours a day, and I went to help her and to say goodbye to my father.

He looked like a skeleton, but when I walked in the door at the start of my visit, he was feeling so good that he winked at me. I thought this must be a false alarm and that my father wasn't really going to die. Not long after that, however, he stopped eating.

We called in hospice to help us with his passing. He was on morphine then. We dripped water into his mouth, as that was the only thing he could swallow. I was in his room right before he passed. You might think he would have said, "You are the best daughter ever, and I love you so much." Instead, my father winked at me and said, "Now I'm going to see who really built the Great Pyramid, and where those gentlemen from outer space are from." And, off he went. Those were his last words to me, and they were profound. My father had top-level security clearance, but he never spoke a word about what he knew until the moment he died.

He had said, however, that no other major advanced civilization like Egypt ever appeared again in that region. He also said that when you look at Earth from outer space, the center of the globe appears to be Egypt. He had read a book about the Great Pyramid and how it predicted so many major things that have happened in the world, like the birth of Christ and World War II. I'm sure that's what he was thinking he'd learn when he died. He still had a mission—he wanted to know *who* designed the pyramids.

I can still picture him sitting at his big desk, studying a strange piece of metal he held in his hand. He had many things on his desk he could be proud of, including a picture of him with President Reagan; a formal letter from Reagan, thanking him for his work and his contribution to America; and other awards he had received as a result of his work. But it was that little piece of metal that fascinated him. I was always curious about that piece of metal too. When I would go into his office, he would take it off the shelf of his bookcase to show it to me. He would place it in my hand and ask me, "What do you think of this?"

I would look at it and say, "Wow, it's really light. It feels weightless." When I pulled it open, it looked like a honeycomb.

He wouldn't say anything. He just wanted to see what I thought of it.

As I've mentioned, my father was one of the designers of the radar-proof covering of the Stealth Bomber, and that covering seemed to be made just like that little piece of metal in my hand. The metal was termed low-observable technology, to make the Stealth Bomber less visible to radar, infrared, sonar, and other detection methods.

Could that piece of metal be a piece of a UFO that my father had studied at Wright-Patterson Air Force Base? The scientists could have duplicated the way the metal was made, using reverse technology. That is what made the Stealth Bomber radar-proof. Remember, my father was the deputy base commander of Wright-Patterson Air Force Base, and he had the highest security clearance. Everything he knew was top secret. Plus, he was an aeronautical engineer and a nuclear physicist who had designed nuclear-powered aircraft and had worked with Albert Einstein in Oak Ridge, Tennessee.

After my dad died, my mom had a dream in which he was giving her an angry look. In her dream, he was unhappy that she was giving away his things, especially his flight helmet with the oxygen mask and his WWII leather jacket, which she had given to me. When I asked her, however, where his special piece of metal was, she had no idea. I thought it was lost forever.

Years later, when my mother died, I found a box with all the things from my father's desk. There it was, tucked away in that cardboard box. I believe solidly in UFOs because not only do I have a piece of one, but my father's last words about the "gentlemen" from outer space gave me an inside perspective. Years later, I found out much more about my father's work by researching him on Google. A lot of things he had worked on had finally been declassified.

* * * *

Stewart and I went on with our lives. I heli-skied all through my late thirties and forties and had a wonderful time. We were thinking about having more children, and we hoped this would happen. At age forty-two, all of a sudden, I started hemorrhaging. There was no pain with this. I just couldn't stop bleeding. I went to the doctor, who told me I had clusters of ovarian cysts. One of them was the size of a grapefruit. We were set to leave on a helicopter ski trip three days after this news from the doctor.

Our helicopter pilot for that week of skiing was Captain Mac again. He was still known for being hysterically funny. One of the things

Captain Mac thought it was funny was to hover the helicopter over the women when we were trying to use the "ladies room." Remember, we were out in the wilderness, skiing all day long, and the women tried to find a private area. The men would ski down the slope ahead of us to wait for us, but Captain Mac loved to find where we were, hover over us in the helicopter, and whip the snow all around us. We eventually skied to the trees, where we could hide from him. This added to the excitement of the heli-ski week!

When the trip ended, I was a bit anxious about what to do about those cysts. My doctor suggested surgery, so I decided to have the cysts removed. I was scheduled for my surgery just two weeks after we came home. I wasn't worried; Stewart was there with me. A few very good friends and our minister came to keep him company during the surgery. Our minister had asked the entire congregation to pray for me.

On the morning of the surgery, I wasn't able to have any tranquilizers. The hospital staff had forgotten to give me the consent forms to sign for the upcoming surgery. They brought me into the pre-surgical area, where I saw other tranquilized patients asleep and ready for their surgeries. I was sitting up and wide-awake. Stewart was there with me.

My doctor came in with a doctor we had never met. He had me sign the consent forms. Out of the blue, he said, "I think you have ovarian cancer. We're going to have to do a total hysterectomy and remove your ovaries too. I'd like you to meet our oncologist."

I was in the pre-surgery room, with all the other unconscious patients on stretchers, and I was told I had cancer and was meeting the oncologist for the first time. I went into shock. Stewart patted my hand and said, "It's going to be okay." Then, my mind went to Gilda Radner and what she'd been through. She had only lived ten years after her diagnosis of ovarian cancer. I thought *There will be new treatments each year. I hope I will be able to live another ten years as well. In ten years, Heidi will be twenty-one, and I will have had all that time to spend with her.*

As they wheeled me into surgery, I asked the minister to ask the church congregation to pray for me again. From my stretcher, I glanced out the window and saw two beautiful white seagulls—in downtown Dallas. It was not what I expected to see when looking out the window. I'll never know where they came from, but in that moment, I felt that everything was going to be fine. The last thing I saw before they put me to sleep was a beautiful cross with Jesus over the door of the operating room. The doctors told me to count backward, and after that, I don't remember a thing.

Post-surgery, I had my first hot flash. As our minister was telling me that the entire congregation had prayed for me, I suddenly felt like somebody had dropped a bucket of water on my head, and I became extremely hot. I threw the covers back and pulled my sweater off. The minister's eyes nearly popped out of his head. He didn't know which way to look. He had no clue what was going on, and neither did I. Then, my doctor came in, and he prescribed Premarin for me. He called it a "magic pumpkin pill" that would help eliminate hot flashes.

I stayed in the hospital about five days and had a follow-up scheduled a few days after that. During that time, I never thought about dying because there was no time for fear. I thought that I would live until Heidi was twenty-one, so I had to focus on the years I would have with her. When we got to the doctor's for the follow-up appointment, I walked past his office on the way to the waiting room and saw him with his head down on his desk.

When we went in to see him, he told me I didn't have cancer. In other words, I had had a full hysterectomy for no reason. They were just cysts. But, I could never have any more children. However, he did tell me something very interesting: I only had one ovary. Having Heidi was a miracle.

He was a very caring doctor, and I was thrilled not to have cancer. Stewart and I felt so blessed to have Heidi. Shortly after that, however, thinking about the abortion bothered me even more, but I kept that to myself. I felt a tremendous sadness and guilt that would stay with me for a long time.

The deeper that sorrow carves into your being, the more joy you can contain.

—Kahlil Gibran

Chapter 11

JUST SAY YES

Open your eyes to life: to see it in the vivid
colors that God gave us as a precious gift to
His children, to enjoy life to the fullest, and
to make it count. Say yes to your life.

—NANCY REAGAN

I've always had a philosophy that I call Just Say Yes. Life is so
busy, and we get so caught up in little things that we forget there's a
wonderful world out there. I realized much later that there is always a
choice between getting caught up or getting out in the world. You can
return home from a trip and spend an entire week inside your house,
going through emails and mail and dealing with your home and the
repairs, cleaning out drawers, etc. There are always so many little things
to do. But if you just walk outside, you could meet somebody who will
brighten your life.

This is my Just Say Yes story:

Dea, my best girlfriend from high school, is a beautiful blonde. In
high school, she dated a very nice college man. They eventually married,
and he became a dentist. I thought her life had turned out lovely. When
I went to my twenty-fifth high school reunion and met her again, I
found out differently. Her husband had been in Vietnam. When he

returned home, he had many problems, including that he never wanted to be away from home for very long. That meant that Dea had never traveled overseas.

I invited Dea and her daughter, Lisse, to go to Mexico with Heidi and me. They accepted and came to Dallas first. At the Dallas airport check-in on our way to Mexico, the agent told us we could not get on the plane—we needed an affidavit from our husbands, stating that we had their permission to take our daughters to Mexico; our daughters were both under eighteen.

I went home and explained the situation to Stewart. As usual, I asked him to do something, and he helped us find a way. We took the girls to Mexico the very next day and had a ball. We stayed in my brother-in-law, Bill's, beautiful condo in Manzanillo and were so excited to be there. We put all of our clothes and jewelry in one bedroom—whoever could fit into whatever they chose could wear it. Sometimes I was in Heidi's, Lisse's, or Dea's clothes. Sometimes they were in mine. We had fun in these fabulous outfits. It seemed as if we four were the only blondes in this lovely Mexican resort during the hottest part of the summer. During the day, we enjoyed iced watermelon drinks. At night, we went to a disco in the condo complex, where we danced.

At this time in their lives, Heidi looked like a model, and Lisse looked like Bo Derek. One day, Lisse wanted to go on a banana-boat ride. The boat would pull a float in the shape of a banana, and the captain would maneuver the boat trying to make us fall off of the float. We were very athletic and had good balance. There we were, four blondes bobbing around in the ocean, laughing a lot, but we never fell off that banana float once. We really did have great balance. Plus, Lisse was terrified of falling because she had watched the movie *Ten* with Bo Derek. We were in the same location where the movie had been filmed. Lisse thought the water might be filled with sharks, just as it was in the movie.

When our ride was finished, a young man in a small boat followed us to shore. He invited us onto his boat for a tour of the bay. Without thinking, I just said yes. Dea was concerned that he might take us out on the ocean, kill us, and drop our bodies into the water.

He called himself Nacho, but his full name was Ignatius. He took us on his small boat to his yacht, where we met his young friends. It ended up being the most fabulous day because of the young people who were so friendly to us.

Afterward, Dea asked how I had known it would be safe and so wonderful. I said, "I never thought he'd do anything bad. That kind of thinking was never in my mind."

I just saw a nice young man offering us a ride, and somehow, I knew it would be fine. I think I was born with faith in the goodness of people. Coming into this world as a blue baby, being saved, and growing up learning to focus on the positive things in life might have something to do with it.

The next day another handsome young Mexican walked over to Dea and me while we were walking though the hotel. He was wearing a starched pale-blue shirt with a button-down collar. He politely introduced himself and asked if we were going to the disco that night. When we told him we were, he asked, "May I have a dance with your daughters?"

Dea and I looked at each other, and I said, "Yes, they would love it."

That night, we got ready to go dancing. We walked into the disco and sat down. Right away, a fifteen-year-old boy came over to our table. Heidi, also fifteen, sat up straight because she thought he was going to ask her to dance.

But he came right up to me and asked, "Would you like to dance?"

When I said yes, Heidi said, "Mom!"

I danced with him, and she was so surprised.

A few minutes later, the handsome young man we had met earlier walked in with a group of his friends. We waved at him. He came over and asked Lisse to dance. While they were dancing, she asked him where he lived. He said, "In a palace." Then, since she was a teenager, she asked him what kind of car he had. He said he had six cars.

"Yeah, right!" she answered. She thought he was leading her on or at least teasing her with his answers.

One of his friends asked Heidi to dance, but Heidi couldn't talk to him because he didn't speak English, and she didn't speak Spanish.

We found out later that he was a famous matador from Spain. He was very good looking too.

Both Lisse and Heidi were asked if they would like to go out the next evening. Lisse asked Heidi if she wanted to go. Heidi said, "No, mine doesn't speak English."

It turned out the boys were not Mexican. Lizzie's dance partner was the son of Juan Carlos, the king of Spain. The prince eventually married a blonde Texan who looked a lot like Lisse.

You just never know. I've learned to follow my instincts and just say yes. Otherwise, you might miss the most extraordinary experience you would ever have.

* * * *

My Just Say Yes philosophy became especially important again in 1995, when my other dear friend, Danielle Smith, who was also called Dee, asked me to join her on a research trip, because she was planning to write her book, "A Cry of Silence" which was set in Alaska and referred to the seagulls' cries. I didn't think twice. I said yes. Dee was dying of a brain tumor, and I wanted to help her any way I could. Our trip to Alaska ended up being one of the most incredible experiences of my life.

We went to Barrow, Alaska, which is the northernmost human settlement on the North American continent. We stayed for several days at the Top of the World Hotel, which is the only hotel in Barrow. We toured Barrow and discovered many things she would be able to write about in her novel. We discovered that when polar bears were spotted, the entire workforce had permission to leave their jobs to go polar bear hunting. It was so interesting to see all the empty office buildings whenever a polar bear was sighted. The men just walked out of their offices. It was a part of their Inupiat culture.

Another fascinating fact is that the Inupiats use their backyards as refrigerators. There is only ice under the tundra. They are able to dig out a pit and put their perishable food items in the pit, just as we use our refrigerators. We looked in these pits and saw frozen game birds hanging on the sides of the pit. Meat also could also be stored on a plank in front of their homes. It was cold enough to keep the meat from perishing, and they didn't have to worry about flies or any other bugs. There were no bugs because there were no trees or grass, just tundra. The dogs were always tied up, so they weren't able to get the neighbors' food that was stored in this way. The meat stored in these natural "refrigerators" stayed just as cold as if they had refrigerators and freezers.

There is no way to dispose of human waste, so the waste from their toilets is piped above the frozen ground into a ravine, which they call Honey Pot Lake. We decided that we didn't have to visit it, though.

Meals were challenging on that trip because Dee was vegetarian, and there weren't many vegetables available. Once, we ordered a vegetarian pizza, which should only have been about six dollars at the time. In Barrow, it was forty-four dollars. Vegetables were expensive.

Another funny fact is that Barrow is a dry city—no alcohol can be sold to tourists. We couldn't even order a glass of wine. Strangely enough, we noticed a lot of men who seemed to have had too much to drink. We found out that the government subsidized the residents because of all the oil on their land. They were all wealthy enough to have their alcohol flown in. They could drink as much as they liked of their flown-in alcohol of choice, but a tourist couldn't buy a glass of wine.

It was on that trip with Dee that I discovered reflexology for the first time. The reflexology practitioner was from China and had won a one-way ticket from China to Barrow, Alaska. He was excited to go to Alaska when he won, but unfortunately, he couldn't afford to fly back.

One day while Dee was resting, I decided to take a walk through downtown Barrow. While I was walking, I saw a sign that read "Reflexology." The reflexologist's office was in an old barbershop with the old-fashioned style of barber chairs. He put a blanket on the floor next to one of those chairs and asked me to lie down. He said that everyone needed this treatment, and he kept repeating, "No pain, no gain!"

Sometimes, it really was extremely painful, but it was miraculous. I went back to our hotel and talked Dee into trying it, which she did. She felt it certainly helped her too. This is another example of how the Just Say Yes philosophy works.

On the last day of our stay, we were fogged in and had to spend one more night in Barrow. We were still at the Top of the World Hotel. The room was not very comfortable, and the blankets felt like orange fiberglass. The next morning after not sleeping well, we decided to go to breakfast at a Quonset hut called Pepe's North of the Border. The owner had beautiful Spanish landscape scenes painted on the inside walls. It felt like a Spanish restaurant. The owner's name was Fran Tate, who was originally from California.

To this day, she sends me a yearly Christmas card. Once for Christmas, she sent me a temperature gauge that measures the outdoor temperature to eighty below zero. I still have this gauge in Cayman.

During the entire trip, Dee was extremely weak and sometimes needed to lean on me to walk. Still, she was taking notes the entire time, gathering information for what would be her last novel. She was full steam ahead and involved in writing that book. I don't really know if she realized she was dying. She may have thought she was beating the disease with her natural remedies. She tried to stay positive as she was fighting the brain tumor. She never gave up fighting and doing everything she believed she was put here to do.

I am so glad I said yes to Dee when she invited me on that trip. She only lived until December 1999. It was at Dee's funeral that her husband, Wilbur, encouraged me to write by giving me the beautiful pen he had meant to give her as soon as her book was published. My Just Say Yes philosophy is the reason you are holding this book.

If somebody offers you an amazing opportunity, but you are not sure that you can do it, just say yes. You can learn how to do it later.

Chapter 12

OUR GERMAN BROTHERHOOD

I cannot even imagine where I would be
today were it not for that handful of friends
who have given me a heart full of joy. Let's
face it; friends make life a lot more fun.

—CHARLES R. SWINDOLL

In 1997, Stewart and I went skiing in Austria with our close German friends, whom we had met on our heli-skiing trips. Horst, Rosie, Willie, Wolfgang, and Ingeborg had all shared the experience of the avalanche with us. They were the ones who helped dig me out of the avalanche and celebrated the first day of my "new" life. After that experience together, we became very close friends. They wanted to introduce us to a magnificent hotel in the Arlberg in St. Christoph, Austria, called the Hospiz. It was originally built in 1386 to provide refuge for mountain wanderers during inclement weather. Later, its owners founded the world's oldest charitable association, the Brotherhood of St. Christoph, or the Bruderschaft St. Christoph. The modern-day owners of this hotel are the Werner family. Their fine chefs, their hospitality, and their generosity are still famous today. King Juan Carlos of Spain is one of their good friends; he loves to ski and stays there quite often. He loves the owners and the snow-covered slopes of the Arlberg. Coincidentally, King Juan Carlos happened to be there the same week as we were, and he happily participated in all the fun evening activities that Adie Werner planned for the guests.

We had enjoyed a beautiful day skiing and were drinking champagne at one of the hotel's outside venues. Stewart looked at his watch and said, "Dianne, it's 5:20 p.m. Do you have a massage at 5:30?"

I had completely forgotten about the time. I skied quickly down to the hotel, where they had a ski valet. I was in such a hurry that I just handed my skis, poles, and ski boots to the valet and started running. I didn't even have time to put my shoes on. The Hospiz has had many additions and passageways added to it in its six-hundred-year history, so it is a very large hotel now. There were so many hallways that I didn't know which way to go as I ran through the passageways in my socks. I was all by myself, with no one to interpret the signs posted on the walls. I had no idea where the massage room was. I kept thinking with every turn, *It must be down this hall.*

I came to a hallway of rooms with a large, beautifully lit room at the end of that hall. I thought I had found the right place. Two men were standing outside their rooms, talking to each other in the corridor. I ran down that hall, passing by the two men. They watched me run down the corridor to that large room. Little did I know that I had run right into Juan Carlos's room—yes, the king of Spain!

I stared right at him and asked, "Is this the massage room?"

He smiled at me and told me it wasn't. At that point, the two men who were in the hall came into the room. It turned out that they were his bodyguards. They had let me run into the king's room; I guess I must have seemed lost. They were all smiling at that point, not saying a word. I can't imagine what they were thinking. I was totally embarrassed; my face must have been bright pink. I was standing in the king's room in my socks and ski suit.

I said, "Please excuse me. I was looking for the massage room, and I don't know where it is."

They smiled and directed me to a tiny door in the wall and opened it. It turned out to be the king's private elevator that led to his personal entrance to the men's shower area and pool. I ducked into that tiny elevator. When the elevator stopped, and the door opened, all I could see were nude men taking showers in front of me. In Germany, nudity is a lot more prevalent than it is in our part of the world. Walking around the bathhouse in the nude is common, but I wasn't used to that. I was so surprised that I said to them, "What are you *doing* here?" They all turned around and looked at me, which made everything much worse. I said, "Oh, my goodness, excuse me. I'm looking for the massage area, and I don't know where it is." I was terribly embarrassed. I know my face was as red as my ski suit.

They pointed in the direction to the massage room. I walked there as fast as I could. As fate would have it, I had been assigned a male therapist. He was annoyed that I was so late. He said, "You're late. Take off your ski suit and get on the table, facedown," as if I would get undressed in front of him.

I put my hands on my hips, looked at him, and said, "I have had just about enough of this! Would you please get out while I get undressed and get under the sheets?" I don't even remember that massage because I was so mortified by the situation leading up to it. I think I was still reeling from walking into the king's room in the first place.

* * * *

Adi Werner organized many celebration weeks throughout the year. On one of those weeks, the whole staff learned, practiced, and then performed *Amadeus* for the guests. They were all so talented and had beautiful voices. The production was amazing.

Adi asked us to wear themed costumes and to dress like Mozart. I wore a white Mozart wig that looked like Dolly Parton's hair, with a great big, black bow. We had white lace jabots and white lace cuffs for our shirts. Stewart also wore a white Mozart wig, with a smaller black bow. It was so much fun, just getting ready for dinner. We had a lot of laughs with our wigs. The waiters and waitresses performed the entire show beautifully. They had fabulous voices, and it was a wonderful evening.

During the week that we were there with King Juan Carlos, Adi organized a toga party. On our beds were fresh new sheets that we could use for our togas, along with some golden ropes to tie around our waists. Our German friends had brought birch wreaths, which we wore on our heads. We looked like Roman citizens in our togas, with the wreaths of leaves on our heads. Adi pronounced himself the emperor. None of us, including the king of Spain, could ever stand if he wasn't standing. And if Adi sat down, we all had to sit down. If Adi lay down on the floor, lounging and eating grapes, we all had to lie down on the floor and eat grapes. It was so much fun. We laughed and enjoyed ourselves very much that evening.

Also that week, Adi planned to hold an induction ceremony for the *Bruderschaft*. We didn't know what to expect, but Stewart and I were among those to receive the honor of being inducted. Because of the language barrier, we had no idea what it was, but we knew that our German friends were excited for us. We were excited about this event too. Finally, it was time for the Bruderschaft induction. We dressed in the best clothes we had with us. Everyone looked handsome and lovely.

That evening, we entered the six-hundred-year-old chapel. Outside the doorway was a nine-hundred-year-old statue of John the Baptist, with the baby Jesus on his shoulder. In front of the door, in a beautiful case, was the ceremonial sword, the Sword of Munich. We all walked in together and sat down behind the prince and princess of Luxembourg, not knowing who they were. Juan Carlos, the king of Spain, was sitting close by as well. Our friends whispered to us, "You are going to be inducted in the Bruderschaft." At that point, we still had no idea what that meant.

Existing members gathered together to watch the newcomers join their ranks. I was called first to walk up to the altar. Adi Werner was the master of ceremonies, and he gave a speech in German. Then, he tapped me on both shoulders with the Sword of Munich and walked me to a special place at the right side of the altar, where there was a large antique book on a gorgeous old table. He asked me to sign my name in this beautiful book.

Then, it was Stewart's turn to do the same thing. Adi tapped him on both shoulders as well. We didn't know what he was saying, but we knew it was something important. Then, to our surprise, the prince and princess of Luxembourg were introduced and went up for their induction. The princess curtsied during her turn, and the prince bowed. Then, the king of Spain went up, and he bowed during his induction.

That is when Stewart leaned over to me and whispered, "Why does King Juan Carlos want to join the ski club?"

I looked at Stewart and said, "I don't think this is a ski club!"

I was right; it wasn't a ski club. It was the Bruderschaft, which is the world's oldest charitable order. We became part of the St. Christoph Brotherhood that was founded in 1386. The organization was started to provide food and shelter for weary mountain travelers who were lost in the heavy snows of the Arlberg. Today, it provides money through our donations for disadvantaged families of the region, particularly for the dependents of road-accident and mountain-accident victims.

Because we were inducted together that day, the king of Spain and the prince and princess of Luxembourg became our brothers and sister. It was quite an honor that our German friends had arranged for us. Later, we also became members of the St. Christoph Ski Club, which is the oldest ski club in the world and is based in the Austrian mountains. Stewart and I are the only members from the Cayman Islands. We donate every year to the Bruderschaft to help the widows and orphans in that area of the mountains.

It was such an honor to be inducted into the Bruderschaft. As members, we were each given a beautiful pin. Because the meaning is so special, we are supposed to always wear the pin. If we are anywhere in the world and another member sees us without the pin, we have to pay that member a hundred dollars. That hundred dollars goes to the Bruderschaft. My "sister" Ingeborg made sure I had a lot of pins.

I guess the next time I see the king of Spain, if he is not wearing his pin, I could ask him for a hundred dollars to donate to the Bruderschaft.

Some of our German friends, Rosi, Wolfgang and Ingeborg

Chapter 13

FISHING WITH FRIENDS ... AND BEARS

The purpose of life is to live it, to taste experiences
to the utmost, to reach out eagerly and without
fear for newer and richer experience.

—ELEANOR ROOSEVELT

Stewart has always loved outdoor sports, especially fly-fishing. So not only did I join him for his helicopter-skiing adventures, but I also traveled along to some of the world's most sensational and remote fly-fishing locations. In 1986, Stewart took me fishing to the Enchanted Lake Lodge, outside of King Salmon, Alaska. Getting there meant taking three flights to Anchorage and another flight to King Salmon. In King Salmon, we finally boarded a floatplane that flew us to the Enchanted Lake Lodge, which is in the middle of forty-four thousand acres of wilderness.

The Enchanted Lake Lodge is in an incredible location. It is up on top of a hill overlooking Nonvianuk Lake and the Enchanted Lake. The main sitting room of the lodge has glass windows all around, which affords everyone a spectacular view. The Enchanted Lake is home to all types of wildlife, including families of loons. You can hear their cries in the morning and in the evening. When we took off on the floatplane, we usually saw them.

Inside the lodge is a beautiful stone fireplace, and there used to be a huge fish tank by the fireplace. The staff would catch a large rainbow trout each week and put it in the tank for the group coming in to observe and enjoy. After the week was over, they would release it back into the lake and get a new rainbow for the next week's guests.

The gorgeous wood paneling in the lodge made it feel so cozy and warm. The sleeping quarters were in smaller duplex cabins, located around the main lodge. Each side had a bedroom and a bathroom for two guests to stay very comfortably. Each suite also had its own door to the outside.

Fishing there was quite exciting. In the mornings after breakfast, we would board a floatplane and land in a lake or large river. We would deplane in the shallow part of the lake and walk over to the tundra, where we would follow the bear trails to the river. On the Moraine River, the riverbank is about forty or fifty feet high, and we would slide down the banks to the river. There, our guide would inflate our rafts, which would hold five of us—four guests and a guide. At times, walking through the rivers, the water would be up to our waists. It was very challenging to walk through a running river, with gravel and large rocks on the riverbed beneath your feet.

After the floatplane dropped us off, there was no communication with the lodge because we were in the wilderness. It was also challenging for me to find someplace in the trees where I could use a washroom during the day that was away from the men and the bears.

The Enchanted Lake Lodge accepts only twelve guests a week. At first, the fishing groups consisted of four guests and one guide. Later, under a new ownership, it changed to two guests and one guide. For my first week of fly-fishing in Alaska, I was the only woman guest in the entire lodge. Stewart and I were paired with Don and Terry, two men from California who were our fishing partners that week. Terry was about six foot four with red hair, and Don was maybe six foot three. In those early days, we had neoprene waders that were a bit difficult to get into. They came all the way up to our chests, with big straps that fastened over our shoulders. At our waists, we wore fishing belts so that if we fell in the river, the neoprene waders wouldn't fill with water. We also wore boots with felt bottoms so we wouldn't slip on the rocks on the riverbed.

Terry didn't know if he'd like fly-fishing in Alaska, so the first day, he came out in his camouflage hunting clothes and very slippery boots. It made it difficult when we were trying to get away from the bears. Once, when we landed and were walking over the tundra, a large female bear took one look at Terry and started jumping up and down. We all were in the water, trying to get away from that bear. Terry was slipping on the rocks in his hunting boots, but he managed not to fall.

At first, I didn't know very much about bears; I didn't know they have an incredible sense of smell. Since it was my first trip to Alaska with Stewart, I decided to bring a new perfume to wear—*Poison*, Elizabeth Taylor's new brand. I thought it would be romantic to take it with me. I also had chocolates in the pockets of my fishing vest, just in case I got hungry. Between the chocolate and the perfume that I wore, all I did was attract the bears.

I always had the many pockets of my vest filled with anything but fishing gear. Since our gloves didn't have fingertips, I thought I could touch up my nails if the fishing wasn't good. So, I had fingernail polish and makeup in the pockets of my fishing vest. I put topcoat on my nails while I was sitting in the back of the floatplane. The pilot thought something was wrong with the engine because he smelled something strange; he almost did an emergency landing. Finally, he figured out what I was doing in the back seat. We all had a good laugh about that.

All day long during our first day in the wilderness, the bears were after us. At one point, the guides decided to put me in the water to try to disguise the smell because I was wearing such a strong perfume. I had my camera in an inside pocket of my neoprene waders, and I was so deep in the water that the camera got wet.

The bears kept following us. Don and Terry were on each side of me. We linked our elbows together to support each other. We were trying to move quickly away from the bears, but Terry kept slipping because he didn't have the right fishing boots. Don kept trying to get over to the bank. Between the two of them, I also was slipping on the rocky, river bottom. I asked Don what in the world he was doing, trying to get over to the edge of the river.

He said, "This morning I put lotion on my face. The bears can smell that, so I'm looking for bear poop to rub all over my face to make myself repulsive to the bears."

I was shocked at that point because I was covered in Jergens lotion and perfume! We spent more time that day trying to get away from the bears than we did fishing. Remember, there was no communication with the lodge or the floatplane until the pickup time at the end of the day. When the floatplane finally arrived at 4:30 p.m., we were happy to get on that plane.

The next year, Terry arrived with the proper fishing clothes and boots.

The three bears came out on the bank right in front of me for this photo!

It was on our second trip to Enchanted Lake in 1987 that we met Wilbur and Danielle Smith from Cape Town, South Africa. We sat directly in front of them on the plane from Anchorage to King Salmon and started our conversations then. We eventually became very good friends. Wilbur is a best-selling author with a specialty in historical fiction, mostly about Africa and the Courtney family. His novels have sold more than 120 million copies around the world. But of course, we had no idea about his occupation when we first met.

When we arrived at the Enchanted Lake Lodge, we were paired with Wilbur and Danielle to fish together that week. One day, the four of us were walking on a bear trail, following bear tracks through the tundra and deep grasses to get to the river. Our guide had warned us that we could never outrun a bear, which made perfect sense. We couldn't even walk properly on the soft, spongy tundra, much less outrun a grizzly bear. Because the tundra is very uneven, it's difficult to walk in a straight line. It's like walking on a huge wet sponge that has deep holes every foot or two.

We were trying to walk in a single file. The guide led, then me, then Danielle, then Wilbur, and finally Stewart. As we went through the tall grass and came closer to the river, right ahead of us was a huge grizzly bear. The salmon were spawning and rainbow trout were swimming among them, feeding on the salmon eggs. This grizzly bear had just caught a big red salmon, and it was eating that salmon in the tall grass right in front of us. We were following its trail and about to run straight into it.

When the bear heard us coming, it got down and hid in the grass. We didn't even see it. This huge bear must have thought we were after its salmon. We had no idea, but the guide who was walking in front of me was only about twenty-five feet from the bear's hiding place.

Suddenly, this huge grizzly bear, with claws as long as the length of my fingers, stood up on its back legs, put its paws and claws up in the air, and roared at us! The bear probably thought that we were trying to steal its fish. Our guide put his arms straight up in the air and yelled, "Whoa, bear!" That's when I turned and ran so fast that I think I dropped everything. I ran right up to Dee, and she started running with me. Wilbur and Stewart saw us racing out of there, and they started running. We all ran away from the river through the grasses on the tundra. Suddenly, I realized we had left our guide back there as a sacrifice.

I heard our guide yelling, "Whoa, bear! Whoa, bear!" I thought he was probably backing away from the bear because that is what we were told to do. When he finally got back to us, he was absolutely livid that I had run away. He said, "What *are* you—a crazy woman? I told you never to run from a bear!" He went into a tirade about it.

We were all completely out of breath. I just looked at him and said, "I'm so sorry. I just forgot."

He had saved our lives by backing slowly away from that bear.

After that experience, Wilbur wrote about it in his novel *A Time to Die*, but he set it in Africa instead of Alaska, and instead of a grizzly bear, it was a lion.

On another day, we walked into a gathering of bears when we arrived at the riverbank very early in the morning. In front of us, bear cubs were just waking up with their mother, and there were bears to the right and the left of us. We counted seventeen bears within our sight at the same time. We just walked very slowly backward toward the plane and waited.

It was early morning, and we had been walking along the top of a cliff that we had to slide down to get into the water for fishing. Right then, by the top of the cliff, two more little bear cubs, who had been sleeping with their mother, popped their heads up to look at us. I looked to the right, and there was their mother too. It turned out that all the bears were waking up just as we got to the river. It was an exciting morning!

Dianne with Grizzly Bear

On later trips, we weren't too afraid of the bears. We discovered that as a group of five or six people, we could stand close together. To the bears, we looked like a great big animal. Also, the bears were getting used to seeing humans fishing there. If we didn't go toward them or into their territory, they wouldn't bother us. We would just look at them and back away slowly to get out of their way. Then, we would wait for them to fish and move away from us down the river.

After having such an enjoyable time fishing with the Smiths, we planned to fish together every year. The land around the Enchanted Lake Lodge is spectacularly beautiful. Sometimes, it even looks like Africa, with huge mountains in the background. The rivers are filled with gravel banks and large rocks. The side banks are beautiful, with overhanging trees and tall grasses. We usually met in September, when the trees were still green and just starting to turn an incredible yellow. The water was crystal clear. We could see red sockeye salmon swimming in the water among the boulders, gravel, and rocks.

When the salmon spawn, the females lay their eggs on the gravel, and the males cover the eggs by pushing the small gravel over the eggs to protect them. This makes the river bottom uneven. There is also a metamorphosis with these salmon because after they spawn, they die.

During this process, their color changes from silver gray to bright red. Their faces then turn black, and the male's upper jaw goes over the lower jaw and hooks down, turning it into a really ugly-looking creature. While the male is covering the eggs, some of the eggs float away. That is what attracts the rainbow trout into the river. The trout gorge on the salmon eggs. The salmon develop whitish spots as they are dying, but they try to stay in the same spot to protect their eggs for as long as they can. During their life span, these young salmon, called smolt go out to the ocean from the river, where they were born, and then swim back upstream to that same riverbed to lay their eggs in the exact spot where they were born. It is quite an amazing feat. It is a miracle how each salmon knows exactly where to return.

Also at this time of year, the bears are getting ready to hibernate by filling up on salmon. They come down to the rivers, which are teaming with salmon. After they have had their fill of salmon, they go up on the banks of the river and have a nap in the tall grasses. With the overhanging trees and tall grasses, you can't even see that they are there. That is why we were told to make plenty of noise when walking through the tall grasses to the rivers. The bears have a keen sense of hearing and poor eyesight, so they will walk away from us when they hear us.

Holding a big rainbow trout

It was very meditative in the silence of the river and nature. It was quiet and peaceful when we were fishing on the river. We could hear the birds chirping and see little otters go by. Swans and hundreds of cranes gathered in the sky and formed groups to fly south. Bald eagles appeared and flew right over our heads. It truly was something to see.

Eagles fly higher than any other bird and are thought to be messengers of God. One day, one appeared on the river and flew right over my head. A large feather floated down onto the gravel. The guide picked it up and was ecstatic because it was considered such a lucky omen. Right after that, I caught the most beautiful rainbow trout. The guide said, "When you find an eagle feather, you need to give it away," so he gave it to me. I took it back to the lodge and have kept it ever since that day. Hopefully, it will always be lucky.

On the river, we were alone with our thoughts, enjoying the peacefulness of being away from civilization. At the lodge, there was no television, no newspapers, no telephones, and no Wi-Fi. We were not in touch with the civilized world, just the world of nature. On one trip, when we went into the wilderness, America had just declared Operation

Desert Shield, and when we came out, it was Desert Storm. To be away from it all is like going through a magical, peaceful passageway. Going back home is like reentry into a very noisy civilization, especially at the airport.

Another large part of the wilderness experience was enjoying the people who were there with us. In the fishing lodge, we ate breakfast together, and dinners were served family-style at long tables. Lively conversations always were a good part of the meals. Everyone felt relaxed and comfortable together.

Lunch was served out on the river. The guides would bring red-checkered tablecloths that they put down on the gravel banks, and delicious lunches were presented to us. They would bring hot soup in thermoses, sandwiches, apples, and homemade cookies or brownies. And there always were Snickers bars and a lot of candy. Nick, one of our guides, knew I liked gummy bears, so he would bring those for me. He likes them too, and we had fun sharing them on the river while we fished.

It was very enjoyable to sit on the riverbanks, having beautiful lunches with different kinds of coffees and teas. I thought it was just like a TV commercial. We were in the wilderness, with choices of tea. "I'll have Earl Grey, please!"

The ultimate compliment to my fishing abilities came when I was in Alaska, fishing with Stewart and my guide, Josh. I was having a great day. The fish were really biting. I was enjoying casting my double-handed spay rod and practicing my C-cast. I was totally amazed because it seemed like I caught a beautiful rainbow trout on every cast.

All of a sudden, my guide scooted up next to me in the river. Josh said in a very low voice, "Dianne, don't look now, but there are four men standing on the gravel bank right behind you. They have been watching you cast for the last thirty minutes."

Of course, I turned around right away to look at them. They had landed on that gravel bank in their floating raft and were not even fishing; they were just watching me. I never heard them because I was so engrossed in the moment. When they saw me turn and look at them, all four men took off their fishing hats and bowed down in front of me, tipping their hats to the river. I was shocked but, at the same time, thrilled. I smiled broadly and thought, *Every woman needs to have men bow down to her. It really feels great. I wonder if Queen Elizabeth feels this way.*

Once when Stewart was on a fly-fishing trip in Russia, he met Alan, who was from Belfast in Northern Ireland. Stewart explained to Alan that he would love fly-fishing in Alaska and might want to join us. On our next trip to the Enchanted Lake Lodge, Alan came along. The first evening when I met Alan, I had an idea that he was thinking, *There's no way this lady will be able to fish very well. She is all dressed up, wears makeup, and has her hair done perfectly every morning and evening.*

We went out in the floatplane the first morning, but Alan wasn't feeling well. He had come down with a horrible cold. That morning was very windy and rough. We were bounced and blown around a lot in the air. I sat back and enjoyed the bouncing, but it made Alan even sicker. He took off his fishing hat and threw up into it. He was in the seat next to the pilot and was so embarrassed. Plus, he would be cold, now that he didn't have a hat. Not only does a hat keep you warm, but it protects you from casting and hooking yourself in your head.

When the plane landed, Alan got out and tried to wash his hat in the cold water.

I said, "Alan, don't worry. I'll get you a new hat."

He probably thought I was crazy because we were in the middle of nowhere, but we had just landed on the Brooks River. He didn't know that a lot of tourists go there to take photos of the bears. It seemed to him that we were in acres of wilderness, but I knew there was a little store for souvenirs. Hundreds of people with their cameras go there from all over the world. The Brooks River is famous for those photos of bears at the falls, catching salmon in their mouths as the salmon try to swim up the falls.

While the men were rigging their fishing lines and deciding which fly to use, I went off to the little store to buy Alan a fishing hat. I had no money, but I told the cashier at the store that I was from the Enchanted Lake Lodge. The lodge takes guests to the Brooks River almost every day. I promised to send the money with the guides the next day. I explained what had happened to my friend, and they sold me a fishing hat. I returned to Alan and handed it over to him like magic. He couldn't believe it! He loved it, and off we went onto the river.

By the end of the day, Alan was flabbergasted by my casting ability. He was also amazed that I could land the fish so easily. Stewart had taken me to Oregon, where I had learned to master a good C-cast. I had a double-handed spay rod, and I would point the tip and line downriver. It is the same cast that was so stunning in the movie *A River Runs Through It*. It's a long cast that seems to catch a fish every time. Alan couldn't believe that this Dallas woman, so beautifully made up, was standing next to him, catching more fish than anyone.

At the end of the week, Alan said to me, "I'm sending you a gift. It's a Kelly Kettle that we use in Northern Ireland. You will be able to have hot tea or coffee anytime on the river." He sent the kettle to me in Dallas, and it's at the Enchanted Lake Lodge even now. They store it there for me every winter.

The Kelly Kettle is constructed with a large opening in the center of a hollow kettle. There is also a removable part on the bottom of the kettle on which you can start a small fire. You pour the water into the hollow part of the kettle through a small spout on the upper outside of the kettle, and put the kettle on the fire. The fire comes up the middle through the large opening, and more wood is put down the center to keep the fire going. This boils the water. The water is much hotter than any thermos could provide. You can choose any teabags you like, put them into paper cups, and have boiling-hot tea. All the guides love it, especially on very cold days. They always ask me to bring the Kelly Kettle.

The tea lady with the Kelly Kettle, Making Earl Grey Tea, A Toast with Hot Tea

We've been making these fly-fishing trips to Alaska for probably twenty-eight years. The same guests would come back to fish with us again and again because we all enjoyed sharing these experiences together We tried to meet every year after that. We had so much fun together and became such good friends. I invented a society into which everyone had to be inducted. I called it the Royal Society of the Canadian Blue Moose. No amount of money could buy your way in. It is a very exclusive club!

Among the people who fished with us that week was Betty Lou, a former television producer who had won an Emmy for *The Meredith MacRae Show*. Her best friend was Meredith MacRae, who starred in *Petticoat Junction* and then *The Meredith MacRae Show*, which was a precursor to *Oprah*. Meredith had been married to Phil, one of the men I later inducted into the Blue Moose Society.

I also started a Silliest Hat contest during our fishing week. All the guides would work on their crazy hats for this contest. There would be hats with corks hanging from them or safari hats studded with fishing hooks. One week, the owner of the lodge thought it would be funny to have a baseball cap with a woman's ponytail at the back. Looking at all their creations, I thought, *Next time, I'm going to win.* So I bought a turquoise Mexican sombrero in Dallas and wore it fishing. Everyone said, "Dianne, you can't wear that hat fishing. First of all, how can you cast?"

I bent my head to the side and said, "Like this!" When I did that, all the silver sparkles on the sombrero caught the light, and everyone thought I'd scare the fish away. Actually, it attracted the rainbow trout, which was so funny!

The Royal Society of the Canadian Blue Moose Club Dance

I left my turquoise sombrero at the Enchanted Lake Lodge, and from that moment on, the last night of each trip became Mexican Fiesta Night. They would place my sombrero on a wooden statue of a bear at the lodge. Margaritas, tacos, and delicious Mexican wedding cake was served. I decided they needed more decorations. The Dallas airport has the best Mexican souvenir shops, so every time I went through Dallas, I would buy more decorations to bring to the lodge, such as small sombreros and colorful, big, incredible paper flowers.

As you walk from the sitting room down the steps into the beautiful dining room at the Enchanted Lake Lodge, it's hung with all the flowers for Mexican Fiesta Night.

The Blue Moose idea was added to our Mexican Fiesta when Keith, a past president of Buena Vista University, took his grandson to a wonderful place for dinner, where they give the kids big blue moose antlers made of foam rubber. Keith collected a number of these blue antlers and gave them to me. He simply said, "Do something with these."

I had no idea what in the world I would do with them, so I stored them for next year with my Kelly Kettle. That year, when we went heli-skiing and landed in the Calgary Airport, I saw bright red T-shirts with a big moose on them in the airport's store. I bought a bunch of those shirts to take to the Enchanted Lake Lodge. The following year when we went to Alaska to fish, Keith had even more of those blue moose antlers. That was when I officially invented the Royal Society of the Canadian Blue Moose Club.

On our flight through Anchorage, we shopped in the airport and bought even more moose paraphernalia, like moose bottle openers, moose pens, and moose-themed checkbook covers—anything with a moose on it. On the evening of our first Blue Moose party, Keith, Stewart, and I walked into the lodge wearing the red T-shirts, and everybody just stared at us. We hid the big blue moose antlers in the sitting room. During dinner, I'm sure the other guests wondered why we were in those red moose shirts. As everyone was eating, and soft music was playing, Stewart, Keith, and I quietly left the room and put on our blue moose antlers in the sitting room. We changed the soft dinner music to "The Stripper," which we decided would be the theme song for our club, and came back in, dancing in a conga line. This fun music, "The Stripper," was playing full volume, and everyone started howling with laughter because we looked so funny, wearing those big blue moose antlers! The atmosphere in the dining room really changed. It was just pure fun! That became the opening ceremony of every Royal Society of the Canadian Blue Moose Club.

I began the first induction ceremony. I stood in front of everyone in my moose T-shirt and my blue moose antlers and said something like, "This is the most exclusive club in the world, and it meets in a very remote region of the world only once a year. No amount of money will enable you to be a member. You have to be inducted into this special club. This year, the first person I would like to induct is Betty Lou, for constantly catching the biggest fish!" I gave a speech about her great fishing abilities and then gave her a red T-shirt with the moose on it and her own set of blue moose antlers to complete her induction ceremony.

When I spoke with her about it later, she said, "Dianne, I won an Emmy, and your induction was nicer."

I also inducted Phil, who was just about to retire. He laughed a lot about those blue moose antlers. Unfortunately, Phil died just two years later. It turned out that this week with us was one of his favorite memories. When he passed away, his family brought his ashes up to the Enchanted Lake, where his son Brian scattered them in his favorite fishing spot. At his funeral, they displayed a picture of him wearing his blue moose antlers at the Enchanted Lake Lodge.

From then on, we'd travel to Anchorage early to buy moose items, such as handmade ceramic moose mugs. I would have the artist put the each of the staff's names on them. We'd give the staff moose mugs, moose pajamas, moose socks, and moose underwear for the pilots—anything "moose" to thank them at our annual moose ceremony. They all looked forward to it because they had about ten people a week up there in the wilderness, and they didn't get a break all season.

A lot of the other weeks' guests were very demanding and probably didn't party that much at the end of their week's fishing. We tried to make the staff feel valued by giving them this party, and I think they loved it. We loved it too! I think at this point, I've inducted almost everybody into the Royal Society of the Canadian Blue Moose.

* * * *

139

From Stewart

We have so many wonderful memories from Enchanted Lake. In the early years, they never planned that women would be there with hair dryers and electric hair rollers. They only had a small generator that was used for the cabin's lights and cooking. If you overloaded it, the breaker would trip, and all the power was lost until they reset the breaker on the generator. Then came Dianne, who always traveled with hair dryer, hot rollers, and everything else she possibly needed. On one of our first trips, she plugged in her hair dryer, and the entire lodge lost electricity! We had to explain to everyone that her hair dryer tripped the breaker. They worked out the time when Dianne could use the hair dryer so they could unload the system another way.

Dianne was the only woman in the men's fishing camp. This lodge was owned by a German man, Dick Matthews. He saw Dianne coming, and you could just hear him say "Oh no" to himself. Dianne was all dolled up and looked like she was going shopping instead of fishing. Our first time in the floatplane, the two of us came down to the dock wearing new waders, new gloves, new boots, and new hats. Dick said we looked like two storefront mannequins going fishing. Over time, Dianne became his favorite client. She is so much fun and never complains. Eighty percent of the other wives are there because their husbands have dragged them, and there is a lot of complaining.

Dianne just loved the experience from the beginning, and all the other men loved her, especially when she showed them her card trick that her father had taught her. She had them pick a card from the deck, put it back in, shuffle the entire deck, and then divvy the cards into piles. All the while, she was planning to magically find their original card. Then, she went through her routine of "I don't know if it will be this card. I'm not sure this is going to work." Finally, it came down to the last card and she said, "It's this one!" And of course it was the card they first pulled out of the deck. The guys were just enthralled. They even stayed up all night trying to figure out how to do it!

Then, there is Dianne's casting ability. Teaching her with longer spay rods made her just spectacular at that. She always shocked the men because she out-fished them.

She also has a waterproof hat with a wide brim, along with all the beautiful feather flies she puts on it. You should see how much Dianne spends on the flies for her hat. To me, it's like buying jewelry that will look good on the hat.

The last evening of these trips is really popular with the staff because it's party night. Most of the crew are just a bunch of fishermen. They really enjoy it when Dianne comes because she always finds out their inside stories, brings funny gifts, and makes presentations for them.

Whenever we travel, even to the wilderness, Dianne always looks glamorous and packs everything she needs to be that way. That could mean several big suitcases for her and just one for me. Over the years, I've suggested limiting things, but Dianne brings what she wants to bring. What happens is that she starts filling up my bag with her things too.

* * * *

Grizzly Bear Fresh Paw Print and my foot!

Stewart is really sweet. He gives me that look sometimes but always ends up letting me put things in his bags. He usually doesn't complain, but once, when we were traveling from Madrid to London, we forgot to tell the travel agent that we were on an international itinerary. She charged us so much for our overweight bags for a local flight we were taking that it cost more for the baggage than it did for the ticket! Stewart told that story for a very long time.

When Stewart first took me on these wilderness trips, I would run out of toiletries, not realizing I couldn't just go to the store and replenish them. Now, I travel with regular sizes of everything, and usually, Stewart ends up using my things, like toothpaste and hairspray. It's been so much fun learning to fly-fish with Stewart and enjoying the wilderness experience with him.

Chapter 14

WHERE THERE'S A BOG

Our greatest glory is not in never falling
but in rising every time we fall.

—CONFUCIUS

When we first met Wilbur and Dee fly-fishing in Alaska, they were sitting behind us on the plane, going to the Enchanted Lake Fishing Lodge. It was such a coincidence, meeting like that, and we instantly became good friends. Wilbur asked if we'd ever gone hunting or shooting in England. We hadn't, but when Stewart was younger, he used to shoot pheasants in the States and Canada with his father. Dee and Wilbur invited us to go with them for shooting in England and Scotland. That's how we began our adventures in the shooting world.

The first grouse shoot we went on was in northern Scotland in 1991. Since I was new to this, Wilbur and Dee suggested that we go to Gleneagles, a five-star luxury hotel in Scotland with a beautiful golf course and spa. There was also an elegant hunting store, where I bought all my stunning shooting clothes. All the clothes were in colors like loden green and brown so that we would blend into the landscape. Wilbur had said my shiny blonde hair would scare the birds away, so I bought a beautiful green hat with pheasant feathers on it. I also bought green Wellington boots because they were made for outdoor use. I could walk through the muck and the mud and then just rinse them off at the end of the day.

At that point, I hadn't bought any shooting skirts. Instead, I bought *breeks*—slacks that only go down to your knees. In America, we call them knickers. In Scotland, they call them breeks. *Knickers* is a rude word for ladies' underwear. My breeks were green tweed, and I bought a beautiful cream-colored sweater with pheasant on the front to wear with my breeks.

Heidi, Hailey, Ashley, Lilly and Stewart at The Gleneagles Hotel

Northern Scotland is very rugged, with lots of rocky outcroppings. The Wellington boots and the breeks made it easier to walk over the rugged landscape. On the first day out on the moors, the sky was gray, and the weather was very cool. I was very proud of my new outfit and wore it when we went on our first walkabout shoot—that means that instead of standing in one place, or "beat," you walk the estate with the gamekeeper. The gamekeeper brings his dogs to find and flush out the grouse. The dogs go on point if they discover a covey of birds.

We were in a vast open area with hills, mountains, and heather everywhere. We were walking over a kind of a spongy, grassy area when the dogs went on point. The dogs had flushed out a covey of grouse, and the men began shooting them.

As it turned out, this shooting estate was owned by a very stingy, Scottish gentleman, who didn't feed his gamekeeper or his dogs very well. They were all starving, but at the time, we didn't know that. We had brought along lovely picnic lunches that the hotel had packed for us. We were enjoying eating them until we realized the gamekeeper and his wife didn't have any food. When I offered them some of our lunch, I have never seen anyone eat so fast in my whole life. The next day, I placed an order for six lunches, which would include a nice lunch for them. The dogs also were starving. When Stewart shot a bird, he had to outrun the dog to pick up the bird before the dog devoured it. The dogs were not supposed to do that. They were supposed to bring the bird gently back to us, but these poor dogs were too hungry to give them up. Once, it looked like Stewart was playing tug-of-war with a dog when he was trying to pick up his grouse. The whole experience was turning into a comedy.

After lunch, we walked the estate again for more shooting. Dee was in front of me, and I was trying to keep up with her. She was in incredibly good shape, and I was in my new Wellingtons that were probably too big for me. I saw a bright-green patch of grass and thought, *I'll just go through here.* I didn't know that I should never step on anything that was bright green because that is usually algae growing on top of a bog. One step, and in I went, new shooting outfit and all. My "Wellies" immediately filled up with bog water. I grabbed at the grasses growing around the side of the bog, and I realized I couldn't feel the bottom of this bog. I was in all the way up to my neck, holding desperately to the grass so I wouldn't get my hair wet. I didn't mind that my whole outfit got wet because the outfit could be cleaned. But I was determined that my hair was going to stay dry.

Stewart was way ahead of us with the dogs, which had just gone on point again. The gamekeeper said to him, "Sir, your wife has just fallen into the bog!" Stewart looked at me, in the bog up to my neck; he looked at the birds and looked back at me again. He decided to take the bird; then he would come back and rescue me.

The gamekeeper came running to me and pulled me out of the bog. I looked at Dee and everybody around me and asked, "Did you get a picture? I was in a bog!" They said no, so I jumped back in while holding on to the grass. I thought *I'm all wet anyway so why don't I go back in for the picture?* I didn't know it, but the bog was like quicksand. When I jumped back in, wearing all my new shooting clothes, everyone screamed—except Dee, who was laughing hysterically as she took the picture.

* * * *

From Stewart

We were grouse shooting, and Wilbur and I were quite some distance in front of the ladies because we were quickly following the dogs. I had forgotten to mention to Dianne not to step on any shiny green surface because you can't see that there is water underneath. The entire surface is green from whatever is growing in there. The dogs had just gone on point to indicate there was a covey of grouse being flushed out when the gamekeeper turned to me and said, "Sir, your wife has fallen into the bog!" I looked back at Dianne; the dogs were still on point, so I asked the gamekeeper to look after her so I could shoot the birds. I knew he would pull her out. Dianne can swim and had enough sense to grab the grass at the sides of the hole. The bogs are like a hundred-gallon oil drum in diameter, which is not a long way to get your arms to the surface to stop from sinking farther in.

The gamekeeper had a thirty-foot rope attached to the dogs as they were going through the heather. We couldn't figure it out. When you shoot the bird down, the dog wanted to tear it apart to eat it, so we had to keep outrunning the dogs to get to the bird. After I fought the dog off the bird, I turned around and walked back toward Dianne, and

146

there she was, jumping right back in the bog for a picture. That time, she was in up to her neck, but Dianne being Dianne, she managed to keep her hair dry.

* * * *

The gamekeeper knew we were with Wilbur Smith, who is a beloved and famous South African author. We all were invited to the gamekeeper's home after the shoot. I had been soaked in peat moss and water and looked like I had little brown twigs all over my new sweater and new breeks. When I was pulled out of the bog, I took my sweater off, and the gamekeeper put a broken tree branch through the arms of the sweater. As we carried it together, it quickly blew dry in the wind, although it still was covered in pieces of brown peat moss. My tweed breeks were meant to get wet, so they dried while I was wearing them, as did my blouse. We dumped the water out of my Wellies and went on with the day.

The gamekeeper lived in one of those old stone houses that dot the landscape in Scotland. When we got to his front door, I asked him where I should leave my boots—I assumed we all would take our boots off before entering his home. He gave me with a surprised look that I didn't understand, but then I learned we could wear our Wellies inside his home.

Earlier in the day, when the gamekeeper had picked up a dead bird that was dripping in blood, he had knocked it on his breeks. I'd looked at him and said, "Now you have to get your breeks cleaned." Wilbur was in hysterics because the way they cleaned them in Scotland was to walk out in the rain and let the rain wash off the blood.

I had the right outfit, but I had no idea of the customs. It was all so different to me. Inside the gamekeeper's house were sheep and chickens that walked in and out of the front door. In his outdoor yard, as I was petting one of the cows, he said, "Don't get too attached to that one. We're having her for dinner tonight." I hoped it was a joke.

We sat down for tea with the gamekeeper and his wife. The gamekeeper had a guest book, and he asked Wilbur to sign it because it would be a famous autograph. Then, he asked me to sign.

I looked at him and said, "I'm nobody."

He said, "I don't care. I want you to sign it anyway."

I signed my name under Wilbur's. I must have made an impression on him by jumping back into that bottomless bog!

Much later in the trip, Wilbur and Dee told me that people drown in those bogs just like they do in quicksand. Stories about people who have died in bogs have been passed down for centuries. Once again, there had been no time for fear. I just thought, *Oh, my gosh, I fell into a bog.* I didn't realize how dangerous it might have been; I only wanted a picture of me in that bog. After everyone's surprise and shock wore off, it became very funny. The gamekeeper said he had never seen anything like it in his life. The whole experience was incredibly crazy, fun, and adventurous.

After that shooting trip with Wilbur and Dee, we traveled together with them every year. First, we would meet in Alaska for fly-fishing. Later, they started introducing us to the most magnificent shooting trips all over the world. We went shooting with them in Zimbabwe, South Africa, Spain, England, and Scotland—that is, the *men* went shooting. Dee and I would never shoot a bird, but we loved watching our men enjoy themselves on these shoots.

On one of the shoots in Northern Ireland, Stewart and I shot with Raymond, a friend who owned Tayto, a national potato chip company. The chips were called Taytos, and the Irish people loved them. The cheese-and-onion potato chips were to die for—they were delicious. When we first moved to the Cayman Islands, a lot of Irish people worked there. I asked Raymond to ship me cases of different flavors of chips to give to our Irish friends. I knew they would love it because it came from their home, and they couldn't get them in Cayman. Today, however, we have an Irish pub on Cayman that serves Taytos.

In Ireland, the men shot pheasants, but at the end of the day, they announced that the last shoot would be ducks. I remembered my baby ducks, Quacky and Lucky, and was horrified. All day long, I was Stewart's "loader," which meant I handed him the cartridges from his leather cartridge bag.

I handed him two cartridges, and Stewart took a shot and hit a duck. It came down and landed right beside me, in the throes of death, flapping its wings next to me. The tears started uncontrollably pouring down my face. I looked at the duck and said, "I can't help you now. The dogs will be here. It's going to be over soon." I looked at Stewart with tears in my eyes, closed his cartridge bag, and sat on it. I don't know what he had paid for the shoot, but he was finished at that point. There was no way I was giving him another cartridge to shoot another duck. Because I was so upset, I don't think he minded.

* * * *

From Stewart

The owners of Tayto have an old castle on their property. One area has duck ponds, so they set up a driven duck shoot. Dianne was my loader. It was her job to hand me the shells so I could put them in the gun. You keep your shells in a cartridge bag that has a top that you can close down. The drive started. Dianne handed me two cartridges. The ducks flew over us, and I shot. One duck fell two yards in front of us, twitching as it died. Dianne looked at it, took the shell bag, and closed it. She put the shell bag on the stool and sat on it with tears in her eyes. Five minutes later, our host didn't know what was happening because the ducks kept coming, but I wasn't shooting. I had to explain that Dianne wouldn't give me any more shells. The rest of that day was pheasant shooting. That was okay because Dianne hadn't had pet pheasants growing up. When I saw her tears, I couldn't get mad at her. There would be no more duck shooting for me.

* * * *

Another time, we were in a field for a driven shoot. Each "gun" is given a certain selected place to stand. There are little seats for the women to sit on behind their men. Each gun has his own loader, who would load one gun while he was shooting with the other one. The gamekeepers and beaters know how to drive the birds over you, a few at a time. They go to the areas where the pheasants are and start beating trees, making lots of noise to move the pheasants out of their hiding places. This scares the birds and causes them to fly very high over you but not in a huge flock. The "guns" shoot; the dogs and their handlers are behind them to pick up the birds that were shot. Stewart had two double-barreled shotguns, so he only had two shots from each gun. Bang-bang. His loader would hand him his other loaded gun as soon as he finished shooting.

At the end of the drive, I saw a big pheasant on the high hill in front of us. I knew that pheasant had been at this game before because he was a mature bird with a long tail. When a bird is fluffing his feathers, he's really comfortable, calm, and happy. But this one was scared to death, and his feathers were plastered to his body. The poor pheasant raced back and forth on the edge of the hill because he didn't want to fly over the guns. He looked behind him. The dogs were coming, and the beaters were coming, so the pheasant finally got up and flew. There were six guns in the field; you can tell it's "your" bird because it flies right over your head. It was flying straight for Stewart, and Stewart's gun went up to shoot the pheasant. I immediately stood up from my chair and said, "If you shoot that pheasant, you'll never be 'lucky' again." As soon as I said that, his gun went down, and he let the bird fly by.

Lately, I have gone shooting with Stewart only in Spain. Stewart loves to shoot at La Cuesta because it is one of the best shooting estates in Spain. Princess Caroline of Monaco loves to shoot there, and the king of Spain is also a frequent guest. The birds are plentiful; there are always thousands of red-winged partridges on this shoot. They fly extremely high and are very fast, so it is challenging for the guns. Stewart is an excellent shot and strives to only take the high birds. He loves the challenge of those high birds. The partridges are delicious and are sold as a delicacy in the shops in that area.

I once saw an antique book, written by a man in the shooting world, titled *My Life as a Pheasant*. The gentleman, who loved to shoot pheasants, came back in his next life in England reincarnated as a pheasant. Lots of times, I've told Stewart, "You know this karma you're building up is really bad. You might come back as a pheasant in England or even a partridge in Spain." We both just laugh.

Pheasant shooting together in England

Being married to Stewart, who takes me on incredible adventures, has been wonderful. I've seen and experienced things I never would have if we had just stayed home. The world is a marvelous place, full of excitement and adventure, and I feel lucky to have experienced so much with him.

Chapter 15

BUTTERFLIES, BULLFIGHTS, AND ANGELS

"I could not have made it this far had
there not been angels along the way."

– DELLA REESE

I've always believed in angels, even before the avalanche. I was once introduced to psychic who was an angel reader. She would self-hypnotize so she could see your angel guide and tell you the name of your angel.

I was at home in Cayman and had set up a phone appointment with this psychic to learn about my angel, but I had forgotten about my appointment and was in the pool when she called. I came inside, dripping wet, to answer the phone and was standing on a towel when we started speaking. The first thing she said to me was, "This is so strange—your angel's wings are dripping wet."

I thought that was amazing! She told me that my angel's name is Mary and that she has long, glorious wings. She said that Mary's shoes were gorgeous—delicate, sparkling, exquisite, and fragile-looking—but the shoes also were so strong that she could walk over anything in them. I guess she needs strong shoes to protect me from all the places I go.

* * * *

I have had a few other near-death experiences that I can only attribute to angels watching over me. In 1990, Stewart was shooting in Argentina with Wilbur Smith, our brother-in-law, and another friend of theirs. I took a trip with my friends Danielle and Maureen and my sister-in-law, Gloria, to Iguazu Falls on the border between Brazil and Argentina. Iguazu Falls is larger than Niagara Falls and quite spectacular.

The four of us signed up for a jungle tour—we would go by boat across the river that emptied into Iguazu Falls. We were walking on a path to get to our boat when a group of lemurs came down from the hilly forest, right onto our path. They looked like a cross between a monkey and a raccoon, with an extremely long striped tail. A whole family of mothers with babies on their backs came right up to us. They were very inquisitive and stopped to examine us. I thought they were cute. One climbed up my leg and grabbed the wrist string on my camera. We had a little tug of war, but I finally rescued my camera. I looked down at my legs and thought, *Oh gosh, now I'm covered in mud*—but it wasn't mud; it was poop!

They didn't climb up on the other women, only me. I was the "lucky" one! Finally, they let go, and we kept walking. When we got to the river, I was able to clean up a little bit.

We got into our little boat, crossed the river, and continued our jungle tour. All of a sudden, we were in the middle of thousands of butterflies. They were so beautiful. Some were as big as my hand, and they flew all around us. It was absolutely stunning. Some were the most gorgeous cobalt blue. Everyone was covered in butterflies. As they landed on our fingers, we took pictures. I said, "Look—I'm walking my butterfly!" It was truly incredible.

We met our boat guide back at the river to go back to our path on the other side. The little boat was a small open boat with just one outboard motor. It sat the four of us comfortably, with our tour guide at the back. The little boat sank slightly into the water when we all got in. We had been ushered into this boat, and when our tour started down the river, we realized that our tour guide didn't speak English.

All of a sudden, we hit a rock, but we didn't know this was unusual—we were talking and admiring the beautiful scenery. We could hear the sound of the falls, and we enjoyed that. We had no idea what was going on, other than how wonderful everything looked and sounded. Our boat guide kept revving up the little engine, and he looked troubled. Unbeknownst to us, the driver was frantically trying to turn the boat around, but it was going one foot backward for every two feet forward.

When we finally got to the other side of the river, our driver literally jumped up out of the boat. All of his companions came running down, and we could hear loud, agitated talking among them. They quickly got us out of the boat and dragged the boat out of the water. When they turned it upside down, I saw that one of the three propellers on the tiny motor had broken off when it hit the rock. We had no idea that we nearly went over the falls. Afterward, they walked us up to a viewing stand, where we could see where we had been. We were absolutely shocked when we saw how close to the falls we had been! Knowing nothing, we had been sitting in that little boat, saying how beautiful it was to hear the sound of the rushing water. We were so lucky!

If you think about it, our angels were protecting us. Maybe they all had really big wings.

* * * *

In 1994, we were in Spain with our friends, Patrick and Catja Mavros from Zimbabwe. Patrick is a world-famous artist who sculpts African animals and jewelry in silver. He has a beautiful store in Harare and also one in London. His silver pieces are amazing and are in some of our most well-known jewelry shops in America. We traveled to Madrid for a few days, and then we went to the countryside to a beautiful estate for more partridge shooting.

The owners of this estate were Samuel and Lily Flores. Samuel was a matador who raised bulls for bullfights in Spain on this estate of thousands of acres. We discovered that the bulls that are bred for the bullfight lack a certain chromosome, which affects their brains. They only interact with a matador one time in their entire lives, and that is in the bullring.

Samuel inherited this estate, which had been in his family since the 1700s. It is absolutely beautiful. Because it has been in his family for hundreds of years, the main living area is full of gorgeous antiques, mementoes, and beautiful furniture. The estate is known all over Spain for the high quality of the bulls.

Before dinner one night, we went out for a walk and heard the bulls behind the big cement walls. We jumped up on a planter to look at them. They stared right at us, and we could tell from the way they looked at us that they were very aggressive. When we went into the formal dining room for dinner, we were amazed to see heads of famous bulls mounted high on the dining room walls. We were told that most of them were missing their ears because the matador was awarded the ears after a great fight. I found it interesting to see this in such a palatial dining room.

Partridge Shooting at La Cuesta

Samuel had a bullring on his fabulous estate, where the young matadors could practice with some of the smaller bulls. It was amazing to see some of the sparkling matador outfits, which Samuel was kind enough to show to me. Then, he showed me the picks and the final dagger, which would be used by the matador at the end of the fight. I have never seen a bullfight, but I was interested in learning about it. In a bullfight, many things go on, all of which look like a dangerous dance. The picadors come into the bullring on their horses and place their picks in the side of the bull's neck. The bulls are so aggressively strong that they still have a lot of dangerous fight left in them.

Samuel then invited me to the bullring to meet a young matador and some of the picadors. They were going to bring a young bull into the ring for this matador to practice some of his moves. It is choreographed just like a dance, and the matador practices beforehand with the red cape. True to my Just Say Yes philosophy, I said, "Yes, I would love to do that." Off I went into the bullring with Samuel.

I met the young matador and some of the picadors. Since I don't speak Spanish, it was difficult to have a conversation. Samuel stayed with me to translate. They pointed to the door where the bull would enter the ring. There were barricades at the edges of the ring to hide behind if the bull became too aggressive. In the middle of the ring, the red cape was on the ground. It isn't just red fabric, as you might think. Underneath the red fabric is a long piece of wood to which the red fabric is attached. When the matador waves the cape, the wood keeps the cape in a straight shape. The matador knows exactly how to use it and wave it so that it flares out beautifully in the fight.

I picked up the red cape; it was heavy. The young matador came over and stood beside me. Samuel told me to hold one end of the cape, and the matador would hold the other one. We would both stand in the center of the ring behind the cape. When the young bull came at us, we would each step to the side and raise the cape for the bull to run through the middle. Then, we were to shout, *"Olé!"*

We practiced this a few times without the bull. All of a sudden, I heard Stewart's voice from a balcony above me; he sounded very stern when he said, *"Dianne, get out of there!"* I looked up at him and smiled. I was enjoying it all, thinking how amazing it would be to do this. It all sounded easy. When the young bull comes out into the bullring and comes toward you, you raise the cape for it to pass, step to the left, and shout Olé! But something in Stewart's voice made me pause.

Our friend Patrick Mavros, who was listening, said, "Dianne, they are about to bring the young bull out. You really should stand behind the barricade, and I will stand with the matador. I would like to try this." Patrick is over six feet tall, very strong, and athletic. He took my place, standing next to the matador and holding the end of the red cape. I turned around to watch from behind the barricade. I was amazed when I saw the "young" bull. It was over four and a half feet tall! It didn't look so small. This bull took one look at the men and quickly charged toward them. They both said Olé and lifted the cape. The bull ran right through the middle of the cape, but then it spun around on a dime and charged back toward them.

No one had told us the *second* step of this scene—what to do when the bull spins around and comes back at you! This time, it came back at Patrick at a very fast speed. It was very strong. Patrick quickly dropped his end of the cape. He leaned forward and grabbed the bull by both horns with his hands. As he was trying to turn the bull's head away from his body, the bull continued to charge. Patrick was so strong that he managed to turn the bull's head sideways, but its horn gored Patrick in his leg.

I can't believe how close I was to staying in the ring and holding the red cape with the young matador. I would have been the one who was gored. In fact, I could have been badly hurt. I have no idea what made Stewart come out exactly at that moment, but right then, he was my angel and probably saved my life.

Old Photo of Spanish Bullfighting.

*Angels are all around us, offering
protection and help. Mine have had a
very busy time of it!*

Chapter 16

HURRICANE IVAN

Life isn't about waiting for the storm to pass.
It's about learning to dance in the rain.

—VIVIAN GREENE

In late summer 2004, we were flying back from another wonderful week of fly-fishing. We had been in forty-four thousand acres of wilderness in Alaska, and there, we had no access to news. When we landed at the airport in Anchorage, we saw the news for the first time in a week on a television station in the airport. The newscasters were talking about Hurricane Ivan, a huge storm that was heading directly for Jamaica. I asked Stewart if we should go home to the Cayman Islands, as the hurricane seemed to be a monster storm.

He said, "The hurricane isn't heading for Cayman. It is heading for Jamaica, which is far from Cayman. It probably won't go over the Cayman Trench because that is the deepest part of the ocean with the coldest water."

Hurricanes don't like cold water; they like warm water. He also reminded me that the last hurricane to hit Cayman had been in 1932.

We thought it would be safe, so we flew from Anchorage to Miami. By the time we got to Miami, Ivan was a very slow-moving hurricane and was still heading toward Jamaica. I asked Stewart again if we should go home, and he still said it would never hit Cayman because of the deep cold water surrounding the Cayman Islands—that's what everyone was saying.

When we got on the plane to go home, we noticed there were only four or five people flying with us from Miami to Cayman. We thought what a shame it was that Cayman was going to have a poor tourism week because of Hurricane Ivan. We still didn't think the hurricane would come close to us.

As we went through immigration in Cayman on September 10, we didn't realize that most of the people on the island were being evacuated. We were just coming in, but airlines such as Air Canada were sending planes in to take the Canadians off of the island, and British Airways had sent planes for the British people to evacuate. Everyone was leaving.

The next day, we realized Hurricane Ivan was a monster storm and that it would be horrible if it made it to Cayman. It was now a category 5 hurricane, with wind gusts up to two hundred miles an hour. Still, we thought it would never go over the cold water of the Cayman Trench.

We had plans for the following Thursday to go Buena Vista University in Storm Lake, Iowa for the Estelle Siebens Science Center dedication. Not only was it a huge honor for my mother-in-law, but it also would a big family reunion. I wanted to look good for the family reunion. My nails had gotten brittle in Alaska from the cold water, and I needed a manicure and pedicure before we flew again to Storm Lake, so I went to a beauty salon. It was closing that day at noon, but I didn't know that was because everyone was evacuating the island.

I had my nails and toes done for our trip to Iowa. I went home with my manicured nails and with massage oil on my feet. I went to my bedroom, which is up two flights of stairs, and decided to put on a pair of new sandals that I had bought in Venice. Then, I heard the news that Ivan had changed course and was now heading straight for the Cayman Islands. I needed to tell our staff to go to the store immediately and buy water, enough to last ten days. I started running down the stairs in the new sandals with my oiled feet, and I slipped right out of the sandals. I fell down the entire flight of marble stairs, shattering both of my kneecaps. My left kneecap was completely broken in half, and my right kneecap was so shattered that the biggest piece that was left was only the size of a quarter. At that point however, I had no idea what I had done to my knees, only that I was in excruciating pain, and my knees were horribly swollen. Each knee had swelled to about twelve inches in diameter.

The raging winds hadn't started yet, but the news we were hearing didn't sound very good. I sent staff out to get water, and I looked at whatever food we had. I had crutches in the attic from other knee surgeries, so Adrian, our estate manager brought them to me. Somehow, I could stand straight-legged without pain, but I could not bend my knees. I had to be carried up and down the stairs, but I used the crutches to get around.

The hospital was now flooded, although I didn't know it at that time. Most doctors had already evacuated the Island. There was nowhere for me to go for help. The rain and winds had become so strong that water was pouring in our house from the light fixtures in the ceiling. Shattered kneecaps or not, we had to try to keep the water out of our home.

Our home has many large windows, and luckily, they stayed in place, even during the two-hundred-mile-an-hour wind gusts. Stewart knew we'd built the house to hurricane category 5 standards, with hurricane-proof windows. The foundation beams went all the way down to bedrock, and stainless steel girders went all the way up to the roof.

Stewart had grown up in the Bahamas and was knowledgeable about hurricanes. When we were building our home, he'd asked the contractors about the last major hurricane, which had hit Cayman in 1932. When they told him that the water had come up ten feet above sea level, he told them to bring our foundation up to eleven feet above sea level with fill and landscaping. That is what saved our home. None of the other homes in our neighborhood survived Hurricane Ivan as well as ours did because they weren't built that high above sea level. With this hurricane, the water came up above ten feet again. Houses were flooded, with water covering their entire first floors.

The slow-moving hurricane started during the night and stayed right on top of us, with category 5 hurricane-force winds, for nearly thirteen hours. I thought we would have a hard time with this, but I had already been through the avalanche, so I wasn't really afraid. I was in a place of acceptance; I just thought, *This is it.*

I somehow knew, in the back of my mind, that we would be okay, even with my shattered kneecaps. I started taking pictures through our bedroom window of the ocean swirling over our lawn. I couldn't see very far, but there was a lot of water swirling in the backyard. The tabletop from our outdoor table was floating back and forth in the waves.

The back of our home   *Devastation everywhere*

We lost our electricity and water supply. When the sun went down, everything turned very dark. The wind gusts were still shaking our house. The staff was in their house on our property. The pressure inside our home was so great that the closed doors were moving back and forth like they were getting ready to blow. The seals around some of the window frames were leaking in places. It looked like somebody outside was using a pressure hose around our windows, and the water was just shooting into the house. The rain came in sideways, nonstop, with two-hundred-mile-an-hour wind gusts. The rainwater pushed under the roof and poured down on us from our light fixtures in our ceiling.

I stood up straight on two shattered kneecaps, with nothing but Tylenol for the pain. We used beach towels to sop up the water from our floors. Our staff, Stewart, and I would squeeze the water from the towels into big garbage cans, so the water didn't collect inside on our floors. Fortunately, we had a small emergency generator that kept our refrigerators, some of our power outlets, and a few of our lights on. However, it was made for small power outages, not for anything like the power outage we had from Hurricane Ivan. We didn't know it at the time, but we would not have electricity or water for months after Ivan. That little generator worked the entire time.

We continued getting rid of the water as best we could until we were too exhausted to keep going. Stewart and I finally went upstairs to bed. It was the middle of the night, and we just couldn't take it anymore. I was in excruciating pain by then. The howling wind continued, and the pressure in our house and on our ears was very strong. It felt as if we were in a pressure cooker and that the doors would blow open at any minute. Stewart held me in his arms and kept saying, "We're going to be fine." I was in such pain and so tired after fighting the hurricane all those hours that I couldn't stay awake. There was nothing else we could do. I fell asleep in his arms and slept through the rest of the hurricane.

Ivan was a huge slow-moving hurricane. The hurricane-force winds continued until about three o'clock the following afternoon. The wind gusts over two hundred miles an hour, which really were mini-tornadoes, wiped out palm trees in their path. On our property alone, we lost eleven palm trees. The winds tore off the roof of condos right across the canal from us. And, cement shingles from our neighbor's roof were implanted into our outside walls at one foot intervals. It looked like those pieces had been shot from a Gatling gun. For a full five hours of Hurricane Ivan, Grand Cayman Island was totally off radar in the entire world. The island experienced a tidal surge of ten feet. In many cases, the roofs and treetops were the only things visible.

The next day, when the hurricane finally stopped, we went outside. The streets were flooded with ten feet of seawater, rainwater, and sewage. Thousands of cars were lost, and the some of those that were left were filled with this tainted water. People's possessions were floating everywhere. There were TVs thrown against washing machines, boats, cars, and trees. Of course, there were thousands of dead fish, which had been thrown out of the ocean and were lying all over the ground.

When the rain stopped, there was no wind. It was extremely hot and humid. The earth was steaming from being covered in water. When the sun finally came out, it was steaming outside. I wouldn't let Stewart open the windows because I knew when the salt air started blowing, it might ruin everything.

We had only coconut water from fallen coconuts to drink. We had no water or electricity. Sweat poured off everyone, and the heat was excruciating. With our little generator working, we had some outlets to plug in dehumidifiers. Those dehumidifiers would gather lots of water, and we used that water to bathe. Also, I could plug in a little fan to keep us cool next to our bed. But after we showered, even five minutes later, we felt as if we needed another shower because it was still so hot and steamy. Luckily, we still could use our microwave. We could warm the water from the dehumidifiers to have a warm shower. We also could cook in small glass containers in the microwave. With no electricity and water, toilets would not work. To use the washroom, we placed a cooler, filled with brackish water from the pool, and a cooking pot next to the toilet. After we used the toilet, we filled the cooking pot with water from the cooler and dumped the water quickly into the toilet to flush it. My knees were so swollen that they wouldn't bend. My triceps got strong, pushing me up and down every time I used the toilet. I later learned that the sewage system wasn't working, so I don't know where the water went that we used to flush our toilets.

A tank full of diesel fuel from a construction project two doors down, had rolled in and landed right next to our house. We were lucky enough to use that fuel to fill our little generator. Our neighbors had evacuated the island. Stewart climbed into their homes through their broken windows. He was able to let out the water in their homes, which had been pooled in their first-floor living areas. I'm sure it saved some of their furniture, which would have been ruined by sitting in that dirty water until they returned.

Somehow, our house was the only one in the neighborhood that didn't lose even one window, much less our roof. Because Stewart's office is lower than the rest of the house, water came up from the electric outlets in his floor. We quickly used the towels to wipe up the water so all the furniture stayed dry.

My friends Viet and Stephanie had brought over their wedding pictures for safekeeping before they evacuated the island with their three little children. It turned out that they lost everything else that was left in their condo. When they returned to the island, they were so happy when we gave their wedding photos back to them.

The entire island was devastated. It looked worse than New Orleans after Hurricane Katrina. To me, it looked like a nuclear bomb had gone off, but our home didn't have enough damage to meet our insurance deductible. Thank goodness Stewart had insisted our home was to be built to hurricane category 5 standards.

Through it all, I wasn't afraid for us, but I was very worried about our best friends, Maggie and Len. They were the only people we knew who had chosen to stay on the island. With telephone and electrical poles knocked to the ground and many damaged cell towers, there was no way to communicate by phone. We had no way to reach them except by car. The island had no electricity or water. Luckily, we had a cistern under the garage, which had been collecting rainwater. The water there was brackish, but we used it to wash things down, one inch at a time.

The next day, I wanted to see our friends, Maggie and Len to see if they were all right. Stewart picked me up and put me in the back of his Ford SUV. At that point, the Ford looked like the Loch Ness monster because it was covered with grass, leaves, and twigs. There was no way we could drive on the roads—they were covered with downed trees, boats, sand, dead fish, and anything else that was displaced from the hurricane—so we drove across the golf course, sidewalks, and anything else, trying to find our way to their house. As we were driving, our beautiful little island looked like it was completely destroyed. The devastation was hard to believe—topless palm trees, no leaves on trees, no flowers anywhere, and piles of sand, antiques, furniture, washing machines, dead fish, cars, and yachts were strewn all over the Island.

When we finally made it to Maggie and Len's, I thought for sure they would be in lots of trouble; their home was right across the street from the ocean. Stewart helped me out of his car, and I stood on my crutches as we knocked on their door. They answered, dripping wet from head to toe. Through the open door, we could see the sky from the *inside* their home; they had lost part of their roof. A lot of the pink insulation, which is usually in the attic, was dangling from their torn ceiling. Water was dripping everywhere. During Hurricane Ivan, they had taken refuge in one of their inside closets. They had pulled the mattress off their bed and pulled it on top of them to protect them from a falling ceiling. I sat down in their hallway, thrilled that they were alive.

Maggie then said, "Would you like some water?"

That is when I finally cried. I knew that we didn't have any water and probably wouldn't have any for a very long time. Maggie's offer of water was so generous and made me realize what we all had been through.

The looting started right away all over the island. Stewart hired an armed guard for our neighborhood, to watch over our home and our neighbors'. On the second day after the hurricane, we realized we could get a phone signal on the highest mound of the golf course while sitting in our car. We drove over the golf course to that high mound and rocked the SUV back and forth until we got a cell phone signal. Anyone who came to our house could recharge their cell phones and computers because we were the only ones who had electricity from our little generator. My neighbor Carol, who had evacuated, somehow managed to call me and asked me to get her special food items from her refrigerator—like her hundred-year-old bird's nest and her shark fins—and keep them in mine. She had a lot of specialty items in her freezer, and our freezers were working. We brought everything of hers over to our house. Between what we had in our pantry and our freezers, we had a lot of food. We could easily thaw things and cook on our outside barbeque because we had that propane tank to fuel the barbeque.

We were fortunate that our home was intact. It seemed as if we were protected by angels. All the other homes in the neighborhood were severely damaged. We hadn't even had time to put up any storm shutters. We found out later that upstairs in a home, which is where we had been sleeping, is exactly where you *don't* want to be in a hurricane. When the roof comes off, the ceiling might come down too. In our neighbor Carol's house, her ceiling which was saturated with water fell onto her bed. If she and her husband had been sleeping when the roof collapsed, they could have been seriously hurt.

My friend Connie, who at that time was working at the University of Miami, wanted to come down with the dean of the Miami Business School to help us. She called us and said, "Donna Shalala insisted that we must go to the Cayman Islands to help the Siebens." Connie stated that the University even has a plane waiting to fly all of them here.

I had to say, "Don't come. There's no comfortable place for you to stay. The toilets don't even work." At that point, there was no way to get rid of sewage. I didn't know where anything was going when I threw water down my toilets. The authorities on Cayman told people to go to the bathroom in paper bags and then put the paper bags out on the streets. The waste management team would come and pick them up because the entire sewage system on the island wasn't working.

I can't explain how I managed with my shattered kneecaps. My knees were both so swollen and still were at least twelve inches around. Later, I could stand without pain, as long as I kept my legs straight. I would need to have both knees replaced. I'd already had seven knee surgeries from helicopter-skiing accidents over the years, so I thought this was it.

By the fourth day after Ivan, the airport runway was cleared. Two of our friends, Ron and Dave offered to evacuate me on their small private plane. Ron was CEO of West Star Cable, the company that supplied Cayman Island with television channels. I always felt that they saved me. The plane could carry only seven passengers, along with the pilot and copilot. They were going to fly me to Miami. From there, I would fly to Dallas to see my orthopedic surgeon, who had done the other knee surgeries.

Fortunately, I was very good with crutches, so I knew I could manage on my own. On the sixth day after Ivan, I packed my ice machine, which I would need for my knees after surgery. I also packed whatever clothes I thought I'd need, since I knew I'd be gone for a while.

It turned out to be a very small plane, restricted by weight. Every seat was taken by people who needed to be helped. Some of them were still in shock; some passengers had to sit on the floor in the aisle of the plane. One woman had lost her entire house and everything she owned. There was also another lady with her cat. Her cat had leukemia, and she was all out of medicine for him. She just sat on the floor of the plane, petting her cat and didn't say another word for the entire flight.

When I arrived at the airport in Cayman, I was told I couldn't take my suitcase. They were evacuating only people, and suitcases added too much extra weight on the plane. Never in my life had I gotten on a plane without a suitcase.

I got on the plane with my crutches, wearing khaki-colored slacks, a white top, and flip-flops. When I was told I couldn't take my suitcase, I looked around at the others and said okay—they all had lost so much. I left everything at the airport with Stewart. I knew I could get whatever I needed when I arrived in Dallas.

I didn't know it at the time, but the plane hadn't come in from Miami; it had weathered the hurricane on Cayman. Later, the owners got into a lot of trouble for flying off the island in that plane because the wind from the hurricane probably had blown sand into the engines, and that meant the plane wasn't safe. It would be dangerous to fly over the ocean to Miami. Also, we were overweight because there were too many passengers. However, we didn't know the circumstances of the plane, and all of us had a desperate need to get to the States for some help. We were just grateful for the chance to fly to Miami.

When I landed in Miami and changed planes to fly to Dallas, I didn't realize how emotionally overwhelming the experience had been for me. Before leaving Cayman, I had showered and washed my hair with the water from the dehumidifier. I thought I was fine. But when I got on the commercial flight to Dallas, I touched the seat. The air conditioning was on, and it felt so good. Luckily, I was in first class. When the flight attendant asked me if I'd like some water, I burst into tears. The man who was sitting next to me scooted as far over to the window as he could. I was on crutches with two broken knees, wearing flip-flops, and crying when asked if I'd like some water. That man didn't talk to me all the way to Dallas. I wonder what he must have thought.

It turned out that people in the States had no idea that Cayman was hit so badly. Cayman managed to keep how much had been damaged by Hurricane Ivan a secret. They didn't want to discourage the tourists because tourism and banking were their only industries.

When we tried to send emails, the emails would not go through. Communication with the outside world was very difficult. It wasn't until we discovered cell phone reception by moving our car back and forth on a mound on the golf course that we finally could call my mother and our daughter, Heidi to let them know we were okay.

The hurricane was a huge lesson in gratitude. People shared and took care of one another. I felt so much gratitude for friends and all people. If I hadn't known Ron and Dave, how would I have gotten off the island? I feel incredibly grateful for what people did for me.

Chapter 17

LADYBUGS TO THE RESCUE

Though small in size, the ladybug is fearless.
The ladybug brings a message of promise and
good fortune, for they get us back in touch
with the joy of living. We must let go of our
fears and go back to our roots, to love.

—INA WOOLCOTT

When I got to Dallas, I stayed with Atlee and Nicole in the guesthouse of their lovely home in Las Colinas. I saw my doctor right away. By then, the pain was so bad that I was begging for knee replacements. It was like I had been on autopilot when dealing with the hurricane, but now my body took back control of my brain.

The doctor said replacements were impossible because he needed a whole kneecap for that. My left kneecap was broken in two pieces, and my right kneecap was completely shattered. The largest piece left on the right kneecap was the size of a quarter. My doctor suggested that I should rehab my kneecaps first by going to physical therapy.

Nicole suggested I call John, a dear friend and former business partner of both our husbands. John had been a bodybuilder and later

170

became a physical therapist, as that was his first love. He had a different method of physical therapy. His goal was to get all the pieces of my kneecap into one flat "plate," so they could mend back together.

I didn't think about how long the therapy would take, but the problem was that Atlee and Nicole's home had so many stairs. From their guesthouse to the kitchen, I had to go up two flights of stairs and then down three to get to the car. All I wanted was to ice my knees because of the pain and swelling. I kept asking Nicole for ice, and she had to keep going up and down the stairs to bring ice to me. Finally, for both of our sakes, she suggested I stay at the Four Seasons. There, I would have room service for the ice and everything else. And it was connected to the Fitness Institute, where I would do my therapy with John.

I checked into the hotel and lived there for three months like a rock star. I had a refrigerator, an electric kettle, a microwave, and a coffeemaker. The hotel sent freshly made cookies every day. Because I had left my suitcase in Cayman, I had to get new clothes. I only bought a few things, but I found that I didn't need very much.

Girlfriends came to stay with me to keep me company. Dr. Choe lived in Dallas, and he came by to treat me almost every day. That was a huge blessing!

One day when I woke up, there were ladybugs all over my room—hundreds of them! I looked out my window to see the air was swarming with ladybugs, so many that I couldn't see through them. It looked like a fog of ladybugs. My window was a sealed hotel window, so I couldn't figure out how they had gotten in—to this day, I don't know how they got in. I've always loved ladybugs and felt like they were good luck but never really knew why. As a child, I let them walk on my hand and would repeat the rhyme, "Ladybug, ladybug, fly away home."

When Dr. Choe came to treat me that day, and I said, "Can you believe the ladybugs all over this hotel?"

He said, "They're nowhere else, Dianne. They're only here in your room and outside of your window."

He was right. They were swarming at my window, with hundreds of them in my room. I smiled because I loved them. Dr. Choe smiled and agreed that they bring good luck.

That weekend, Heidi came to keep me company, and she felt a little scared by them. "Oh, my gosh!" she said. "I'm afraid to go to sleep. There are so many ladybugs all over the walls. They're going to fall in my mouth while I am sleeping!"

Of course, I assured her that they wouldn't. I didn't know it at the time, but she and her husband were trying to get pregnant. She spent the entire weekend with all of those ladybugs and me. About a week after she went home, I got a telephone call. "Mom, we're pregnant!" My first grandchild was on the way!

We now have three granddaughters, and we buy ladybug clothes for them in memory of those lucky ladybugs. The ones in my hotel room gradually went away. I don't know how. I never tried to get rid of them, and I never complained about them to the hotel staff. I've never seen so many at one time, before or since.

While I didn't know it at the time, I've since learned that ladybugs bring luck and are messages of abundance, a letting go of fear, and a return to love. It's no coincidence that they came to me after surviving the devastation and loss of Hurricane Ivan and shattering both my kneecaps. Looking back, I can't think of a better time in my life for them to have shown up.

After about six weeks, when things finally got better on Cayman and the airport reopened, Stewart started visiting me on weekends. The first time he came, he walked right past me in the lobby. I didn't even recognize him. I was sitting in the lobby, reading, and I looked up. He saw me and walked over to me. His hair was very long. Cayman still had no public electricity or water, and there was nowhere for him to get a haircut. He had pulled his hair into a ponytail and had shaved, but that was about it. He had been on the island since I'd left, protecting our home and all of our friends' homes too. Stewart and our staff had spent every day cleaning up our home and garden.

Stewart told me more details about the hurricane and what had been happening since. They'd had to clean up the island by bulldozing all the rubble out of the way, putting it on barges, and shipping it away for disposal. England had sent a warship to assist in protecting the homes and businesses. Looting had started during the hurricane at the jewelry stores and in abandoned homes. The police had enforced curfew on the entire island. Everyone had to be in their homes by 6:00 p.m., and no one was allowed out after that. Around 5:00 p.m., people would take their soap and towels and walk into the ocean for their baths. Everyone shared the food and water that they had with everybody else.

Our house manager, Adrian was living in our guesthouse because the home where he lived had been destroyed in the storm. At first, private planes were the only flights taking people out and bringing in food, water, and generators. Commercial planes still weren't flying. There was no water or electricity, and the airport personnel had to deal with cleaning out their own homes.

After Ivan, the island looked like it had been hit with a huge bomb. There was not a flower or leaf left anywhere. Only a few palm trees still had their tops. I don't remember seeing one blade of grass. It was all dirt, paper, debris, and twigs. Birds had been smashed against houses, along with leaves and branches. We learned later that two people had died. It looked like more than that to the rescue workers because graveyards had flooded and gravestones had washed away. Because of all the flooding, some graves had been pushed up from the ground. Someone told me it was difficult to tell the difference between the skulls and floating coconuts.

In some cases, people had ten feet of water inside their homes. To escape the water inside their houses during the hurricane, they had climbed on top of refrigerators or bookcases. They were afraid to move through the water because of all the electrical outlets—they didn't know there was no electricity.

One grocery store opened and gave food away because they didn't have air conditioning or refrigeration for the food. People stood in line at the water company with gallon containers to get drinking water.

Wherever they could, people set up places to cook, and little lines formed to buy food. People called their friends in the States for help. At the beginning, food, water, and portable generators were sent by private planes. Everyone who remained took care of each other.

By December, about three months after Ivan, life had gotten somewhat back to normal. I had been away that entire time, doing physical therapy with John. I came back for Christmas. It turned out that I didn't need knee replacements after my kneecaps mended. I was so lucky.

At Christmas parties that year, conversations were very different. Instead of saying, "Oh, that's a beautiful dress you are wearing," people asked, "Oh, what did you do for water?" Everyone's perspective had changed, and water had become a precious commodity because you couldn't live without it.

By the time I returned home, almost everything had been cleaned up. I was amazed that every single person had worked so hard at clearing up the debris on the island. I was also amazed by what people could accomplish. The rebuilding made the island look better than it had before the hurricane. All the places that were rebuilt were freshly painted and clean. And people made a point to improve their homes by making sure they were now hurricane-proof.

A new Ritz-Carlton was built. All the new hotels and condos were built to "Hurricane 5" standards now. As of this writing, there is still a lot of work to do, but the improvements are remarkable. It's a beautiful little island, like a phoenix rising from the ashes. Looking back, I believe the ladybugs were a reminder to help everyone on Cayman let go of fear, reconnect, rebuild, and appreciate the simple joys and luck of living on such a beautiful island.

When Ivan was all said and done, I looked around my beautiful home. I could appreciate the beauty of it but understood that although it was very nice, it wasn't necessary to my happiness. We don't need all of the things we acquire. Anyone can be happy in a tiny room with very few possessions. It's amazing!

Chapter 18

CROSSING OVER
WITH LOVE

No fear is the ultimate joy. When you have the insight
of no fear, you are free. And like the great beings,
you ride serenely on the waves of birth and death.

—THICH NHAT HANH

*My mother at Temple
University on her
boyfriend's car!*

My mom's original name was Wilhelmina Cornelia Fazekas, but she changed it—to be more "American"—to Wilma Faze. She was born in 1917 and lived to be ninety-two years of age. For my entire life, she was my "prayer warrior." Whenever anything was wrong, she would pray, and somehow, everything would become right again. She spent a lot of time praying for me, especially after she heard about the avalanche. At first, I didn't want to tell her what had happened because she would worry so much. But, she must have overheard it somehow, since all of

176

my girlfriends knew about it and talked about it. She hadn't wanted me to go helicopter skiing in the first place, and later, she never asked me about my near-death experience in that avalanche. We never talked about it until just before she died.

When my dad died in 1982, my mom was left completely on her own in California. We decided to ask her to move from California to Dallas to be near to us. She became the grandmother who enjoyed Heidi's growing-up years. She had a home in Dallas only seven minutes from our house, so we enjoyed many happy family times with her. She loved to stay with Heidi whenever Stewart and I took some of our trips, and she became very close to Heidi. She had been a teacher all of her life and retired when she was sixty-five, but standing all day in heels put a heavy burden on her knees. Eventually, she had to have both knees replaced when Heidi was only eight years old. About ten years later, she couldn't walk very well and needed to be in a wheelchair. I think it was because she didn't exercise and didn't want to do her physical therapy programs.

A few years later, Stewart and I decided to move from Dallas to the Cayman Islands to build our dream home. By the time we decided to move to Cayman, it was time for my mother to be in an assisted-living place in Dallas. We made sure she had a two-bedroom apartment so she could keep as much of her beautiful furniture as she wanted. As an interior designer, I helped my mother decorate her new living quarters very elegantly. She loved the experience of picking out fabrics, trims, and wallpapers with me for her new home. Whenever I visited her, we always went shopping. She loved having pretty clothes and looking elegant. The ladies in her assisted-living place were always dressed beautifully. It helped that North Park Shopping Center, with Neiman-Marcus was right across the street from where they lived.

My mother and I talked almost every day on the phone, and whenever we spoke, I asked her how she was. She always said, "Just fine." Then, she would tell me that nothing hurt as long as she didn't have to move. I knew that not moving was unhealthy, but she had given up trying to exercise.

I asked my best friend John Lane to visit her three times a week and help her do chair exercises. He had been Stewart's business partner, but his love for physical therapy made him seek a new path. He spent many hours with her encouraging her to do some exercise. I think she loved being with him because he was always so nice to her.

Every month, I flew to Dallas from Cayman to see her. I didn't want her to feel she was left alone. It was my turn to be in the "sandwich generation," with my one parent needing me just as much as my husband and daughter needed me. From not exercising, my mother eventually needed to be on oxygen. She would spend all day sitting in her wheelchair or sitting up in her bed, but she still loved to go out to see all the pretty new things in the stores. When I visited, I got a portable oxygen tank, put her in her wheelchair, and wheeled her into the shopping center at North Park in Dallas. Her favorite store was Neiman-Marcus. Even though she could hardly see because of her macular degeneration, she loved being in the stores.

My mother was heavyset her entire life. At her lowest weight, she was on Nutrisystem. She went down to a size fourteen or sixteen, but she was always a big lady. Toward the end of her life, she weighed almost three hundred pounds and couldn't walk. Her only joy at that stage in life was eating. Even though I tried to control what she was given, I couldn't. She loved to eat bacon, eggs, toast, and jam every morning, and I thought of how unhealthy that was. I once told her, "You're not allowed to have any more bacon with your breakfast."

She was very smart, however, and she called the security guard to have the bacon delivered to her. There was no stopping her when she made her mind up to have something. She also loved chocolates—I mean, she really loved them. She had her cupboards filled with Reese's Peanut Butter Cups and Hershey's Kisses! There was nothing I could do to stop it. No matter who I hired to take care of her, she would ask them to bring her all kinds of chocolates, and they would.

Stewart would say to me, "Dianne, see that wall over there? Go stand against it, and bang your head on it." That's how he saw my struggle to make my mother eat healthier. He knew I couldn't control her.

Earlier, when she had been more physically able, I had taken her to La Costa Spa and signed her into the Life Fitness programs, where

Oprah and Barbara Walters would go. Stewart said, "You've taken your mom to La Costa and bought her all kinds of cookbooks on eating and cooking healthily. You know she's just going to do what she wants to do." He was right, but I still kept trying because I wanted her to be healthier.

When my friends visited my mother with me, they would ask, "Dianne, how do you handle your mother? Doesn't her behavior bother you?"

I would look at them, not even understanding what they meant. For example, my mom had macular degeneration and could hardly see. When we were in the car, driving, my mom would tell me where to stop and when to go. I would just follow her instructions. She was my mother, and I loved her. Her behavior did not bother me.

She was stubborn and refused to wear the emergency beeper around her neck that they gave her at the retirement home. She would rather wear a beautiful necklace. She was very independent. She once got up by herself in the middle of the night to use the bathroom. When she came back to her bed, the mattress had been pushed back from the edge of the bed. Because of her macular degeneration, she didn't see that. When she tried to sit down on the edge of the bed, she missed the bed and fell, landing directly on her ankle, breaking it in seventeen places. Some bones came out through her skin.

She crawled across the floor to find that beeper. When help finally arrived at her apartment, she said, "I'm okay; just put me back in bed!"

She was taken to the hospital and had to have seventeen pins put in her ankle. When I got the call from her assisted-living place about her fall, I had just finished a fly-fishing trip in Alaska and was going home to unpack and repack to go to our niece's wedding in Banff, Canada. I very much wanted to go to the wedding, but of course, I flew to Dallas to be with my mother in the hospital.

She was relieved when I got there. And with a lot of hands-on therapy, she managed to recover. She could not walk any distance at that point, but she could manage to get from the wheelchair to her car or to her shower by taking a few steps at a time.

Unfortunately, a few years later, she had a massive stroke. I flew to Dallas immediately; it was clear she was going to die. She couldn't speak, open her mouth to eat, or even move. She only could squeeze my hand with one of hers. It was then that I learned how afraid she was of dying. She was the daughter of a Baptist minister and my prayer warrior, yet she was still afraid to go. She wanted me to stay beside her and hold her hand every minute. She didn't want to be alone.

Although she was in the hospital, I hired ladies to be with her twenty-four hours a day. The nursing staff was overworked and couldn't be with the patients all the time. I thought that at the end of her life, it would be reassuring to know that someone always was there. I was there with her every day for as long as I could. From her home, I brought my mother a red heart-shaped pillow that she loved. She had dislocated her shoulder years ago, and this pillow was a huge comfort for her because it lifted her arm comfortably when she was lying down. I also brought her a small dolphin stuffed toy that she loved. I made sure that beautiful music was played in her room. I tried to keep her transition as peaceful as I could. I filled the room with beautiful scents, with white flowers everywhere—Casablanca lilies, roses, and orchids. Casablanca lilies have the most beautiful fragrance. I thought, *Why have them at the funeral? Why not let her enjoy them while she's alive?* I sat and held her hand and enjoyed being with her.

With Heidi, Stewart, and my Mom and Dad

The hospital was in Dallas. My mother had a corner room on the seventh floor with floor-to-ceiling windows. It had been about five days since she'd had the stroke, and she was clearly not recovering. Suddenly, an eagle came right to the window and circled around the windows, flying so close that I couldn't believe it. I immediately thought, *That's my father!* As an air force colonel, his insignia was an eagle. I always thought that eagles were my protectors and good luck talismans. And out of nowhere came this beautiful eagle, circling my mother's windows.

I told her, "You don't have to be afraid to go. You will never be alone. All those who have loved you and who went before you will be right there to welcome you into their arms with so much love. It will be absolutely beautiful. Your mother and grandmother will be there. Your grandfather and father will be there. And Dad is there. He is waiting for you."

I also told her how beautifully peaceful and loving it would be. "Anything that has bothered you during this lifetime melts away in an instant, and all that is left is unconditional love and peace. All those things that made you uncomfortable will just melt away, and I promise you will feel only unconditional love." But, she was still wary and didn't want to go. I think she wanted to stay and be my prayer warrior and protect me. It wasn't until I said, "I will be right behind you. I'll be there with you soon," that she loosened her grip and relaxed.

She died that evening. It was February 12, 2009. My daughter, Heidi, had given birth to our second granddaughter, Ashley, on February 9, 2009. My mother was able to hear about Ashley's birth, and she smiled with her eyes.

I went to her apartment to get a caftan that she could wear to be cremated. I chose a beautiful rainbow caftan for her. That is when I found a lot of Hershey's Kisses and Reese's Peanut Butter Cups hidden all over her apartment. I grabbed two handfuls of those to put in her hands, to be cremated with her, because she loved them so much. Later, I also found receipts in her apartment for all of the sparkly bracelets she wore when she was in her hospital gown. I had thought they were cubic zirconia, but it turned out they were real diamonds. My mother went on her way with her chocolate and diamonds, which I know made her happy.

Her funeral was held in Dallas, and we turned it into a celebration of her life. We had a private viewing room and put her urn inside a beautiful casket. There were beautiful flowers draped over the casket, and we played her favorite music. In this viewing room was a television screen that ran photos of her during different periods of her life, from childhood through her adult life. I decided to serve the famous Cayman Island rum cake while everyone told wonderful stories about my mother.

Coincidentally, Mickey Mantle's wife's funeral was being held at the same time in the chapel of this funeral home. Whitey Ford and other Yankee baseball players were in the chapel, paying their respects to Mrs. Mantle. After her service was over, they came to my mother's room and enjoyed the music and rum cakes. The funeral director was going to tell them that this was a private party, but I thought she would have liked to have those famous baseball players there. It was a true celebration of her life.

Just after my mother passed, I had a session with a spiritual guide in Dallas. He had a remarkable gift for communicating with spirit beings. He only needed to touch you with one finger, and that would connect him with your energy and theirs. When we were in the process of communicating with my mother, he saw a tornado of white light coming out of me. It was so powerful that I fell over backward.

It was my mother. She had just passed away and was enjoying being out of her body. Now, she was free from pain and enjoying herself too much to move on. He said my mother hadn't gone all the way to the white light yet. She was enjoying the freedom of not having a body encumbered by pain.

My mother's sister, Elsa would always say, "If Wilma prayed for you, you knew everything was going to be all right. She hasn't moved on yet. She's still around, and she's still praying for you." My mother became my new guardian angel.

The following May, I went back to one of my favorite spas in California, the Golden Door. It is a very spiritual place. One of my favorite rooms there is right next to the Prayer Rock. Buddhist monks honored this huge rock by tying a rope around it because it is the largest boulder in the entire area. Prayers were written on paper and then were pinned to the rope, in hope that these prayers would be answered. Near the Prayer Rock are an antique Japanese stone lantern and a Japanese statue of a mother frog with her baby on her back. I scattered some of my mother's ashes on all of these.

She was my prayer warrior in life, and she continues to be. Whenever I am there at the Prayer Rock, I can feel my mother's love and her presence.

* * * *

Another time, I'd been away on a trip to Chicago, and the minute I got home to Cayman, I received a phone call from my girlfriend Shelley, whose husband is our doctor. They both are originally from South Africa. Shelley's mother, Joyce had become my friend as well. Joyce would come to my home and give me Guinot facials. She was the loveliest lady and taught me how to take better care of my skin. Her facials were fabulous.

Shelley had some bad news for me. Her mother was in the hospital, and her family was all around her. I was surprised to hear that Joyce had gone into a coma, as it was completely unexpected. Then, Shelley said, "My mother's dying, and we're at the hospital."

I had just walked in the house with my suitcase, but I turned around and drove straight to the hospital to find Shelley. Her sister, Helene had flown in from South Africa. Helene's son was there as well, along with Joyce's husband, Danny. It was sad to see Joyce like that, and I could tell that everyone had been crying a lot.

Shelley came out in the hall to talk to me. "I fixed my mother up," she said. "She looks so pretty." Shelley had brought in a manicurist, pedicurist, and a hairstylist for Joyce. Shelley had dressed Joyce in a beautiful Victoria's Secret nightgown, instead of a hospital gown. Joyce was curled up tightly in a fetal position. I went in, sat down next to Joyce, and took her hand, which was tightly closed in a knot.

I held her hand gently and spoke to her of things that I had heard from *Graceful Passages*, a CD set with the most beautiful messages that are an inspiration for living as well as dying. The CDs were given to me by a woman named Carol, whom I met on my first visit to a spa in Southern California almost twenty years ago. I still listen to *Graceful Passages* every day, to remind me that we all are love.

I talked quietly to Shelley's mom about her transition. I told her, "Everyone you ever loved who has already passed will be on the other side, waiting for you. There is nothing to fear. It will be so full of the most beautiful peace and unconditional love where you're going. You're not alone and never will be. Your angels are always with you, as well as everyone who has gone before you. Your mother, father, grandmother, and grandfather will be waiting for you, and they will surround you in the most amazing feeling of love that anyone could ever imagine. It has been a privilege to know you and to have had the honor of calling you my friend."

Then, I talked about what I experienced in the avalanche when I went into the white light. "I discovered that everything we worry about on earth melts away in a second. All those worries and fears disappear, just like that. Soon, you will be surrounded by angels and will be in a beautiful, sparkling white light. You will experience an incredible feeling of peace and love." When I said that, I could feel her hand loosen up a tiny bit. Her hand didn't open, but I definitely felt her relax.

As I kept softly talking to her, I realized that everyone else in that room had stopped crying and were listening to me. Finally, I said goodbye to Joyce and left the hospital.

That evening, she passed away peacefully. Later, Shelley told me that I had come to the hospital to be an angel for her whole family. In my mind, I had just come to say goodbye to Joyce and tell her what a beautiful thing she was about to experience. To me, I was simply giving and sharing love by telling her how thankful I was to have known her and to have become her friend. Shelley never forgot that, and it was incredibly rewarding to me to hear from her how I had helped her family.

I am grateful to have had the words I needed when I was comforting Joyce. I wasn't crying or saying how sorry I was that this was happening. I felt very peaceful, and it was beautiful to help her transition. It felt like that when my mother transitioned too. I wasn't crying. I had placed beautiful flowers in my mother's room and played soft music for her, and I had spoken very gently about all that I had experienced when I was in the white light. I know it made my mother's transition very peaceful.

Looking back, I can see that my experience with the avalanche gave me a new perspective on death that I was able to use to help my mother and Shelley's mother through their passings. I knew that dying was not an end at all but the most beautiful, loving new beginning.

Chapter 19

A MESSAGE FROM ABOVE

Everything will be all right in the end, and if
it's not all right, then it's not yet the end.

—TRADITIONAL INDIAN SAYING

It was September 2012, and Stewart and I were on our annual fishing trip to the Enchanted Lake Lodge in Alaska. We had an exciting schedule planned. We were going straight from fishing in Alaska to Fashion Week in London, as guests of John Rocha, one of the top clothing designers. I was excited because I had never been to a Fashion Week in London. I had a stylish white suit made just for the occasion. After London, we returned to Cayman for a couple of weeks. Then, we flew to Spain to La Cuesta, where Stewart would do his annual Spanish partridge shooting trip, and I would always accompany him there.

The first day of our Alaskan fishing trip happened to be the coldest day of the year. I don't remember the exact temperature, but it was very cold and rainy. We could see that it was snowing on the top of the mountains, and it was raining on us as we stood in the river. The cold was so intense that I didn't realize that one of the legs of my waders was filling up with water. The outside temperature was just as cold as the water temperature

When the TSA closed my duffel bag after inspecting it during their security check, they caught my waders with the zipper, which put a hole in my waders. I didn't realize that my waders had a hole when I'd put them on that morning; I hadn't checked because Stewart had checked them for holes before we left for our trip. That day on the river, I was so numb from the cold that I never knew the right leg in my waders was filling up with cold water. I guess the outside temperature might have been 46 decrees, and the temperature of the water that was filling up my waders was also 46 degrees.

At lunchtime, I realized that one leg was filled as high as the four-foot-deep water I had been standing in. I got out of the water right away and emptied the water from my waders. I was absolutely freezing, and it was still raining, but the floatplane was not scheduled to pick us up until four thirty that afternoon. There was no way to contact them to come earlier. By that evening, hypothermia had set in. I couldn't stop shaking. Even after a hot shower, I was still shaking. This continued throughout dinner, and I had to put my feet up on the bar under the table just to stabilize myself and try not to shake.

It was an entire week before we were to leave Alaska for London, with a plan to stop in Cayman for two days. It was a lot of traveling. On the fourth day in Alaska, my chest and neck would burn when I took a shower. A rash appeared at the top of my chest near my neck. At the time, I didn't know that it was Shingles, which had been triggered by the hypothermia. I had little red dots with red connections all over my neck. I kept taking showers, even though it was painful. If I wasn't showering, it wasn't painful.

But then the back of my neck started aching badly. I thought, *Oh, great, now I'm getting arthritis in my neck.* Because I didn't realize what was going on, I never saw a doctor in Alaska or did anything about it. When we got back to Cayman, I went to a dermatologist to check on the rash on my neck. She gave me cortisone cream for the week, as she thought it was just a rash.

We headed to London for Fashion Week. I was looking forward to getting all dressed up. We were going to stay at Claridge's, a very famous hotel. Claridge's has a private elevator that's 150 years old and has a sofa in it. A lot of people involved with Fashion Week were staying there. It was all very exciting.

Stewart and I went out to dinner with John Rocha and our friend, Suladda, who is from Cayman also. John took us to one of his favorite restaurants, which was really lovely. I wore my all-white suit and white silk top that I'd had made especially for the trip. I still had the rash, but I wasn't paying attention to it because the dermatologist didn't think it was anything to be concerned about. It was only my neck and ear that hurt, and I kept thinking I was getting arthritis. I didn't think about it and really enjoyed being in London for Fashion Week.

From London, Stewart and I flew home to Cayman, and soon after that, we flew to Madrid, Spain, to go partridge shooting in the countryside. Alaska, Cayman, London, and Spain—all within a three-week period. It was difficult to pack for that holiday because it included a week of fly-fishing in Alaska, Fashion Week in London, and then a week of Spanish partridge shooting at the beautiful estate, La Cuesta. For Spanish partridge shooting, the shooting clothes were a much lighter weight than the English shooting clothes and were so stylish and elegant. I wore a lot of leather and suede in Spain.

Evenings at La Cuesta were very elegant. The men wore jackets and ties for dinner. At night, the chandeliers and candlelight sparkled. The dinner table was set so lovely, and the food and Spanish wine was delicious. I was excited to be there that week because Princess Caroline of Monaco and her shooting party were joining us. I had always admired her mother, Princess Grace. The owners of la Cuesta had built a brand-new wing, and they showed me where Princess Caroline would be staying. She would have a large bedroom, a huge new bathroom, and a beautiful outdoor patio that overlooked the countryside. The view continued as far as the eye could see, with lines of olive trees dotting the rolling hills.

Soon the pain in my neck and ear got so bad that when we were driving on bumpy country roads to go shooting, I could hardly stand it. But, I kept going. On our last night there, something began changing with my face. My phone had rung in the middle of the night, and I picked it up while I was half asleep. It was my youngest granddaughter,

Lilly playing with my daughter's phone. When I heard the giggling and laughing, I decided it must be Lilly because she didn't answer when I spoke. I went back to sleep.

When I woke up in the morning, I looked at myself in the mirror, and my face looked very strange. I looked really tired. I noticed I was having a hard time putting on makeup, but I as was getting dressed, I felt in horrible pain from my ear and neck. Stewart gave me Tylenol with codeine, called 222, for the pain. I usually don't take them, but that morning, I took two.

The pills took the edge off the pain, so I headed down for breakfast. Everyone in the dining room looked so elegant in their shooting clothes. I picked up my cup and tried to sip my coffee, but the coffee wouldn't stay in my mouth. My mouth had fallen on one side, and the coffee had poured down the front of my clothes! Everyone at the table was staring, wide-eyed, at me. My friend, Linda said, "Dianne, something's really wrong." I think she thought I was having a stroke. Everyone at the breakfast table decided that I should go to a doctor right away to see what was happening.

Anything I tried to eat fell out of my mouth. I couldn't eat, drink, or even sip through a straw. My mouth had dropped completely open. My eyes and the entire right side of my face had dropped down, while the left side of my face somehow went up. My neck and ear were now killing me. It felt like I was being stabbed by an ice pick through my ear. My face also felt strange, like a tightening of the muscles on the right side. I thought I might be having a reaction to the pills.

Stewart and I don't speak Spanish, so one of the owners of La Cuesta, Maria took me to a little walled town where there was a hospital and a doctor she knew. Maria interpreted everything the doctor said. He was wonderful and gave me steroids pills, pain medication, and anti-inflammatory shots. He told Maria that in addition to the shingles inside my ear, I had Bell's palsy. He told me to relax because it would go away. I wasn't scared because I always had Dr. Choe, who would help me, but the pain was excruciating. It went through my ear and half my head, around to the back of my neck, and down my shoulder and arms.

189

By then, the shingles had settled in my ear, which was swollen and bleeding from the inside out. The right side of my face not only had dropped but also was swollen. The only shingles scab I had ever had was at the back of my right ear. That was extremely painful. If I just touched that spot, it felt like a burning match was touching the skin on the back of my ear. Because of the pain from the shingles, all I could do was hold my ear and lie down. I forgot about meeting the princess.

We had to leave La Cuesta that evening. After spending the night in a smaller town, the next day, our driver took us to Villa Magna Hotel in downtown Madrid, which was three hours away from La Cuesta. The hotel called their doctor the next morning. He gave me shots for the pain and told me to relax because this was Bell's palsy, and it would go away. He also gave me more pills to take, but he told me not to take the pills unless the shots didn't take the pain away. Because the shots worked, I never took those pills. They were probably some kind of painkillers. I found out later what they were and that they could cause cancer. I'm glad I never took them. I had no idea what the painkiller shots were, but the pain had become unbearable, so I'm glad I had those. The doctor told me to go home and get to a doctor as soon as possible.

We took an afternoon flight from Madrid to New York. I don't remember much about it except lying down and holding my ear the whole time. I slept most all the way to New York from the shots I had been given. Stewart was helpful and supportive. He held me, carried my suitcases, and lay next to me quietly. We were both happy to be going to New York because we knew we could get to a neurosurgeon. I felt comforted, knowing that help was just around the corner.

What we didn't know at the time was that we were flying straight into the arms of Hurricane Sandy.

* * * *

From Stewart

Dianne was moving quite slowly that morning in Spain, so I went downstairs early for coffee. When she came to the dining room, I could see that the side of her face had dropped a little. I thought she hadn't slept well. I was at one end of the dining table, and she was at the other. When she tried to drink or eat, nothing worked correctly. We had no idea what was going on, and, of course, I was very concerned. We thought maybe she'd slept wrong, and it was something temporary. That's when the owner of the shoot called his sister, Maria to take Dianne to the local doctor, which she did. Dianne came back in the afternoon with a diagnosis of Bell's palsy. The last morning, we were going to shoot from the hotel and leave for Madrid. Among the friends who were shooting with us was a gentleman whose wife had been a nurse. She started to do research on her computer and went to Dianne to explain what had brought on Bell's palsy.

I didn't shoot that last morning. Instead, I got us to Madrid as quickly as possible. Dianne's ear was hurting her terribly, and it was extremely swollen. The doctor in Madrid gave her another shot so she could fly home. We boarded the plane to New York, where we were going to meet our daughter and grandchildren to visit with them in Greenwich, Connecticut. Little did we know that Hurricane Sandy was on her way to New York also. Dianne couldn't get to a doctor for a few days. Bell's palsy was really settling into her face at that time, and the pain kept getting worse.

Ladybugs teach us to restore our trust and faith in the universe, reminding us to get over our egos, go with the flow, and allow life to take its course. When my face dropped and the pain hit, I had no other choice.

Chapter 20

COMING HOME

The only courage that matters is the kind that
gets you from one minute to the next.

—MIGNON MCLAUGHLIN

Bell's palsy—four months later

I was lying down on the plane from Madrid to New York in the most horrific pain imaginable. I had no idea that we were flying right into the arms of Super Storm Sandy, the most destructive hurricane of the 2012 Atlantic hurricane season. Even though we were hurricane veterans, we weren't prepared for the complications the storm created for us.

Our plane landed at La Guardia Airport in New York that evening just ahead of the hurricane. A car picked us up at the airport, and we headed for Heidi's house in Connecticut. By the time we got there, trees had fallen down, and all the power was out in our daughter's home.

She didn't have a generator, so we scrambled to find a place to stay that had electricity. It was very cold, with freezing rain and wind gusts up to 115 miles per hour.

Instead of worrying about my Bell's palsy and the pain, we worried about where we could take three children, a ninety-pound golden retriever, and four adults. There was no time to worry about what was going on with me. Also, I didn't want to worry, in case that would make the Bell's palsy worse. I believed it would go away, as the doctors had said, but I didn't know how long it would take for that to happen.

Heidi made reservations at a small hotel near Greenwich for the next night. We left our luggage from Europe at Heidi's house and just packed enough for the hotel. We had two adjoining rooms for four adults, our three little granddaughters (one was still a baby), and Heidi's golden retriever. The storm was just beginning as we checked into the hotel. The sky was dark gray, and everything seemed to be blowing around. Trees were falling everywhere and were knocking down power lines.

Just when I thought things couldn't get any worse, our hotel lost all power in the middle of the night. An excruciatingly loud alarm went off, and the pain in my head was unbelievable. All I could do during the alarm was lie on my bed and put a pillow over my head so I wouldn't hear it. By that time, I was in horrible pain. With no power, we had to leave that hotel, but we didn't know where to go. The next morning, we tried to maneuver down three flights of steps with a ninety-pound dog and three little girls by using flashlights in total darkness.

Luckily, Catherine, a friend of Heidi's called and offered to let us stay at her parents' home in Greenwich, which was very close by. Her parents just happened to be away on an extended trip, and their house had a huge generator. Everything was working in that home, and we were so grateful to be there. Catherine and her husband, Blake were our angels. The house had everything we needed. It was a huge home with six bedrooms. I went into one bedroom to lie down and mainly stayed there.

Heidi, Catherine, and I went shopping for food. I bought things like cupcakes, chips, and other snacks for the kids, not realizing that Catherine, Blake, and their two daughters only ate very healthy food.

We brought the food home and combined everything., including all my unhealthy purchases. Other friends of Catherine and Blake stayed there as well. Their homes also had no power, and they were very grateful to be there too. All in all, there were eight adults and six children living together. Because the pain was so horrible, I spent most of my time in the bedroom, trying to sleep. We were there for about six days. I stayed in my bedroom, and everyone would cook and bring me food.

Finally, I said to Stewart, "This isn't getting any better. I really need to see a doctor." The only hospital we could get to at that point was in Greenwich. It had power, so we headed to the Greenwich Emergency Hospital. There, the doctors decided to do a head scan to make sure I wasn't suffering from a stroke. They confirmed it was Bell's palsy. The doctors gave me more steroids to take. The directions were to take six one day, then five the next, then four, then three, then two, and then one. I think they gave me double packages because, by that time, Bell's palsy had fully set in. We hadn't known we should have gone in immediately. We had been so caught up in the storm and finding a place to stay with the children that it hadn't been a priority.

The doctor there told me that Bell's palsy might last for two days, two weeks, two months, two years, or twenty years! I thought, *Okay, I will take the two weeks.* When two weeks passed, and I wasn't getting any better, I said, "All right, two months." Then, two months passed, and I thought, *I'll give it a year.* I later learned I actually had Ramsay Hunt syndrome, which causes extreme pain and is more difficult to heal.

We finally flew back to Cayman. It was a full month before I could see Dr. Choe and Dr. Jung, my doctors from Korea. They flew to Cayman from Dallas and stayed in our guesthouse. They told me not to put on any makeup in the morning and started working on me from 9:00 a.m. to 5:00 p.m. every single day. We would go into the exercise room, and I would lie down on the exercise mat. Dr. Jung would start massaging my face, while Dr. Choe did circulation and energy work for my entire body. They walked on my back and massaged around my spinal cord. Dr. Jung did deep-tissue massage all around my clavicle and squeezed the nerves in my neck and ear. They constantly helped with circulation and energy points, massaging my face and mouth muscles and working on closing my right eye.

We would eat lunch together and then go back to the exercise room for more work. Dr. Choe would go to sleep in our guesthouse when the sun went down and wake up when the sun rose in the morning. It probably was a very healthy thing to do.

Dr. Jung left early each morning to go to the markets and shop for organic food for both of them to enjoy. They stayed with me for two weeks and worked on me all day, every day. Finally, I began seeing changes. They actually got my eye to close. Dr. Choe kept telling me it would get better. What happened to my facial nerve was the result of an infected nerve in my ear canal from the shingles in my ear. The facial nerve had died from the infection, and it had to regenerate. The problem was that it only regenerated the width of a hair at a time.

The ear nerves are intertwined with the facial nerve. I was able to stay calm because I knew it was temporary, and I trusted Dr. Choe's and Dr. Jung's help. I had seen them cure things in other people that no one else could cure, and I was grateful they'd come to help me.

With Dr. Choe, Dr. Jung, and Gracie—my angels

I believe Bell's palsy was meant as a message for me to slow down. After all those years of traveling all over the world, suddenly I couldn't travel. It was simply too painful for me. Before I developed Bell's palsy, we would be gone from our Cayman home for three weeks a month on a regular basis. It was just our habit, and we enjoyed ourselves. But our friends on Cayman would say, "You're never home. Aren't you tired of traveling?"

Sometimes when I did the packing, I felt that it was too much. But then, as soon as we arrived at our travel destination, I loved it. Whatever we did and wherever we went, it was always fun and exciting. And that's why it never occurred to me to slow down. Don't forget—I spent the first weeks of my life in an airplane.

Later on, I met Alex, an astrologer at a famous spa in California, and thought it would be interesting to have an astrology reading. I had never had my horoscope read. The first thing she said was, "Dianne, you don't have a home."

I was a little surprised. I thought, *I've wasted an hour for this reading. If she doesn't think I have a home, she should come to Cayman and see my home.*

She then said, "The world is your home. You were born to travel."

Then, I listened very carefully to everything she said. It was so accurate that I asked Alex to do Stewart's chart as well. When she did, the same thing proved true for him.

But now, Bell's palsy made me see that the time had come to travel easier. In other words, don't do an overseas one-day trip, come home a day later, and leave the next day for another overseas flight. My body just told me, *That's it.* I had to give up the extreme sports, like helicopter skiing and fly-fishing in remote areas of the world. It was time to slow down and enjoy the peace and positive energy in our Cayman home, which we called the Owl's Nest.

When we are home, we enjoy the simple things, like sitting outside the first thing in the morning, enjoying a cup of coffee, and watching the green parrots in our back garden with our dog, Gracie. She is so full of love and happiness. It's just the three of us, enjoying the morning together. It feels wonderful.

> *The luck of the ladybug brings fearlessness, regeneration, rebirth, and renewal, which is a perfect reminder for everyone's life.*

Part 2
WISDOM

Chapter 21

WE ARE ONE

Strangers are just friends waiting to happen.

—ROD MCKUEN

During the helicopter-skiing week when I was in the avalanche, I met some wonderful people from Germany: Ingeborg, Wolfgang, Horst, Volker, and Willy. We had such fun getting to know each other, laughing, and learning to understand each other. Many funny jokes were told while we waited for the helicopter. Stewart and I didn't speak German, so we used our hands a lot when we talked. Thank goodness, they were good with English. We became very good friends, and they ended up "adopting" me. After the avalanche rescue, they toasted to the first day of my new life. We became like family.

Ingeborg said, "Come to Frankfurt or send your daughter to Frankfurt. We'll teach her how to speak German and go skiing together."

Eventually, we did go to Frankfurt and had the most wonderful time in Germany and traveling to Austria for beautiful ski trips. It was the start of a wonderful friendship that continues through today.

When you travel the world and your heart is open, you realize how wonderful friends are. There are so many interesting and exciting things to learn from these new friends and explore the world with them. So many exciting experiences will await you, especially when you explore this world together.

On other ski trips, we met people from Switzerland and Japan, and it was wonderful learning from them too. I skied with a Japanese girl named Midori. She and I skied the "powder eights" in perfect tandem. I learned to shout *"Banzai!"*—a Japanese battle cry—when we started our ski runs. We would start together at the top of the mountain and follow each other all the way down. Every day, they'd all say *ohayou*, which means "good morning." They also taught me to say *domo arigato*, which is "thank you very much," and *doitashimashite*, which means, "You are welcome."

Sometime later, I boarded a plane and was looking for my seat. A Japanese lady had boarded with me. She had a special cake she wanted to put in the overhead compartment, but she was too short to reach the compartment. I motioned to her that I could help, and she smiled and nodded. I put the cake in the compartment for her and sat down.

She said to me, "Domo arigato."

I replied, "Doistashimashite."

Her smile brightened, and she started talking to me a thousand miles an hour in Japanese. I laughed and tried to tell her I didn't really understand the Japanese language. She smiled. It was a happy experience.

When you are at the helicopter lodge, you will meet people from all over the world. At the end of the week of skiing, there is usually a fun costume party, in which everyone loves to participate. Three days after the avalanche, the costume party was unusually festive. Someone videotaped the event, and there I was, in the middle of the crowd, introducing everyone to everyone else. It was truly a celebration of life. There was a lot of joy and love.

Raiding the costume closet for the Friday night party. "Elvis and Fan"

* * * *

There is a story of the Golden Buddha, the world's largest gold statue, that was made around the thirteenth century. To prevent the Golden Buddha from being stolen by the invading army, the monks covered it with mud and plaster so no one could see that it was solid gold. During the raid, all the monks were killed. That gold statue was forgotten for a full two hundred years. One day, when this Buddha statue was being moved, it fell to the ground. Some of the plaster and mud chipped off, and the beautiful Golden Buddha was revealed again.

Just like the Golden Buddha, everyone has a golden light inside.

My very first spa experience was the Greenhouse Spa in Dallas, which I loved. I went with my friend Deanna. We had such a wonderful time that we decided to go to the Golden Door Spa in Escondido, California, which we had heard was very special. This spa offers one thing that most other spas don't—a highly spiritual dimension. They had exercises for the mind, body, and spirit. They also trained guests to have a healthier way of living. Over the years, I have met wonderful instructors and amazing women from around the world at this spa. From them, I have learned new spiritual practices that have changed my life.

Over the course of the first few days at the spa, everybody becomes friends and begins to open up. With new friends, you discover so much deep wisdom and sisterhood. You also discover so much support, comfort, and love from women who were strangers to you at the beginning of the week.

Deejay is the Tai Chi instructor at this spa. During my first session with him, I realized he possessed much wisdom. He has given me many insights over the years. One of the first things I heard him say was, "Men would have blown the world up long ago if it hadn't been for women. All that men know is fight or flight. Women give men something soft and comforting to soothe them when they come home after a hard day at work. If it weren't for women, this world wouldn't be here."

I found those words to be profound. When I heard Deejay speak, I thought, *I need to hear more.* I made sure I went to every one of Deejay's classes and encouraged everyone else to go too. *You know the truth when you hear it.* When I heard Deejay's wisdom, I started listening. My connection to Deejay was special, right from the beginning.

During one of my first visits, I went out for a walk in the morning, and a coyote suddenly appeared and sat down right in front of me on my path. The coyote and I locked eyes for a few minutes. It was completely mesmerizing. I headed straight to Tai Chi, feeling very excited about that encounter. After the Tai Chi session ended and everyone had left, Deejay and I walked out together, and I told him, "I had the most amazing experience on my walk before class. A coyote stopped on my path and sat down right in front of me. We just stared at each other for a few moments."

Exactly at the moment I was telling the story, the same coyote appeared again and sat down right in front of us, stared for almost a full minute, and walked away. We were both floored! It turned out that when coyotes appear like that, they are teachers of hidden wisdom, but they also teach with a sense of humor. The spirit of the coyote can remind you to not take things too seriously and to bring more balance into your life with both wisdom and playfulness. That experience with Deejay will always stay in my mind.

* * * *

From Deejay

Dianne is an incredible lady. She is like a light that keeps on shining and a gift that keeps on giving. I have been teaching for close to twenty-seven years. I have met a lot of people, and Dianne is among the top in terms of being a genuine person with a truly beautiful spirit. She is connected to healers all around the world. Whenever she discovers that anyone needs help, she does everything in her power to help them.

Many people have to work at being good to others. Dianne naturally exudes goodness in a quiet, sweet, and peaceful way. She doesn't have to put any effort into being the light that she is. She just has "it" and wants it for everyone else. Guests aren't normally like that. For years, we had Tai Chi classes that were very specifically forty-five minutes long, enabling the ladies to get to their next activity. Every class is that way. Dianne enjoyed my class so much that she would tell everyone about it, and they were then encouraged to come. She then told the activities director that we needed more time for the spiritual practices and that the class had to be extended by fifteen minutes. We were able to try it out. The full hour became so popular that we just went with it because of the demand. We then had the additional time to do some of the spiritual self-defense of Tai Chi. That extra time was exclusively because of her.

Dianne was also instrumental in getting women to go on the meditation hike. When ladies come to spas for the first time, they like to learn from women who have been there previously. The night before the meditation hike, the director would pass around a sheet describing the hike. Dianne would stand up and say, "Yes, you really want to do this!" She would explain it from her heart in a way that the ladies understood its value. We ended up doing different phases of the hike. First, we would slowly hike up the mountain in silence, do Tai Chi movements at the very top of the mountain, and then find a special rock on which to sit for silent meditation. We would then walk silently down the mountain to the labyrinth. After walking the labyrinth, we'd have a silent breakfast and then break the silence to discuss our discoveries. That's when the spiritual awareness happens.

So many people come to this spa, and someone always says something to try to influence the others. Dianne always did it differently. She opens things up in a way that helps people give themselves permission to express their true feelings, often the spiritual things that they don't realize they need. So many of them worry about what people will think. Dianne exudes her spiritual beauty naturally, and over the years, people have gravitated toward her.

There are no accidents in our lives, and a lot of what I have grown into as a teacher is because Dianne either spearheaded it, gave me the idea, or talked to other people about it. She is an incredible lady. I see her as a spiritual entity. Early on, she and I would go into specifics about spiritual things that were uncomfortable for so many people. She is like a magnet. If you have any kind of spirituality/awareness and you are around her, you begin to notice something very genuine and different about her. But unless you are willing to be quiet enough to see it, you could miss it.

Dianne has done so many things in the world that I cannot possibly imagine, yet she is incredibly humble. When you use the word *beauty*, hers shines way beyond the physical. We all have to live in two worlds. Dianne has a practical, grounded, human side, yet quietly, she is the light that shines. That is part of her beauty.

I'm very grateful for Dianne. My own personal growth has a lot to do with knowing people like her. She has done so much for me. Because she visited us so much, I can look back and see where I was when I met her and where I am now, with regard to my personal expansion. Often, I'm looked at as the teacher or the facilitator. Around Dianne, I'm like a guest. We are all students until we leave this planet, and she has been a real teacher for me. I'm glad to be her student, instead of she being mine.

* * * *

> We don't meet people by accident.
> They are meant to cross our paths for a reason.

Chapter 22

THE ART OF HELPING

There is no small act of kindness. Every
compassionate act makes large the world.

—MARY ANNE RADMACHER

Throughout my life, even before the avalanche, I always felt there was nothing more wonderful than helping other people. It's so rewarding to see the results of that help. I've been very fortunate to meet many truly incredible people in this world who make a difference by improving others' lives. Whenever this happens, I am grateful to see that miracles actually take place.

In 1989, we were skiing in Aspen, Colorado. One night, we took Rob, our ski instructor out to dinner. He told us about Amanda, a lady he wanted us to meet. Amanda was a beautiful blonde who had been paralyzed in a skiing accident. When we all had dinner together, Amanda shared her story with us.

She had been skiing when she had a bad fall, resulting in her becoming a paraplegic. Her spinal cord hadn't been severed, but the fall had fractured four of her vertebrae, which immediately left her paralyzed from the waist down. Just a few weeks later, she was told she would never walk again. Her husband left her shortly after that happened, but Amanda is such a special woman that she somehow stayed positive throughout the whole thing. We discovered she was now skiing in a mono-ski, and we asked if she would like to ski with us the next day.

Amanda was in the process of starting Challenge Aspen, a nonprofit organization devoted to helping paraplegic, quadriplegic, and blind people to ski again. When we met the next morning, she was in her mono-ski, which is an apparatus that fits tightly on your hips. To steer, she used outriggers, which are like arm-fitted, short crutches with small skis on the bottom. Amanda's mono-ski didn't fit her properly; she had to add padding and use duct tape to make her mono-ski fit. Afterward, we decided to buy Amanda a custom mono-ski, which would fit her properly.

That week, we were so impressed with Amanda and what she accomplished that we also funded Challenge Aspen, which has helped so many people enjoy skiing again. They say they love to feel the wind on their faces again while they are skiing down the slopes. In a wheelchair, that feeling doesn't happen very often.

The first event we helped sponsor was when Amanda and the founders of the program went to Walter Reed Army Medical Center in Washington, DC. Walter Reed cares for America's wounded soldiers. By coincidence, that is where I was born. Challenge Aspen asked a group of wounded young men, who had just served in Afghanistan, "Who would like to come to Snowmass, feel the wind in your face again, and ski?" Every hand in the room went up.

There wasn't enough funding to bring everyone, so decisions were based on their physical capabilities. For the entire week of that event, I was privileged to ski with all the vets who were chosen to come to Snowmass. I'll never forget one who was snowboarding with one leg. He was having so much fun that until he stopped, he didn't realize he was bleeding all the way down to his prosthesis, and it was covered in blood.

It just so happened that I had had a knee surgery and couldn't ski that week with my family. Amanda solved that. She put me in a mono-ski and asked Houston, a Challenge Aspen director, to volunteer to help me. He skied behind me holding onto a rope, which was connected to my mono-ski. He could help me turn and also hold me back from going too quickly down the slopes. He also showed me how to get into a chairlift while in the mono-ski. When you are in a mono-ski, you are actually strapped to the chairlift because the safety bar will not come down over the mono-ski.

In the mono-ski, my knees were strapped tightly together and bent in a ninety-degree angle. By the time we got to the top, my knees were killing me from being in that position. I just had to get out of that mono-ski, and I wanted to stand up for a minute. When we got off of the chairlift, Houston helped me out of the mono-ski, and we walked a little ahead. At that moment, Amanda screamed, "It's a miracle!" Then, the poor veterans who were right behind me on the chairlift in their mono-skis couldn't help but look at me and completely fell over on their sides as they were getting off the chairlift.

Luckily, no one got hurt, and we all were laughing so hard, especially Amanda. It was a great example of Amanda's playfulness, fun, and positivity. She reminded me of a quote: "Don't take life too seriously. With childlike wonder and joy, always be on the lookout for the wonderful opportunities the universe provides. You will be amazed at how much joy will come into your life."

Blind men and paralyzed vets were all skiing. Each one had a volunteer, like Houston, to look after them and help them down the slopes. All of Snowmass opened up their hearts to them. Bo Derek donated her time there and volunteered to have her photo taken with each of the young veterans. Her father was paralyzed, and she wanted to be there to honor the young men who had so bravely defended us. It was incredible.

Rock climbing was also part of the program, and another young man who had lost both legs in the war could still climb. He was unbelievable. He knew that Stewart and I were among the sponsors. He saw us from his wheelchair, where he was sitting with his young wife and his little boy. He wheeled himself over to us and started thanking us. It was really hard to say "You're welcome" to him, knowing all that he had given up. I couldn't help but have tears in my eyes for what he lost for all of us.

We take so much of our freedom for granted. These men gave so much, tirelessly and willingly, and so many of us don't appreciate what they have sacrificed. To me, it is so important to give back to them.

Our whole family skiing with Amanda

Amanda and me

* * * *

211

From Amanda

I met Dianne only one year after my fall, and she has been a beautiful, gorgeous influence on my life from that very first moment. She emanates a radiant light that was obvious to me immediately. The first day we skied together, she was so sweet and funny. We were on the chairlift together, singing at the top of our lungs. She told me her story of being buried in the avalanche, seeing the light, and surviving. On one hand, Dianne is very much a girl and loves to giggle and have fun. The other side of her is deeply connected in the euphoric realms. We resonated immediately as kindred spirits, with a deep level of understanding one another. I've always talked about seeing and calling in the angels, and Dianne does too.

To be gifted with the mono-ski was divinely beautiful. It freed me in a way that proved I could accomplish the one thing that broke my back but not my spirit. I could ski again! That restored my life, helping me leave my empty wheelchair behind. It was extremely liberating to be able to go out in nature with friends and family, do something I loved, and say a prayer to the wind. It was beyond anything I'd ever dreamed of doing again. Skiing again made me understand my own potential and helped me be all that I wanted to be for Challenge Aspen. By becoming the "face" for these efforts, I showed everyone, "If I can do it, you can do it too!" From that point on, in everything I did, I became Challenge Aspen. I am so happy to say that Challenge Aspen has helped so many people and made me into the woman that I am today.

Dianne is also amazing in the way she has learned about so many healing modalities. She's always explored all kinds of alternate therapies and played a huge part in helping me understand my own potential to heal, way beyond what any Western doctor ever told me. She also gifted me with the ability to work with Dr. Choe. Between working with him and the stem cell therapy I was undergoing, I understood that I could restore life through alternate therapies. Dianne was so convincing and full of hope, light, and possibility that I just went with it. Her belief that I would heal infused with me new energy, and there is so much to be said for that. She was an integral part of keeping hope alive for me, which is as powerful as every breath we take.

I've always had an uncanny insight that my legs will support me again. It might be through bionic technology, which is a suit that is an exoskeleton, and it will enable me to actually stand up and walk again. This reminds my muscles and nerves how to work again. I've learned that acceptance and hope can and must coexist, and I see that in Dianne too. Even though she fell down a marble staircase and shattered her knees, she restored full mobility to her body with knees that simply shouldn't be functioning. She's recovered beautifully from Bell's palsy, never thinking for one moment that she wouldn't. Dianne defies odds and lives miracles. While many of us underestimate the power of our minds, prayer, and spirits, Dianne lives and emanates it. She understands something I never would have known. We are so much bigger than our physicality, and our spirits have no limitations. Dianne is a wonderful influence on my life, and I will be grateful to her forever.

* * * *

Another experience began at the spa in Southern California, where an incredible man named Dave Towe was the Watsu (Water Shiatsu) practitioner there. The staff described the treatment as water massage and said it was good for arthritis, so I signed up. I headed to the spot where Dave was supposed to meet me. Around the corner came a gorgeous, six-foot-four Navy SEAL–looking man.

I had no idea what to expect. I also didn't know I was about to experience what is called WaterDance, the underwater, deeper version of Watsu.

The water in the pool is kept at exactly ninety-six degrees, which is body temperature. The water temperature and the gently rocking movements put me right into a meditative state. Other than the initial instructions, the entire experience takes place in complete silence. Your eyes are closed, and there are water floats around your knees to keep your legs buoyant. The first twenty minutes are done on the surface of the water, with Dave gently pulling you through the water. After that, Dave taps you silently three times to signal that he is about to take you underwater. I had no fear. I was in a deeply meditative state and actually forgot I was underwater.

You release all tension as Dave pulls you through the water, stretching your arms and legs. Dave's underwater moves propelled me through the water, and I felt as if I was swimming like a dolphin. In my meditative state, we both became amphibious forms, not human anymore. In my mind, I just saw our smiles. It was so therapeutic and magical at the same time.

I later flew Dave to Cayman, so that Stewart could experience it. Stewart saw the benefits of the relaxation techniques and enjoyed the experience.

One of my spa instructors told me that Dave had a beautiful quartz-crystal pool at his home in San Diego and that I should try a session there, if I ever had the chance. It just so happened that Stewart and my dear friend, Suladda and her husband, John were going to spend a week together at the spa. We made arrangements to go to Dave's pool, which he called the Four Elements Lagoon. It was during that visit that Dave told us about his vision to help veterans overcome post-traumatic stress disorder by providing Watsu therapy to them. Through that first discussion and from experiencing our Watsu therapies, Stewart and I decided to help Dave secure his funding to begin a San Diego–based program called the Wave Academy. Working with veterans and helping them heal from post-traumatic stress disorder is now a very important focus of his life. It's an incredible program that helped so many heal, and I am so grateful to have had a hand in starting it.

Dave Towe, my Watsu practitioner

From Dave

In my life, there are no coincidences. I look and listen very carefully to every experience, always staying present to understand each relationship at the time it appears in my life. When I first met Dianne, I knew immediately there was someone in my presence who was a kindred spirit. After two minutes in the water together, I understood that her being was at a much higher level than most. I knew she was a very old soul with great knowledge and experience. She is such an evolved entity that she is beyond human, with an incredibly powerful, angelic presence. She was playful like a dolphin. Being with her felt like we were kids again in the water, swimming around and blowing bubbles. She has an extraordinary ability to connect with you right away, in a powerful and beautiful way, through her unique sense of curiosity. Dianne possesses the ability to achieve a deep, beautiful level of human understanding.

I had the opportunity to work with both Dianne and Stewart, providing this unique blend of aquatic therapy, a multidimensional conscious experience. WaterDance and Watsu therapy help individuals peel away the different aspects of their selves so they can experience remembering who they are. The pool is specifically ninety-six degrees, the same temperature of embryonic fluid. Being in that temperature of water is like a memory "reboot" for your consciousness, bringing you back to the pre-birth state. After about twenty minutes, your skin, which is also ninety-six degrees, cannot differentiate where water and skin begin and end. At that point, the nervous system begins to let go and quiet down, the chatter goes away, and you begin a journey of rediscovery in the water. It is a different journey for everyone. Some go off into space and have experiences with deceased loved ones or angels. Others speak with ancestors, animals, or creatures in the sea.

Many people I work with experience awakenings, where they "wake up" to information that has been covered by layers. Some of these awakenings can be tearful and painful. Some can be joyful. Because we carry unresolved emotions in our muscles, many people have a full emotional release. One to two percent have a full-blown rebirth. They go into a fetal position, turn blue, stop breathing, and then start breathing again. There is always some kind of transformational moment that is quite sacred for me. Whenever anyone finishes a session, something is changed in their being. There is no good or bad. It is always perfect.

When I first met Dianne, my focus had become to work with veterans from Afghanistan who suffered with PTSD. Tragically, they have a suicide rate of twenty-two lives a day. They suffer from what is defined as "moral injury." They've gone off to war and killed young children. Then, they come home to their own young kids and wives and have a very hard time understanding what they did. The Wave Academy brings them back, first to their bodies, then back to themselves, and then to their lives and their communities.

Without Dianne's help, my vision and dream would still be only that. Instead, we are now a thriving nonprofit. Hundreds of individuals have benefited from our program, and that number is increasing every single week. We have no idea what the ripple effect of this will be, not only on the vets but also on their families and the world around them. Our seven-year goal and dream is to design and build a nationally recognized aquatic learning campus, where Wave Academy will conduct research, provide education, and bring more people into the warm water. We aim to be the center of understanding on how this therapeutic experience impacts all different aspects of the human condition. This journey would not be happening without Stewart and Dianne.

Dianne is such a joyful, interactive spirit. We are very much kin to the ocean. She is definitely a dolphin! I will always be incredibly grateful to her and Stewart for their generosity and support. Many other "angels" have arrived to support Wave Academy in helping these young men and women who have given their lives for us. We are honored to help them "come home" again. I love Dianne and Stewart so much. They are a great inspiration, and many lives have been touched because of them.

* * * *

Another wonderful program that I am proud to be part of also originated in at a spa in San Diego, when I invited Jennifer Ables to have lunch with me there. In 2012, our dear friend from university days, Doc called my cell phone just as I was landing in San Diego.

Doc was a two-star rear admiral and the base commander in San Diego. He said, "Dianne, there is someone I would like you to meet. Her name is Jennifer Ables. She is a salsa instructor at Mary Murphy's dance academy in San Diego. Mary is one of the judges on the television show *So You Think You Can Dance*. They are both involved with a group called Soldiers Who Salsa. Mary and Jennifer had an idea to teach wounded vets with post-traumatic stress how to help them recover and heal, one step at a time, through dancing. Would you like to meet her?"

I was excited to meet her, so I invited Jennifer for lunch, and she told me about their dream for Soldiers Who Salsa. They wanted to help marines and soldiers who had been traumatized by war to reconnect with their wives and girlfriends through dance. They already had a board of directors, and Doc was involved because of his connection on the military board.

Like most little boys, these soldiers had been told all their lives, "Don't pull that little girl's pigtails, and don't pull the puppy's tail." Then they are trained to shoot and kill someone. We can't imagine how that would affect a person. The soldiers find that it's hard for them to forget, much less freely hug their wives and girlfriends when they come back.

Jennifer teaches them salsa dancing and the fox-trot too. They eventually ask, "Can I bring my wife or girlfriend to the dance studio?" Her answer is always yes because that's exactly what she wants to have happen. She wants them to remember how nice it feels to hold their loved ones again. The beautiful music that plays is a romantic Bee Gees song. And as they listen, they eventually want to dance with their arms around their wives or girlfriends.

Again, as my plane was landing in San Diego, I was delighted to receive a call from Jennifer, inviting me to Mary Murphy's tenth anniversary dance academy party. Of course, I said yes, but there were two problems: I was in San Diego, going to a spa, so I didn't have any clothes to go to a ballroom dance party. And, I didn't have a dance partner.

When I arrived at the spa, I asked anybody I saw if they could come with me. I wasn't even thinking of what I was going to wear. I just thought I needed to find a dance partner. I asked one massage therapist, but he couldn't go.

One of the instructors said, "Why don't you ask the chef? He is an entertainer who sings, and he also loves to dance." I hardly knew the chef, but I went right into the kitchen and invited him. He was willing to go!

Then, I was immediately called into the director's office. The director said to me, "Dianne, the guests are not allowed to date the staff." It was completely innocent—I was just looking for a dance partner—but I didn't want to get anyone in trouble, so I gave up on that idea. I decided to go without a partner. And then I thought, *Just say yes!*

The next problem was what to wear. I asked one of the fitness instructors, Suzie, to lend me her black frilly pants, which she wore in one of our fun costume classes. She lent them to me, and I wore them with my black Lulu Lemon exercise top. The jewelry designer from the shop at the spa kindly and generously loaned me jewelry to wear, which made my outfit complete. I was ready for the dance, and I ordered a limo in this crazy outfit to take me to Mary Murphy's party.

That night I met Louis van Amstel, who was one of the ballroom dance instructors on *Dancing with the Stars*. He asked me to dance with him. He thought I knew how to dance, and as we were dancing, he would call out dance steps. I had to say, "Sorry, but I don't know these steps." We still had so much fun, laughing and dancing.

I also danced with other handsome ballroom dancers. I didn't know who they were, but it was an incredible experience, which I would have missed if I had worried about not having a dance partner or party clothes. That evening, Jennifer introduced me to Mary Murphy. We had a chance to talk about the program Soldiers Who Salsa, and I was very impressed.

Later, I danced some of the marines involved with this program. There was only one soldier who didn't dance, but he did seem to enjoy the music. I could see that he was suffering emotionally. It was very moving. The other eight soldiers had smiles on their faces, and they were excellent salsa dancers. This is a testament to the important work being done by this program. Each one asked me to dance, which was very sweet. It was a lovely evening. I was so excited when I got back to the spa and was happy that I had decided to go.

Me. In my Lulu Lemon top Mary Murphy, and Jennifer Ables at Mary's 10th Anniversary Dance party.

I first met Eleanor at a party in Cayman. She is an accomplished underwater macro photographer, who reproduces her photos of tiny sections of fish and coral into beautiful, colorful, wall-sized artwork. Later, we were both sitting next to each other on a plane to Los Angeles, where she was going to have medical tests. She had her little Shih Tzu, Ruby with her in her travel case, and she tucked the case under her seat. We started talking, and after about thirty minutes, the stewardess came up to us and said, "I hope you don't mind, but your dog is curled up asleep on the pilot's lap." We had no idea—we just thought Ruby was being really quiet! She must have crawled out of her bag and had gone into the cockpit before the plane took off. The stewardess asked Elle if she was okay with that, but Elle wanted Ruby back. I held her on my lap for the rest of the trip, petting her, and keeping her calm. I had no idea at that point that Elle was ill. She looked so vibrant and healthy. She told me she was having some tests done, but I didn't get the whole story.

During the next months, we saw each other at parties, and she looked gorgeous. Then one day, I was driving by her home, which is fairly close to mine, and I saw her in a wheelchair, wearing a breathing apparatus. Ruby was in her lap. Elle had deteriorated to almost nothing. She smiled at me, and I stopped immediately. That is when she told me she had Sudeck's atrophy, a chronic, systemic disease that comes with severe pain, swelling, and, over time, complete physical deterioration. It is similar to Lou Gehrig's disease, but instead of muscle deterioration, Sudeck's atrophy affects the organs. The doctors had already told her that she had only a few months to live and that they would only be able to keep her comfortable with pain medication.

I was completely shocked! She was only thirty-nine years old and just beautiful.

I immediately thought of Dr. Choe, who I knew would be able to help Elle. By some miracle, Dr. Choe was in Cayman, treating my neighbor, and I introduced him to Elle. I knew he could help her, so Stewart and I decided to pay for her first treatments. Almost thirteen years have passed, and she is now beautiful and healthy. It's truly a miracle!

* * * *

From Eleanor

Twice before, I'd had episodes of Sudeck's. The first time was about nineteen years earlier. It can't be cured with Western medicine, but it was something that could be managed with quite aggressive therapy. The illness is basically a short-circuiting of the sympathetic nervous system that occurs after an injury. It is also called reflexive dystrophy. When it occurs, your blood supply is compromised because blood isn't getting to where it should go in your body. It causes complex regional pain.

When I met Dianne, I was in the middle of my third episode. Sudeck's atrophy is so rare that doctors have not been able to do viable studies on it because not enough people have suffered from it. The first occurrence took ten months to diagnose in the UK. The doctor who diagnosed me hadn't seen it for two years.

I had been overdoing weights at the gym and likely had strained something. That caused an affliction in my right hand, which was awful, as I am extremely right-handed. My entire hand was blue, and I couldn't pick up a pen for ten months.

My second attack came after a fall. I was in a department store, buying a kettle, and was wearing high heels. Someone had dropped some packs of butter on the floor, and I skidded in the butter and did the splits. I stiffened up to hold on to the kettle and also to anything that was near to me.

I had to have surgery on my shoulder, and the orthopedic surgeon wasn't able to reconnect the ball and socket joint. He shaved that joint and damaged the blood flow to the clavicle. I went to see him a couple of weeks after the surgery because my bra straps kept falling down. I didn't connect this injury with Sudeck's because it had been years since my first episode. During my examination, I mentioned that I had Sudeck's, and he immediately sent me for an ultrasound. In just two weeks, my trapezius muscle, which had been about six inches thick had shrunk to half a centimeter (less than one inch). I also had a big hole in the back of my shoulder. It became an extremely long and drawn-out episode because it was global, rather than affecting only one half of my body.

Then, the third episode started with an extremely minor surgery I had in Cayman. At my worst, I was seventy-seven pounds, in a wheelchair, and on oxygen. The long and the short of it is that my having had this illness led to my extraordinary relationship with this extraordinary woman, who literally saved my life.

After meeting Dianne on the plane, it was over a matter of months that I became the incredible shrinking woman. Dianne had been away, so she didn't see any of this happening. I was becoming more and more immobile. I couldn't drive or see very well. It was horrible. Farther down the line, my breathing became more and more problematic. I never vocalized how sick I was to anyone. I didn't even tell my family in the UK. I told them I wasn't well, but I didn't want to tell them just how sick I was, as we have a complex family dynamic. The degree of anxiety it would have caused me to tell them, particularly when my breathing became problematic, wasn't worth it. I believe telling them would have shortened my life. At that point, I'd been given only three months to live.

When Dianne found out how sick I was, she was on my case all the time, saying, "You need to go to Dallas to see Dr. Choe." I just kept thinking, *Why would I go to Dallas?* Then, I was given the three-months-left-to-live diagnosis. I was turning forty, and I remember my fortieth birthday very clearly. I felt like I was at my own wake. It was horrible. Nobody recognized me.

On December 17, after my birthday, I thought, *I need to find a way to be okay with this diagnosis.* I thought I needed to accept my lot. I had done all that I could do. I was just back from LA and was out walking Ruby when Carol drove past and saw me.

Carol stopped her car and said, "Look, we have flown in Dr. Choe from Dallas to treat my husband. Please take my number and call me so he can see you too."

I said, "Okay, okay," all the time thinking that I couldn't remember ever paying such blatant lip service to someone. I felt like I had to call it quits and come to terms with whatever was left.

I stopped taking all my medication. I decided I'd rather feel every ounce of pain I could feel. I thought, *It's about serendipity and the cosmic universe. You get what you need, not what you want.* Then, on New Year's Eve, I had a very odd dream. I was standing at the side of the road and saw my dad standing on the pedestrian island in the middle. He had passed away, but in my dream, he was about fifty-one, and I could feel myself walking into his arms.

He said, "Elle, I know what's wrong with you. You are going to be okay, and I'm going to make you better." He said this to me three times. He sat down on the curb, saying, "I've just got to make a phone call." He pulled out a Nokia flip-phone and called my brother, with whom I'm not particularly close. He left him a message, saying, "Mike, I just want you to know I'm with Elle, and she's going to be okay. I know what's wrong with her, and I know how to make her better."

Then I woke up. It was 9:14 on New Year's Day. I called Dianne and told her about my dream. She told me about her near-death experience and that I had to believe what my dad had said: I was going to be fine. I phoned Dr. Choe, and at six o'clock that evening, he and Dr. Jung came to see me.

I didn't know what kind of doctors they were. I had no idea if they would even want a full medical history. But they didn't want to know anything. They just wanted to get to work on me. They worked on my face and my left bicep because if I picked up my arm, there was no muscle left. Dianne kept coaxing me to continue seeing them, and she paid for my first visits. Those visits were a true gift of love from her.

The fact was that whatever Dr. Choe and Dr. Jung were doing, it was working. I had to keep going to see them. The only asset I had was a house in London. I called agents there and said, "Sell it for whatever you can get. I need the money now!" They did just that. I paid off my mortgage, took whatever cash was left, and gave it all to Dr. Choe. I flew to Dallas, stayed for a month, and was treated seven days a week for five hours a day. It was horrifyingly painful, and I was in tears every single day. I went straight from Dallas to Cedars-Sinai Medical Center in Los Angeles, where they would measure me to gauge how much I was shrinking. By May of that year, my rib cage was four inches bigger than it had been in December. From there, it took several years, but I made a complete recovery.

With Eleanor, at the Chaine des Rôtisseurs Black Tie and Cowboy Boots Ball

I still carry the disease, but I'm never going to get ill again. It's just not going to happen! Being treated by Dr. Choe because of Dianne was absolutely a miracle. Every last breath I take, I take with Dianne. I don't say that lightly. Dianne gave me back my life. Honestly, there's nothing I've ever experienced that will ever touch that in significance. I wouldn't be here if it weren't for her. I wouldn't have had my wedding day, which took place in her backyard. It's impossible to thank somebody for that.

* * * *

When I saw beautiful Elle in a wheelchair and on oxygen, I couldn't believe it. I knew Dr. Choe was in Cayman at that time, and I just wanted Elle to see him and start treatments. Stewart and I gladly paid for the first week of treatments, and it was so wonderful to see Elle respond so positively. We should all look for opportunities to "connect" people. It is such a rewarding experience.

Chapter 23

SACRED GEOMETRY, SACRED LIFE: THE LABYRINTH

The path to our destination is
not always a straight one.

—BARBARA HALL

The first time I walked on a labyrinth was during my first visit to the spa in Southern California. It was the early 1990s and an incredible trip. I was with Dr. Christiane Northrup, who is a true visionary when it comes to women's wellness, and Ina Garten, who is the host of the Food Network program *Barefoot Contessa*.

At orientation, I learned that this spa had a labyrinth. The staff described it as ancient sacred architecture, a circular structure on the ground with patterns that are aligned with the moon and stars. You walk it as a form of meditation.

They said, "We encourage you to walk the labyrinth on your own and also walk it with a small group. At the end of the week, we will have a labyrinth ceremony, and we will walk it with all the guests together."

I thought, *Who has time to walk the labyrinth on their own, much less with a small group? With our schedules, we don't even have time to wash our hair!* So I never walked the labyrinth on my own or even saw it until our last evening, when we all walked it together.

On our last evening, as promised, we had a labyrinth ceremony. It was so beautiful! The entire outer edge of the labyrinth was surrounded by candlelit lanterns. There was a full moon overhead, and soft, soothing music was echoing through the trees. We were instructed to walk the path to the labyrinth in silence. We stepped onto it, one by one. With the first step, it was magical. It was so serene and peaceful.

That particular week, I had met an elegant, powerful woman who had the most gorgeous blue eyes and blonde hair. When she saw that we were coming straight at one another on the labyrinth, she just put her arms around me and gave me the biggest hug—her hug felt so good that it brought tears to my eyes.

Walking the labyrinth made it clear to me that we're all on the same path of life, yet we each walk our own way. We are all connected.

The ceremony was on a Saturday night, and I went home the next day. I walked into the house, sat down at the computer, and looked up "labyrinth makers." I thought it would be nice to share this experience of a labyrinth with my friends in Cayman. I knew most of them would never go to a spa and have a labyrinth ceremony. I decided to order one.

I didn't know anything about labyrinths, except that I had walked one. When I looked up labyrinth makers on the Internet, I found the name Robert Ferre. I picked up the phone and called him. He agreed to make a portable one for me out of canvas. It would be thirty-five feet in diameter, with grommet holes around the edges so we could stake it to the ground. He asked me what color I wanted. Although purple is not usually my color, that's what I chose. It turned out to be the color of the Pran chakra, which is the highest of all the chakras. Before I knew it, I had purchased a purple, hand-painted canvas labyrinth, and it was soon en route to Cayman.

When it arrived, Stewart got the call that it was held in customs; it was packed in a cooler! Stewart went to the Customs Office and paid the duty that customs charged. When he came back, he had "the look" on his face. He asked, "Dianne, *what* is a labyrinth, and why do we have one?"

I said, "Oh, you're going to love it!"

He looked at the labyrinth with his arms crossed in front of him with the body language of *I'm not having anything to do with it.* I don't think he was a happy camper.

I realized I hadn't even planned where I was going to place it. Somehow, just like it was meant to be, the labyrinth fit in my garden just perfectly between all of our palm trees. We set it up and invited about ten of our friends to an evening candlelit ceremony, where we would walk the labyrinth under the palm trees and full moon.

Everyone dressed in white, even Stewart. I chose to play the music from *Graceful Passages.* I read the opening quote from the *Graceful Passages* book, which is one of my very favorites. "No matter who you are, no matter where you're from, no matter what tradition guides your way, there comes a time to be touched through the heart." The music seemed to put everybody in a most peaceful state.

Before stepping onto the labyrinth, I gave everyone a small piece of paper and asked each person to write down the one thing they didn't want in their lives anymore. Then, each one of us would burn those notes in the center of the labyrinth as part of the ceremony. Afterward, we walked out of the labyrinth, free of what we no longer wanted in our lives. On the way out of the labyrinth, we imagined what that would actually feel like. Everybody loved it, even Stewart.

From that first ceremony on, I began having labyrinth ceremonies under a full moon because everyone enjoyed it so much. More and more friends wanted to come. These gatherings soon turned into labyrinth parties. People started bringing cookies, cheese, and goodies. We started serving wine and tea and having full labyrinth evenings. We'd leave the food in the kitchen and then walk the labyrinth. Afterward, we would talk about our experiences. I did that as often as I could during the times we were at home. It was always meaningful to everyone.

Our dogs, Kiki and Goodness, realized the labyrinth was something special. Somehow, they knew never to run across it. They would always lie down next to it to be with us while we were walking it, but they never got on top of it. A Catholic priest who lived on Cayman, Father Michael, came and blessed it. I also had a space-clearer from Bali sprinkle it with sacred holy water and place a "bubble of blessing" over it, so that nothing bad could ever enter.

After Hurricane Ivan, I thought that my friends in Cayman really would benefit from a labyrinth ceremony. We were all in severe shock at the devastation on the island, which was still very barren. There were no leaves anywhere. You could see the airport from my backyard because so many of the trees were gone. The island looked as if an atomic bomb had hit us.

I invited twelve people for our Ivan Hurricane walk. For the theme of the ceremony, I asked everyone to walk the path into the center of the labyrinth while thinking of what Cayman had been like before the hurricane, with all the beautiful palm trees and foliage. In the center of the labyrinth, we stopped to think about what Cayman looked like at that very moment, after all the destruction. But when we walked out, I wanted us to think of what it could become in the future. It was very moving, and I think it did a lot to support everyone's healing.

After the avalanche, I became even more aware of the endless possibilities in helping and connecting people, and the labyrinth became another incredible way to do that. One especially meaningful experience was with Igor Burdenko, the famous Russian swimming coach who pioneered aquatic therapy. Igor defected to America with his family in 1981 and started the Burdenko Institute in Boston, Massachusetts. He hardly spoke English when he arrived in the United States, but he became so well known in America that when Tonya Harding hit Nancy Kerrigan in the knee, Nancy went to Igor for help. Nancy did all her therapy in the pool with him. She skated her entire Olympic routine in the water. Igor has been a training consultant to numerous athletes from the NBA, NFL, and NHL; the US and Russian Olympic teams;

members of the US Paralympics team; and top international dancers and figure skaters.

I met Igor one day on the beach in Cayman. He helped me with some exercises for my knee in my pool, and we became friends. I also met his wife, Irina, and their daughter. One night when I was having a labyrinth evening, the doorbell rang. There stood Igor. I was so surprised. He didn't really know what a labyrinth was, but he had heard I was having a labyrinth evening and wanted to experience it for himself. He had just arrived in Cayman from Walter Reed Army Medical Center in Washington, DC, where he had been invited to present a water-exercise program for the wounded vets who had lost their legs or arms. In the water, they were able to be upright and free of their wheelchairs.

That evening, the music from *Graceful Passages* was playing, and we walked the labyrinth by candlelight. There was a full moon, and it was such a peaceful walk. When Igor got to the center of the labyrinth, he knelt down because he felt so much emotion. When he finished walking out of the labyrinth, he said, "Dianne, that was such a gift. I was walking the labyrinth for all those men who have lost their legs." He had decided to pray for them in the center because they would never be able to walk a labyrinth.

Igor wanted to give me a gift in exchange. He taught me a healthy breathing practice to improve my life and told me to do it every single day. To do this, you inhale, inhale, and inhale. And when you think you can't inhale anymore, you inhale even more, until it hurts. Then you exhale slowly. You do the inhalations five times standing, five times sitting, and five times lying down on the bed. You immediately notice how shallow your breath normally is. When you take very deep breaths, it is very healing and restorative.

One day I was thinking about how wonderful it would be to have more people experience the benefits of a labyrinth walk. I thought we should have a permanent labyrinth in Cayman. The National Art Gallery was still in the design stage, and I thought it would be a perfect place to build a labyrinth. I called the director of the National Gallery, and she agreed it would be a welcome addition.

Once the National Gallery of the Cayman Islands was built, I contacted Chuck Hunter and Marty Kermeen to build a permanent labyrinth. They design and build labyrinths all over the world. In fact, one of their designs had been installed at Walter Reed Medical Center, where the patients in wheelchairs were able to "walk" a labyrinth. We designed the one at the National Gallery in Cayman based on the famous labyrinth at the Chartres Cathedral in France. This is the same design that I had first walked at the spa in California and had so much meaning.

The Cayman labyrinth project took about a year to plan and complete. Suddenly, I was struck with Ramsay Hunt syndrome of Bell's palsy and in excruciating pain. When the installation finally began, my Bell's palsy was at its worse. At that point, the nerves had pulled my face so tight that my right eye could not even close. It was so severe that the doctors wanted to sew my eye shut. My whole face was completely drooping.

The project had taken so long already that I couldn't imagine delaying the installation any further. I said, "Well, let's go ahead and do it anyway."

When I finally met Chuck and Marty, my eye was taped shut, with cotton and gauze over it. I looked like a World War I hospital patient, but I didn't care because I was so excited about the labyrinth. When you are busy and inspired, it's easy not to think about what you look like.

Dave Towe, my Watsu instructor, had given me beautiful quartz crystals. White quartz crystals are known to amplify intentions, so I thought it would be good to install them in the labyrinth. I took the crystals in the ocean to "clear" them. The labyrinth builders had created a stainless-steel grid, which was beautiful on its own. This was to protect the labyrinth from being destroyed by hurricanes. I placed the crystals in the steel grid all around the path of the labyrinth. The concrete was poured right over the crystals. The labyrinth design was then hand-painted over the concrete in a light bluish-gray color.

When the labyrinth was finally done, we had a small ceremony with the director of the National Gallery, the labyrinth makers, and a small group of friends who had come to the labyrinth evenings in my garden. Before the ceremony, I took the bandages off my eye and face. I looked so awful. I noticed it was hard for some of my friends to look at me, but it didn't bother me at all. I was so excited that the labyrinth was finally done, and I was grateful to be able to gift it to the National Gallery in Cayman.

For the official dedication, the staff at the National Gallery was kind enough to wait until I was feeling and looking better. The dedication was a few months later, and I invited Chuck and Marty to come back the following May for the official dedication. Chuck had made a metal medallion to put in the center that read "The Dianne Siebens Labyrinth." That was his gift to me.

The ceremony took place at twilight, and every mosquito in the world had just hatched. During the beautiful prayer, dedication, and gratitude, we were all jumping around and putting on bug spray. We finally walked the Cayman labyrinth, and I was so happy. It was an amazing walk that was filled with love and gratitude.

Dedication of the Cayman labyrinth

We are not human beings having a spiritual experience. We are spiritual beings having a human experience.

—Wayne Dyer

Chapter 24

EARTH ANGELS

Until one has loved an animal, a part of
one's soul remains unawakened.

—ANATOLE FRANCE

Our plan was to name our home Paradise by the Sea because of all the surrounding palm trees. I had a logo planned for our stationery with a beautiful palm tree in the center. Then, while we were building, an owl family moved into one of our air conditioning ducts. We didn't have the windows in yet, and the mother owl swooped down every night to hunt and came back every morning. Each day during our construction, I would see her sitting on the top of the scaffolding, looking down at me. I'd say hello to her in the morning, and she would sit there through all the jackhammer noise and everything else going on. Then, she would swoop down at night to find food to feed her two babies.

One day, all the workers came to us because they thought they'd found a baby chicken on the floor. Stewart said, "That's not a chicken; that's an owl." We'd had no idea, but the mother owl had made a nest inside the air conditioning duct. We picked up the baby, got a very tall ladder, looked into the duct, and found another baby. It turned out that the bigger, one who had hatched first, had pushed the little one out of the nest. We had to move both of them out of the duct and replace the forty feet of it because the mother owl had filled it with mice and rats to feed her babies. Because of that, we named our home the Owl's Nest.

Once we replaced the forty feet of air conditioning duct, we had to find the owls a home. There was a man on the island named Cardinal D, who had a bird farm. He trained peacocks to sound like Elvis Presley. They would say, "Thank you very much," copying Elvis's voice when you gave them a treat. Cardinal D had all kinds of parrots and birds, so we took the two baby owls over to him. We gave him money to buy raw hamburger and other things for them to eat. He ended up raising the babies, while the mother owl flew all around the farm and even visited her babies.

Over the years, we have been blessed to have all kinds of animals everywhere on the property, from iguanas to butterflies and beautiful green parrots. I notice even the tiniest ones and am always sure to take a moment and say thank you to them for being part of our lives.

Whenever we fished in Alaska, so many mother bears were attracted to me. I decided it was because they knew, somehow, that they could trust me. During one trip, a mother bear left her three little cubs on the bank in front of me and went downriver to catch salmon for them. It was like she told them not to move because I was watching them. They just stayed there, playing across the river, waiting for her to come back, letting me "bear-sit" them. When the mother came back with a big salmon, there was a lot of soft grunting while they feasted on their salmon. It was amazing to see.

Babysitting the bears

Bears are magnificent. It is certainly a privilege to see them in their natural habitat. The wilderness belongs to them; it isn't ours. Whenever we went fishing and got too close to the bears, we would just back out of the river and wait for them to go by. They understood that we respected their environment and always left us alone.

I have always believed that dogs are our very special angels. They show such unconditional love, loyalty, and devotion, no matter what is done to them. They go above and beyond the call of duty. They become our therapy when we need them, and they turn our thoughts from despair to joy. I think there is much to learn from this.

In my own life, dogs of all kinds have always completely trusted me. Because it has always been this way, I never thought it was unusual. They come straight to me, even when people say, "Oh, don't touch him. He doesn't like people or strangers."

One time I was with a group of working dogs in Greenland. I was told not to pet these dogs, but one came right up to me and put his head on my knee. Of course, I petted him as soon as his head was on my knee.

After my dad died, Stewart and I brought my mother to live in Dallas to be close to us. We bought her a little Shih Tzu puppy to be her new companion. We trained the puppy, so the puppy was already housebroken when my mother first moved to Dallas. My mother immediately fell in love with that Shih Tzu and named her Lady. One day, my mother went to a picnic with her friends and saw a darling little cocker spaniel puppy. She thought this puppy was so cute and that it would make a great playmate for Lady. The problem was that the cocker spaniel wasn't even housebroken, and my mother had no idea how to train a puppy.

Because the puppy wasn't housebroken, Stewart and I suddenly had a new puppy. Taffy moved in with us and became the first dog that we had as a family. It was 1985, and Heidi already had a Siamese cat named Kitty. Kitty had no claws but could scare Taffy away from her by scratching at her. Later, when they relaxed with each other, they got along beautifully.

People say that a dog picks you. Taffy always loved me the most. She was my "Velcro dog" and would never leave my side. If she fell asleep and I left the room, she'd wake up and start to cry. When I went out, she would lie down by the door and stay there until I came home. When we left Dallas to move to Cayman, Taffy and Kitty were still with us. By that time, Heidi had graduated high school and had started university. When she went to university, her boyfriend gave her a beautiful husky named Kiki, whom we inherited in 1998, when Heidi graduated and got her first job. When Heidi got married in 2001, Taffy walked down the aisle wearing pearls, Kiki had a collar made of flowers, and Goodness had on a collar that had a black bow tie.

In 2010, Stewart and I went to Greenland. He wanted to try heli-skiing in the untracked glaciers in Greenland. I wasn't able to heli-ski anymore, so I decided it would be wonderful to go out on my own in a dog sled, to travel over the pack ice and touch a glacier. I wanted to touch, walk on, and photograph ice that was thousands and thousands of years old. The guides made arrangements for me to go out to a glacier with a dog sled team. The sled was a homemade sled. The driver made it comfortable for me and padded it with blankets. My driver stood on the rudders extending out behind the sleigh. I sat on the sleigh, and he offered to cover me with blankets. For extra protection from the cold, the driver gave me one of his parkas to put over my ski suit. I wore goggles, a face scarf, and the Inuit's parka.

There were ten dogs pulling the sled, running parallel to each other, on one lead. My driver had taken this team over the pack ice that morning to hunt for seals where the pack ice had started to melt and open, so the dogs were somewhat tired. I was happy about this because the team pulled us a little slower than usual. The scenery was spectacular, and my driver would slow the team down to point out amazing icebergs and unforgettable scenery.

I was warned not to touch the sled dogs because, supposedly, these dogs were not tame. They were working dogs that had received very little love or affection from people. They were definitely not treated the same way Stewart and I treated Kiki and Taffy, but they were a husky mix and reminded me of Kiki, our beloved husky.

Leading the sled was a beautiful white Malamute female, who seemed to want to come to me. When we stopped at the glacier, all the dogs lay down on the ice, but she came and put her head in my lap. Even though I was told not to pet her, I just started petting her. She was so sweet. My Inuit driver smiled and said nothing.

I got out of the sled and walked across the pack ice, right up to the glacier. It was vast. I knelt down and touched the edge of the glacier. It looked like a frozen blanket of ice cascading right down to the pack ice. It was almost unbelievable to think I was touching something that was thousands and thousands of years old. I wondered, *Oh, my gosh. What does this glacier know?* Later that week, while I was walking through town, I saw the white Malamute outside of a little hut. She was chained to the ice by a pick. When she saw me, she sat up and howled like a wolf. I wanted to go over to her, but I couldn't walk that far. It was very touching.

Dog sledding to the glacier in KULUSUK, Greenland

Malamute chained in the snow

Helicopter skiing in Kulusuk, Greenland

At the end of the trip, I was at the airport in Greenland with Mad Max, one of our heli-skiing guides. Max was the national Russian snowboarding champion from Kamchatka, Russia. I went into the duty-free shop, which was a small shop and filled with things that the Inuits had made. Then, I spotted a rack of furs. I tried on a beautiful fur vest that was supposedly made of wolf furs. Mad Max gave me a wolf whistle. That whistle really made me feel great, so I bought the fur vest.

When I returned home and looked at it, I realized it looked just like Kiki's fur. Of course, a wolf's and a husky's fur coats do look alike. I started to think it was made from the sled dog's fur. Because of that, I never wore it. I brought it to Heidi, but she didn't want to wear it either. It was beautiful, though. I ended up giving it to a beautiful friend of Heidi's, who still enjoys wearing it to this day.

Heidi and Kiki

It was February 1998 when Goodness came into our lives. Stewart and I were in Cayman, walking Kiki and Taffy. By then, Kiki was about four, and Taffy was thirteen. All of a sudden, something came up behind me and licked at my little finger. I had no idea what it was. When I turned around, I saw a stray dog in terrible shape. He had long reddish hair, like an Irish setter, and the shape of his face was like a collie's. He was very matted and emaciated and had clearly been abused and abandoned. I very gently said, "Hello," and he ran away into the bushes. He was petrified. After that, we looked for him for a while but couldn't find him. When we continued walking, he decided to come out and follow us all the way home. Kiki really liked him and started kissing his face. His tail wagged for the very first time.

Stewart said we should try to feed him. The dog was clearly starving. We could see every bone in his body, and when we started to pet him, his spine felt like the back of a knife blade. I touched his back and said, "Oh, my goodness!"

Adrian, our house manager, heard me and asked, "Oh, Miss Dianne, shall we feed Goodness?" And, that is how Goodness got his name. We fed him and later took him to the vet. We learned later that not only was he starving, but he was full of worms, every kind a dog can have. He even had heartworm. The vet didn't think he'd survive the treatment, but Goodness held on. We kept him outside because Stewart had agreed to keep him as long as he would be an "outside" dog. Goodness lived outside but would never leave our property. He played with Kiki every time we took her outside. They formed a bond right away. At night, when we would go upstairs to bed, he had the saddest face. He would look at us through the glass doors and bark. Then, he would press himself against the French doors and watch us go up the stairs. Kiki, Taffy, Stewart, and I would look at him and say good night. I felt sorry that we couldn't let him inside.

The next time Stewart went away on a trip, I opened the door and let Goodness in. He ran straight up to my gorgeous yellow-silk sofa and went to the bathroom all over it. I screamed at him and scared him so much that he flopped onto the floor and got soaked in his own urine. He never did that again. That trained him immediately, and he would watch Taffy and especially Kiki whenever they wanted to go out. He followed their lead.

The next thing he knew, Adrian was giving him a bath, and I'd never seen a happier dog! It turned out that his hair was fluffy and soft. The vet said he had the softest ears she had ever felt. Goodness had a beautiful white star on his chest that we hadn't seen before his bath.

Kiki and Goodness

When Stew came home from his trip, Goodness took one look at him and fell in love. From that moment on, wherever Stewart went, Goodness went too. They became best buddies, and it was true love both ways. If Stewart was working in his office, and friends came over and tried to walk into Stewart's room, Goodness would bark and not let them in. He was guarding Stewart. Goodness would jump in the car with Stewart to go get the mail. Kiki was also madly in love with Goodness. Wherever she went, there was Goodness. Kiki was his angel. When they were outside, all you could see were two long, floppy tails running together all over the garden. It was true love. They were always together.

The Humane Society held a fund-raiser to show how beautiful and tame the stray and abandoned dogs would become with a loving home and a family. We hired a video team to video Goodness in and out of our home. The song that played in the background of this video was "If My Friends Could See Me Now." I'm sure no one would believe the change in Goodness from the moment we saw him to what he had become. That dog had so much love to give, and we gave it right back to him. He was a beautiful addition to our family. He never jumped on the furniture or made a mess a second time. So much for Stewart's idea that Goodness should be our outside dog!

The first year Goodness was with us, we went on a trip. When we returned to Cayman, we couldn't find Goodness anywhere. When we asked our staff where he was, they told us they thought he had run away. We were all devastated, especially Kiki. We put his picture in the paper and offered a reward in our ad. We got some calls from concerned people who had found a stray red dog, but it was never Goodness. We would go searching for him in Stewart's Ford Explorer, and Kiki would sit in the front seat, looking all over for Goodness. She was in mourning. She wouldn't eat and was getting black circles on the white area under her beautiful blue eyes.

We were out walking one day about four weeks later and heard dogs barking. We thought it was the neighbor's dogs. A lady lived across from us on the canal, and she had six dogs. Those dogs usually barked when they saw us. But Kiki started going crazy, so we let her off her leash. She ran over to the canal and kept barking. Stewart went over to see what she was making her bark so much. There was Goodness under the canal, standing on a coral ledge under the boat docks!

We think he might have encountered some workmen and probably barked at them, and they must have gotten upset and threw him in the canal. There was no way for him to get out. There wasn't even a boat ramp for him to climb out of that canal. Somehow, he had survived under those boat docks by eating the plants, snails, and crabs he could find. There were also rats underneath the ledges of the canal and places where rainwater could have been trapped for him to drink. It was sad to think that when the tide came in at night, his feet and lower body must have been completely underwater.

When Stewart saw that Goodness was on the ledge under the boat docks and realized he couldn't get out, Stewart immediately jumped into the canal with his shoes on and his wallet in his pocket. Everything got soaking wet, but he rescued Goodness. It had been an entire month that Goodness had been gone, and he was really emaciated again, but Goodness was so happy to see Kiki and Stewart. Even though he was so weak, his tail wagged a million miles an hour. We had walked by him every night, not knowing that the barking was coming from him. We had assumed the barking came from our neighbor's six dogs. Poor Goodness!

In 2002, a few years after we found Goodness, Taffy wasn't doing very well. She was sixteen years old. She had always loved to eat, and I would get her Vienna sausages as a treat. One day I offered her one, and she turned her head away. When she did that, we saw the huge lump on her throat and discovered she was very sick. The vet came to our home, examined her, and said it was her time to go. Our whole family gathered around her. We lit scented candles and played beautiful soft music. Taffy could hardly walk, so I picked her up and placed her on a fluffy peach rug. The vet came to our house, which was so nice and considerate of him. Everyone cried as I put my head on her head, holding her as she was put to sleep. I kept telling her that I would see her again at the Rainbow Bridge. It was so loving and peaceful that Stewart said he wanted to go the same way.

Kiki was about four when Goodness came into our lives, and the two of them had many wonderful years together. When Kiki was about sixteen, she got an infection in her front paw. She also had arthritis in her hips, and we could tell she was in pain when she tried to walk. We had a harness with a handle for her that we used to walk her up the stairs at night to sleep with us and walk her down every morning. Goodness never left her side; he slept right next to her.

Finally, Kiki couldn't take it anymore. I was away at the spa in California when I got a call from Adrian, who was at our home with the vet. Adrian said to me, "It's time. Kiki is suffering so much."

I was crying with my head down on the desk, talking to Kiki over the phone. I said, "I love you, Kiki. I'll see you soon. I'll see you at the Rainbow Bridge." I could hear her breathing, and I kept talking through my tears. Finally, I heard a small little yelp, and Kiki was gone.

I was devastated and couldn't help but cry. I took a walk around the property at the spa and picked some beautiful camellia flowers. Coincidentally, there was another lady there that week whose dog had also passed away. The two of us put flowers on the Prayer Rock for our new "angels." The staff at the spa was so lovely and caring. They hugged us and sent orange-blossom candles to each of our rooms.

Goodness was now completely in mourning. He wouldn't eat and seemed to want to sleep all the time. We decided to get another dog to cheer him up. We started looking on the internet at Cayman CARE, an agency that takes in abandoned dogs and finds them homes. We saw a picture of a beautiful little white puppy that they had posted. Stewart called CARE but was told she had been adopted. He said, "That's a shame. She looked like a sweet puppy."

A few days later, we got a call from CARE to see if we were still interested. Apparently, they didn't like the conditions at the place where the puppy was now living. They wanted to come to our home first to see if the conditions around our home were suitable for this adorable white puppy. Goodness loved her right away, and Gracie has been part of our family ever since.

When she arrived, she was covered in fleas and ticks. I knew she must not have been in a caring home. I pulled eleven ticks off her and put her in a flea bath. She was so happy afterward.

Goodness was only one or two when we found him. He had such a worried and frightened look in his eyes, and he didn't know how to play with toys; in fact, he was petrified if we threw something for him to play with. Thankfully, that worried look changed to total happiness and smiles. We never had to train him. He did that all by himself after I yelled at him. He always tried to be such a good boy. He lived a long, wonderful life. When he was sixteen, it was time to put him down. He loved Gracie, but he was still heartbroken about losing Kiki. His body had had enough. He would lie all day long next to Stewart while Stewart was in his office, not even lifting his head. Gracie would tease him with a toy, he'd grab it, and she'd pull him up. He played a little with her, but he was ready to leave and be with Kiki.

Stewart had a trip to Canada planned. As soon as Stewart left with his suitcases, Goodness refused to stand up. I think Stewart knew when he left that it would be the last time he would see Goodness. We had used the same harness we'd had for Kiki to pick him up and help Goodness upstairs to the bedroom because he wanted to sleep with us. After a few days with Stewart gone, I had a "dog whisperer" come in and communicate with Goodness.

I asked, "Is it time to put him to sleep?"

She said, "It was time last week. He is so ready to go."

I held Goodness in my arms by the French doors with the doors wide open so he could see outside. He loved our back garden so much. As he was being put to sleep, our beautiful green parrots flew over to our tree to say goodbye.

Now, it's just us with Gracie. She is amazing. She is full of so much love and trust. Since she came to live with us as a little puppy, no one has ever hurt her. She's just pure love. When Stewart is gone, she is with me all the time. When we are inside, she follows me everywhere. If I am sitting down, she has her head in my lap, or she cuddles right up against me. She gets me to take her out and play because, somehow, she knows when other people are out with their dogs. She is such a happy little spirit. You just look at her and smile.

When I had Ramsey Hunt syndrome, the horrible pain always got worse at night when the sun went down and the atmospheric pressure changed. I would have to lie on the white sofa in our family room and put my head back on it because the pain was excruciating. Gracie would always lie down right next to me and never leave my side. I have no doubt that her love and sweet spirit helped me heal.

All our dogs showed us unconditional love. I said to our vet that I thought God hadn't planned this right. Our dogs die too young. She said to me that sometimes the way some poor dogs are abused, they couldn't take that treatment anymore. She said it was a blessing for them to go. I look forward to seeing Taffy, Kiki, and Goodness again at the Rainbow Bridge.

Gracie's touching me is so calming and healing. She keeps smiling. I am sure she in an angel.

Chapter 25

LOVE AND MARRIAGE

In the end nothing we do or say in this lifetime will matter as much as the way we have loved one another.

—DAPHNE ROSE KINGMA

The moment I first met Stewart, I was attracted to him. Maybe it was love at first sight. I looked forward to all our dates with such excitement. Whenever he took me out for a beautiful dinner date, I could hardly eat. He was so wonderful. Later in our relationship, when we were away from each other for the summer vacations, I would run to the mailbox every day to see if I had received a letter from him. And, I usually found one because he would write almost every day. Whenever he would call, I would be so happy to talk to him. He would call me in California from Nassau, Bahamas, so the calls were very special because long-distance calls were expensive for us back then. By the time we graduated from university, we were both so in love. We couldn't wait to be married. We thought we were so mature. I was only twenty-one, and Stewart was twenty-two when we married on October 5, 1968 in Toronto, Ontario.

We did everything together after we were married. Stewart and I loved skiing together and would take ski vacations with friends. We went to various ski areas like Vail, Snowmass, and Lake Louise in

Canada. We also took other vacations and made sure to visit our parents in California and Lyford Cay at least twice a year.

Years later, when we were living in our temporary home in Dallas, we had finally earned enough points with American Airlines for a free trip. I said, "Oh boy, Hawaii!" and Stewart said, "Oh boy, Alaska!" The next thing I knew, I was enrolled in an Orvis fly-fishing school in Houston, Texas. There, we both stood by a pond outside the Houston Galleria, taking fly-fishing lessons from a fly-fishing instructor. The weather was really warm, and I kept thinking that I would love to be inside the Galleria, shopping. But, I also was enjoying learning how to cast.

Stewart then took me to New England, and while we were there, he arranged more fly-fishing lessons, followed by a private shopping spree in the Orvis store to outfit me in my new fishing gear for our first Alaskan trip. The store clerk brought me my first pair of neoprene waders, felt-bottomed fishing boots, a fishing vest with lots of pockets, a fishing jacket, and fishing gloves that had no fingertips. I realized that was so I could tie my flies onto the fishing lines without having to remove my gloves.

But, when he placed the duck-billed hat with the flip-down earflaps on my head, I said, "I'm getting my own hat!" When we returned to Dallas, I went hat shopping and picked out a Sherlock Holmes–style hat with a bow on top. Then, I found a fly-fishing shop in Dallas and picked out the most colorful fly in the store and pinned it to the middle of the hat brim. I was ready for our big adventure of sport fly-fishing in Alaska.

Stewart then ordered two large green Orvis duffel bags for us. I had no idea how to pack one. I kept trying to lay everything down flat, and I told Stewart that my things would not fit into that duffel bag. Finally, Stewart showed me how to pack a duffel bag. If I had continued packing my way, I wouldn't have been able to close the bag. I also packed electric curlers and an electric hair dryer. Stewart taught me how to roll my clothes and to fit them in the corners of that duffel bag. Our wilderness adventures to Alaska would now begin.

* * * *

Previously at a spa, Deejay, my Tai Chi instructor had shared a wonderful proverb with me about two monks. I think it is a helpful story for all relationships but especially for marriage. It goes like this:

There was a wise old monk and a young novice monk. The novice monk came to the old monk and said, "Sir, I'd love to train with you to learn some of your wisdom. Would you please teach me whatever you can?"

The old monk thought about it and said, "Yes, I will teach you, but would you be willing to go on a journey to learn from me?" The novice monk happily agreed. Then, the wise monk said, "During this journey there are just two things I will ask of you. The first is that there will be no talking at all. Not one word must be uttered to me or to anyone we see. The second is that during this journey, you can never touch or speak to anyone." The young monk agreed and said he was excited about what the wise monk would teach him.

Off they went on the journey. For days and days, they walked, not uttering a word. Much later, they came upon a river. A beautiful woman was standing by the river, looking very perplexed. The wise old monk said to the beautiful lady, "Excuse me, may I help you?"

The woman replied, "Oh yes, thank you. I need to get across this river, but my shoes aren't made to get wet."

The wise monk looked at her, picked her up, carried her across the river, and put her down. The two monks then continued on their journey.

The young monk was walking and thinking about that encounter, nonstop. A few weeks later, he couldn't stand it anymore and said, "Excuse me, sir. I need to ask you one question."

The wise monk said, "Yes, what is it?"

The young monk said, "You told me we were never to speak to anyone, yet you spoke to that woman. You also told me we were never to touch anyone, yet you picked her up and carried her across the river."

The wise monk looked at the young monk and said, "I put her down at the river weeks ago! Why are you still carrying her?"

I shared this story with all of my friends. Now, when someone complains about something that someone did or something that happened to her or him, we just say, "Leave it at the river! Let it go. It's over, and there is nothing you can do about it."

Whatever irritates you happens in a moment. Then, it's over. You can't change what happened. We tend to keep it in our minds and go over and over it, until we become really irritated. The wise monk taught the young monk that how we choose to think about things determines how we feel. The best thing to do is to let it go.

If you keep going over the bad things that happen to you, you certainly will not be calm or happy; you will be just the opposite. And most likely, the person who irritated you in the first place will have forgotten about it. Remember to leave it at the river. You will find peace and happiness instead of stress and worry.

* * * *

Stewart is an incredible husband. He is a man of few words, but each word has deep meaning. He is a truly gentle soul and shows his love in unusual and beautiful ways. In all the years we've been together, I can't remember his every saying *no* to me. In fact, he is constantly full of romantic surprises.

One of my favorite examples of this amazing side of Stewart happened in 1993. We went helicopter skiing, and I had a bad fall. I could not walk and went to see my *friend*, the orthopedic surgeon, again. I needed another difficult knee surgery.

It began with the doctor removing a five-inch screw and bolt from an earlier surgery that was holding down the top of my tibia—I broke that in an earlier skiing accident. This time, he not only removed the top of the tibia, the five-inch screw, and the bolt, but he also removed my posterior cruciate ligament at the same time. After that surgery, I had to be in bed for one month and on a machine almost twenty-four hours a day that continuously bent my knee to a ninety-degree angle. I could only get up by using crutches. I wasn't allowed to put any weight on my leg.

My Dallas girlfriends had decorated my crutches, entirely covering them in pearls, with shocking-pink and royal-blue ribbons. At the hand grips, they made huge bows, with bunches of pearls dangling down. They were the prettiest crutches I had ever seen and were perfect for Dallas.

Finally, after what felt like forever on that machine and lying in bed, I was able to go outside. It felt so great, not being on that machine. I put on a bikini and went to our pool to enjoy some sunshine and fresh air. I was listening to the Bee Gees and thoroughly enjoying the music and the warm sun. Stewart walked outside to see me and asked if I wanted to go for a ride. I was thrilled to be going somewhere after being in bed for such a long time. I grabbed a cover-up and threw on my flip-flops, and off I went on my crutches with him. I thought it was a beautiful day for a ride, and I was so happy to be off that machine and going out with Stewart.

We drove for a while and soon were in downtown Dallas. Stewart pulled into a parking lot and said, "Let's get out!"

Obviously, I wasn't dressed for being downtown—I was in a bikini, cover-up, and flip-flops, and I would have to walk with those beautifully decorated crutches. I said, "Are you crazy?"

He kept insisting that I get out of the car, and I kept saying, "Are you crazy?" Finally, he convinced me to get out. He walked me to a corner and stopped.

All of a sudden, every two-seater 500 SL Mercedes convertible was paraded in front of me as I stood on that street corner. There were blue, silver, red, black, cream, gold, and white Mercedes, with every different interior combination possible. There were so many that I couldn't count them. Stewart looked at me, smiled, and said, "What color would you like?"

Again, all I could say was, "Are you crazy?"

He was excited, but because I was so embarrassed by my outfit, I only looked quickly before saying, "The red one!"

Stewart was happy, and I was thrilled. The salesman drove the red Mercedes to me right there on the street corner. I got in the red

Mercedes and started it up. I waited while Stewart went in to pay for it. We were laughing as I followed him home, each of us in separate cars. I was still in shock and couldn't believe it. During the entire ride back, I couldn't stop thinking of all of the amazing things that Stewart had done for me.

As I pulled into the garage in the new red Mercedes, however, I couldn't get the gold one with gold trim out of my mind. I had been so embarrassed at the moment when he asked me what color I would like that I'd just picked the red one, which was right in front of me at that second. Of course, the minute I'd said *red*, I couldn't stop thinking about the gold 500 SL.

Stewart took the red one right back to the dealer and came home with the gold one. I was beyond thrilled.

That was one of the most romantic and thoughtful things Stewart ever did. I loved him, and I loved that car. When it came time to license it, my Texas license plate read "R U CRZY."

A few years later, we moved to the Cayman Islands. I loved my R U CRZY car and wanted to bring it to Cayman. I had to get a Cayman license plate, but I kept the Texas R U CRZY plate for myself. It had a lot of meaning to me.

At that time, there was a restaurant in Cayman called the Lone Star Bar and Grill. The owner was a man who had attended Texas A&M University. On the ceiling of the restaurant were different university T-shirts, hanging as banners, especially Texas ones. On the walls were Texas license plates. I gave him my R U CRZY Texas license plate, and he hung it up on the wall with all the others. It brought back beautiful memories, and it was always fun to go there and see it. Unfortunately, Hurricane Ivan destroyed that restaurant, and my R U CRZY license plate was washed out to sea.

Going through that surgery and long recovery was really hard, but Stewart made the end of the recovery so incredibly special. What a silver lining that was.

So Happy Together

Whenever we are apart, Stewart sends me the most beautiful roses. One time when I was at a spa, the roses were so tall and the vase so large that the poor man delivering the arrangement was sweating bullets by the time he got to my room. The card with the flowers read, "From Russia, with love." Stewart was in Russia, fly-fishing, while I was at the spa. One of the ladies who worked at the spa asked if she could have the vase to use as a fish tank. When I left at the end of the week, I gave her the vase and the flowers, too.

Stew's father died suddenly in 1989. Obviously, it was a huge shock to everyone. When it happened, Stewart and I had long before booked a ski trip for the two of us. In fact, the limo was at the door, ready to take us to the airport to go to Aspen when we received the call about his father. My mother was on her way to our home to take care of Heidi while we were gone. Since Heidi was in high school and needed to attend classes, she couldn't go with us.

We postponed our trip. Then, we had the idea of bringing Stewart's mother to Dallas to stay with Heidi and my mother. We thought this was a good idea, as my mother had lost her husband a few years earlier.

We thought she would help Stewart's mother through this difficult time. In hindsight, this was much too soon for Stewart's mother. She was still suffering from Harold's sudden death.

When we got home, we were shocked. Our two mothers were fighting. World War III was going on. Stewart's mother stayed upstairs, and mine stayed downstairs. They weren't even speaking to each other. Poor Heidi was in the middle of this unfortunate fight. I don't know exactly what had happened, but it wasn't at all what we had expected. Heidi was an angel and tried to help them communicate. Later, after they both had returned home, they finally calmed down and realized how silly they had been. It took a few months, but they finally spoke nicely to each other again. The story of "Leave It at the River" applied here as well.

Stewart and I had silly fights early in our marriage—everyone does. I think part of that was just our being young. Probably the biggest fight we ever had was when we were living in Toronto in our tiny one-bedroom apartment. I was working at my first teaching job, where I sensed that some of the other teachers were envious of my education. I had double-majored in early childhood education and elementary education in a four-year honors program. The other teachers had attended a three-year program at a teacher's college in Canada.

The principal was a chauvinist. One day at a staff meeting, the principal asked a question. I didn't raise my hand; I just started to answer. He put his hand right in front of my face, and I immediately stopped talking. I thought that was so rude! I went home, steaming, and told Stewart what the principal had done. Stewart just sat there, calmly reading the newspaper. I got so mad that he wasn't reacting to what I said that I grabbed the paper right out of his hands and ripped it up.

He just picked up a book and began reading that. He was wearing gold-rimmed glasses, and I pulled them right off his head and broke them by twisting them over and over in my hands. Then, I stormed into the bedroom and slammed the door so hard that it broke the molding around the door—all that because the principal was rude to me, and Stewart wouldn't listen to me, or so I thought. I just went crazy! Stewart stayed calm, even after I ripped the paper out of his hands, broke his glasses, and ruined the door. What a silly thing for me to do. I took out my pent-up anger on the man I loved most in the entire world.

His reaction after all of my stomping around was to calmly say to me, "Well, we need to call the superintendent and have the door molding fixed."

I was still angry, so I stomped around in the bedroom. Then, I got hungry and went out into the living room after I calmed down. I started to fix dinner, and Stewart came over and hugged me. That is all I really needed in the first place. I definitely could not leave it by the river at that time in my life. My ego took over and caused me to react in a ridiculous way.

Before the avalanche, I was a perfectionist. I didn't know how to leave anything at the river. Everything in our home had to be perfect, twenty-four hours a day. I would spend so much time polishing the silver and making sure everything looked perfect, including me. Sometimes, when we had planned dinner parties, I spent so much time on those things that the food wasn't ready when our guests arrived—but our place looked beautiful.

We were living in Dallas and had gone to the Festival of Trees, which was a fund-raiser for our community hospital. Each designer donated a beautifully decorated Christmas tree, which was on display for a week. The festival was a black-tie auction, where everyone would bid on the trees, and it was a lovely affair. The money that was raised went to the Irving Community Hospital.

Stewart and I chose to bid on a twelve-foot tree that was decorated with gorgeous Waterford ornaments and what looked like a thousand tiny white lights. We were so excited when we won the bidding. The tree not only came with those lovely Waterford crystal decorations, but it also came with gifts—a limousine evening that would take eight of us to different restaurants for a four-course progressive dinner; a tuxedo for Stewart; and a white fur jacket for me.

I didn't realize the tree would be delivered totally decorated. The decorations were so tightly wired to the tree that it was impossible to remove them.

At the time, we were building our dream home in Dallas and living in a small temporary home during the construction. The tree arrived, and we were delighted to get it before Christmas. It was beautiful through the holidays and even through January. After that, I realized we had no place to store it. February came, so I decorated it with red hearts for Valentine's Day. At Easter, I decorated it with Easter eggs.

Stewart's parents were coming to visit, and I began cleaning the place to make everything perfect. I thought, *What am I going to do with this Christmas tree?* Stewart was supposed to take it to his office warehouse, but he hadn't gotten around to it. Their visit made me feel very nervous. I convinced myself that I had to have everything looking perfect before my in-laws arrived. I thought I really needed Stewart to take the tree out of our house.

Stewart rented a flatbed truck and hired four men to sit in the back and hold the beautifully decorated tree to transport it from our house to his office warehouse space. What a sight that was on the road, with four grown men sitting on the back of a flatbed truck, traveling at twenty miles an hour, holding a fully decorated, twelve-foot Christmas tree in April! And since this worked out so well, we continued to transport that tree back and forth from the office to our home for many Christmases after that.

I needed to learn to leave things at the river. I was so caught up with how things looked that I almost went crazy with Stewart again, all about a Christmas tree. In the years to come, we would giggle when we watched our tree transported on the flatbed truck, with four men holding it. I wanted everything to look so perfect for my in-laws that I almost made myself so upset about a Christmas tree in our living room. It probably wouldn't have mattered to them one bit. This just shows how you can overreact to the tiniest thing.

Just be natural and be who you are, and things will work out, just as they are supposed to.

* * * *

Every year, we went helicopter skiing in Canada with Canadian Mountain Holidays. Stewart still continues this tradition and now has more than seven million vertical feet of helicopter skiing. I skied three million vertical feet with CMH. We loved these holidays together, but when I fell down our marble stairs during Hurricane Ivan and shattered my kneecaps, that ended my helicopter skiing. I guess the universe was telling me to slow down. I now enjoy our family trips with our granddaughters on our ski trips to Colorado.

* * * *

One day in 2002, Stewart wanted to surprise me with a different adventure. He called our good friends, Connie and Eddie from Miami and said to Eddie, "Dianne and I have traveled all over the world, fly-fishing, helicopter skiing, and pheasant shooting, but I've never taken her on a relaxing vacation." They decided we should go on a cruise from Venice to Rome.

The four of us had a fabulous time on that cruise, and we have continued to have special trips together every year. Now, our favorite place to go is Capri, Italy. We all love it so much. We have cruised to St. Petersburg and traveled to Scotland, Portugal, and back to Venice, Italy. Most recently, we flew to Capri and enjoyed a week together before discovering a new place. It has turned into a very special time for the four of us.

Every March, we take our daughter and granddaughters to Aspen and Snowmass for a family ski trip. The girls are becoming great skiers and love it. So, with family skiing trips, time in Capri with our friends, and partridge and pheasant shooting in England and Spain, Stewart and I still enjoy our adventures together. Unfortunately, my Bell's palsy has prevented me from fly-fishing in Alaska, which I really loved. Stewart still continues the party I started at the Enchanted Lake Lodge, the Royal Society of the Canadian Blue Moose. He has so much fun dancing in the conga line to the song "The Stripper," with the other guests. Stewart also continues to take special moose gifts to the wonderful staff. I'm happy to have started such a joyful tradition at such a beautiful fly-fishing lodge in Alaska.

* * * *

At the beginning of our marriage, we did absolutely everything together. Now, when Stewart says he is planning another helicopter-skiing trip, I plan a trip to a wonderful spa or a trip to Connecticut to visit Heidi and the girls. At first, I wasn't sure I would like to do things on my own, without Stewart, but then I thought, *Go alone, without fear!* Now, I really enjoy my girls' trips. I have been lucky to meet amazing new friends. The trips to the spas are sometimes for two consecutive weeks. These are places where I am ensconced in beauty, with lovely landscaping, fun exercise classes, fabulous beauty treatments, and wonderful people who have helped me awaken and become who I am today.

When Stewart and I both return home, we have so much to talk about and share with each other because each of us has had a fabulous time. It really is wonderful. Certainly, we are not one of those old married couples you sometimes see having dinner in restaurants, with nothing to say to each other, sometimes never saying even one word to each other. Maybe they haven't had any wonderful experiences on their own. They might have been too full of fear to travel alone.

When Stewart and I get back together after a week or two apart, each having done something we love, we have so much to talk about. I feel very lucky to be able to go off on my own and have such fascinating experiences. I started doing more things on my own without fear, which has been wonderful for our marriage. My advice is to do the things you love that will make you happy. This might mean that you will travel alone, and that is perfectly okay. Remember—no time for fear!

I think the fact that I almost died also showed Stewart how fragile life can be. After the avalanche, he wanted us to build our dream home right away. He still sends me cards that read, "I love you. You are my best friend." Our special song has always been "Unforgettable" by Nat King Cole. To this day, we both feel the words:

> That's why, darling, it's incredible
> That someone so unforgettable
> Thinks that I am
> Unforgettable too

With all of our adventures, our entire life has been unforgettable—and full of love too.

Enjoying a "Leather and Lace" party in England

* * * *

From Stewart

Dianne and I grew up together. When we found each other, we were just eighteen and nineteen years old. You think you are a mature person at that age. When you grow up with a person over so many years, you grow together.

Our connection is very caring, and we've always looked out for each other, like best friends. Early in a relationship, most people have a desire to always be together every minute; Dianne and I were like that too. Like everyone else, as we gained more self-confidence, we became more confident in our relationship, and our connection matured to where we respect each other's desire to do different things, which means that we aren't always together. I like sending Dianne flowers from wherever I am because I know she loves the beauty in her room. And it keeps us connected.

The avalanche definitely changed how Dianne viewed life. I was more of an observer, watching these changes take place over time. She was always a loving, giving, and compassionate people-person, but after the avalanche, she began to enjoy the spiritual side of things. What is between us is so enduring and loving after all of these years. We are very lucky to have each other.

STEWART, GRACIE AND I AT CHRISTMAS IN OUR HOME IN GRAND CAYMAN

Always treat your partner the way you would like to be treated. It's just the Golden Rule.

Chapter 26

AWAKENED

When you change the way you look at
things, the things you look at change.

—WAYNE DYER

The avalanche was not only a life-changing experience; it was a
true gift, full of blessings and lessons that I still experience every day. I
discovered that I no longer feared death. It was so peaceful and loving.
Death is just another new beginning. In an instant, you have no more
pain. Like a flash, everything you ever worried about, any fights you
had, any sorrow you've experienced in this life just melts away. And,
you are surrounded by the most incredible unconditional love and joy.

After the avalanche, I really *saw* the world for the first time. I could
truly appreciate the beauty of everything in a new way. Flowers were
beyond beautiful. I could see the love that God put on this earth for
us everywhere in the beauty of nature. I also realized the full power
that nature has to heal us. It's so obvious when you've been somewhere
incredible that is pure and quiet, away from all the sounds, telephones,
and emails.

Stewart and I have experienced this deep silence while helicopter
skiing down the powder slopes and also when fly-fishing in Alaska. In
places like that, you realize how magnificent the earth is, and you soak

in the beauty and silence of it all. Taking moments to enjoy the beauty of nature around you will take you away from the stresses of life. The worries of life fall away, and thoughts come with extreme clarity.

After only a week at a spa, with a focus on inner work, it is disturbing to return to real life. Immediately, at the airport in San Diego, the announcements, the loud beeping of those electric transportation carts, and the crowds of noisy people take away the peace and beauty that always surrounds you. When you've been immersed in nature, going on meditative walks, with no television or radio, you come back in a very altered state—I feel complete peace and see the beauty of God's love everywhere.

You don't have to go to a spa, to Alaska, or helicopter skiing to experience this. Take a long walk outside and embrace the beauty that surrounds you. Go to a beautiful park and look at the flowers, watch the birds, listen to a running stream, and really observe. Immerse yourself in what's going on around you. *Listen* to the sounds. Feel the breeze. Hear the wind. Look at all the incredible colors in nature. Taking time to do this will help you feel more connected and peaceful than ever before.

Besides my deeper appreciation for nature, another gift that came out of the avalanche was a new sense of what is important in life. I have a much greater compassion and tolerance for myself and others. I used to be very shy and quiet and always was very concerned about what people thought about me, to the point where I almost didn't talk. If somebody would say something that I thought was critical of me, I would be disturbed. My reaction was that I would start repeating it to myself and to my girlfriends, constantly saying, "Can you believe so-and-so said this?" Dee Jay's wisdom in teaching me the proverb with the two monks by the river helped me realize how silly it was to allow something that someone said make me unhappy. As the wise old monk said, why was I still carrying the disturbance when the other person probably had forgotten it already and had gone on happily to enjoy the rest of the day? It was never significant to begin with, but I was upsetting myself by the way I allowed myself to react to it.

The avalanche helped me fully realize that it doesn't matter what anyone else thinks. Everybody's going to have a different opinion anyway, and it's much too hard to try to please everyone. It's a huge waste of energy to go through life by trying to show people only what you think they want to see and making big deals out of nothing. It's what we humans tend to do—make things bigger than life and sometimes even getting depressed about it. You have no control over other people's opinions, so there is no point in carrying them around and beating yourself up. You will harm your relationship with friends by continually focusing on those things. It's much better to let things go and leave them at the river. And, talk with your friends about happy things.

The avalanche awakened a new sense of what appearances really meant. I have always appreciated all kinds of beauty and still do. I've always cared so much about how things looked—maybe that's why I love art and interior design. But, it went beyond that for me. It was always very important to have things look picture-perfect, no matter what. If someone came over while I was decorating the Christmas tree and the boxes were out, I would take time to hide them. Now, I couldn't care less about the boxes. It's much more important to be present with whoever is with you than to waste time worrying about how the house looks or what that person thinks. It also frees up energy that you can devote to noticing the beauty of nature or spending time with those you love.

That doesn't mean that I think it's not important to take good care of oneself. When you look in the mirror, you want to be the best you can be because it makes you feel better. In my entire life, before and after the avalanche, through Bell's palsy and all of my injuries, I never thought of doing anything different than I did while growing up. Fixing my makeup, doing my hair, and wearing nice clothes is what I have always done. It must be part of my spiritual path, since that part of me has never changed. No matter how bad I have felt, I always tried to look my best. When I was a girl, there was a popular movie called *Flower Drum Song*, starring the beautiful Nancy Kwan. In the movie, she sang a song called "I Enjoy Being a Girl." I really do enjoy being a girl who tries to always look her best.

Here I am, in the "pink" for Christmas!

All of that aside, the true beauty I experienced as a result of the avalanche was internal. I learned, at a very deep level, that you can never judge anyone by what they look like, and it doesn't matter if someone says something hurtful. What matters is knowing in your heart that many people are in pain, so it's best to try to understand where they are coming from and see if there is a way you can help. We each have inner light, and that is what counts the most. There is nothing like the sparkle in someone's eyes when they smile at you authentically. That is what defines true beauty.

If I'd had Bell's palsy before the avalanche, I would have responded completely differently. I would have been so concerned about the way I looked that I probably never would have left the house. I wouldn't have wanted people to see me with half of my face hanging down. Yet, that first New Year's Eve after developing Bell's palsy, my dear friend Susan invited me to the Cayman Cookout, which is a very big event. I thought it was so nice of her to invite me. I went with my face drooping, and I tried to look as good as I could. I noticed a lot of people had a hard time looking at me, but I had a wonderful time. Susan said I was very brave to attend. It was such a blessing to understand that other people's reaction to what I looked like had nothing to do with the "real" me.

It's been a few years since I came down with Bell's palsy. While it is almost completely gone now, as I look back, I realize I would have missed many wonderful experiences, trips, and time with friends and family if I had cared about my appearance.

The privilege of a lifetime is to become who you truly are.

—C. G. Jung

Chapter 27

GIVING THE GIFT OF LOVE

Happiness doesn't result from what
we get, but from what we give.

—BEN CARSON

A friend once told me that my gift to the world is the help I provide by connecting people to each other—matching those in need with those who have the power to heal or share knowledge, skills, or resources. My life has been blessed with the great opportunity of meeting incredible people with gifts of healing, and I've been able to extend this to others. I think it comes from my deep desire to help people.

Since the avalanche, I've been much more aware of this. Now, when I see someone who needs help, and I know someone who can help, I put them in touch with each other. I feel so grateful and humbled when I can do something for another person because I know it isn't really "me" doing this. I'm just the connector, making the introduction of people who might never have met or known about each other. I am so grateful when I hear someone say, "You helped me feel so much better," or "What you did saved my life!" We all have the capacity to do this. Too many people choose to ignore the needs of others, instead of offering whatever they can to help another human being.

Our three lovely granddaughters: Lilly, Ashley, and Hailey

I've been blessed to live an amazing life. Sadly many other people who have lived a lifestyle similar to mine aren't happy. I believe my happiness comes from deep gratitude and appreciation. Because of what happened to me, I was able to look at the world with new eyes and became aware of all the beauty around us.

The truth is that we are spiritual beings. No amount of material things will make us truly content. It's not that we can't have wealth and feel spiritually connected; we absolutely can. Many people in this world have great affluence, but they hardly use it to help others.

I find that when people give, and they give *love* at the same time, that is when giving really helps. It makes all the difference in the world.

I am also so grateful to have met and shared incredible experiences with very powerful souls, who are transforming the world exactly that way—by using their affluence to influence others. People like Dr. Choe, Dr. Jung, Werner Erhard, Igor Burdenko, and Christiane Northrup are all examples of highly successful people who exist very much in the material world but are on a spiritual path of helping. Dr. Choe and Dr. Jung help with their Sugi practice. Igor Burdenko does it through water therapy. Christiane is a visionary and best-selling author, who has helped millions of women understand themselves. Werner helps through the Landmark Forum and EST. During my time with them, I believe I take in their healing energy and then pass it along and share it with others who haven't had such opportunities. In this way, I feel that I have been able to touch many lives.

> As James Taylor sang,
>> When you're down and troubled
>> And you need a helping hand
>> And nothing is going right
>> Close your eyes and think of me
>> And soon I will be there
>> To brighten up even your darkest night
>> You just call out my name
>> And you know wherever I am
>> I'll come running ...
>> I'll be there
>> You've got a friend

Afterword

If you want to tap into what life has to offer,
let love be your primary mode of being, not
fear. Fear closes us down and makes us retreat.
It locks doors and limits opportunities. Love is
about opening to possibilities. It is seeing the
world with new eyes. It widens our heart and
mind. Fear Incarcerates, but love liberates.

—JOHN MARK GREEN

I honestly believe that the path to happiness lies in helping others
and treating other people the way you would want to be treated. It is
the Golden Rule. I have learned that everyone is born with the ability
to offer love, help, and hope to others in some way, big or small. We all
have an incredible light inside of us, much like the Golden Buddha that
was covered in plaster to protect it—its true light was hidden. We need
to peel away our own layers of protection that we applied to our hearts
to prevent ourselves from being hurt again. We need to show our love
and let our light shine through.

I am grateful for the challenges I had, mainly because they shaped
me into the person I am today. The avalanche took me to a new level,
helping me achieve a true awakening, with an incredible feeling of
love and peace that has never left my heart. It's always there, and it has
impacted all of my behaviors and responses to everything since then.

Obviously, not everyone will have a near-death experience, but everyone has lessons that deeply affect their hearts. When you recognize that you are here to learn from these lessons, you become more confident and grow wiser.

Life challenges us all the time. We become ill, we lose loved ones, or the earth suffers natural disasters. We are called to step straight into all of these things because once we do, our fears will go away, and we will find the strength to get through them. If you never take that first step forward, you will stay terrified, heartbroken, and stuck, believing that you can't go on. Actually, the opposite is true. You will become stronger, wiser, and more grateful for everyone and everything when you take the steps to face your fears.

You will discover that there is no time for fear—only *love*!
—Dianne Siebens, 2021

Acknowledgements

This book has had a life of its own. When Wilbur Smith gave me that beautiful malachite pen and simply said, "Write," he gave me the idea to write this book. I have had a lot of unusual experiences, which I wanted to share my granddaughters.

One day at a spa, I was sitting down for lunch with three other ladies I had just met. We had nametags with only our first names on them. One of our fitness trainers came over to our table and said, "Dianne, have you told these ladies about your avalanche?" She knew who they were, but I didn't. They wanted to hear my story. After I finished telling my story about the avalanche, I found out that the lady sitting next to me was an author, and she helped me to start writing this book. Also, sitting at my table was a television writer and producer who told me, "If this book is any good, send it to me, and I'll write a screenplay!" We all laughed because, after all, I was writing this for my granddaughters. But then, the fourth lady sitting at our table said, "If you are writing a screenplay, send it to me. I'll get my best friend, who is a famous actress, to star in it!" She then asked me, "Dianne, when you were in the avalanche, what were you thinking? Were you petrified?"

I answered, "No, there was no time for fear."

She pointed to me from across the table and said, "That is the title of your book."

That's how this book started.

I am so happy that, one day, my granddaughters will read this book and learn there is no time for fear. I hope they will learn to leave things at the river and live their lives with much love and gratitude in their hearts.

This book and all these adventures would never have been possible without my husband, Stewart. Little did I know when we first met in university that I would become a helicopter skier, a fly-fishing woman, and a lady who would enjoy the adventures and travels of the shooting world. Stewart, thank you so much for opening up all these worlds of adventure for me. I will love you forever.

And my daughter, Heidi, you have always been the sweetest love in my heart. Every time we are together, my heart not only fills up with love, but it actually swells with pride. You have been such a special gift to your dad and me. Thank you for being the kind of daughter everyone dreams about and for giving us our three amazing granddaughters.

And lastly, this book would never have been possible without the help of my incredible friend, Connie Kazanjian. Connie helped me in every way possible, even suggesting she would help with all the rewrites, which took a lot of her precious time. Her help with everything concerning Balboa Press and her encouragement all along the way of the process of writing this book will always be much appreciated by me. Thank you so very much! I love you, Connie, and I will always be grateful for everything you did.

Thank you, Maggie Jackson, for the cover photo of me and for all your help with all the photos in this book. We spent many hours with the photos, and I'll always be grateful for all of your help.

And thank you so very much, Christjian Laturner, for your beautiful cover photo of Mount Sir Sandford and all the other helicopter-skiing photos in this book.

Also, I want to thank everyone who contributed their stories along with mine. Your friendships will always be so dear to me.

Remember, there is *no time for fear* as we live this adventure called life. Instead, always keep love and gratitude in your hearts.

"Love is the Goal. Life is the Journey." – Osho

Stewart and I – at our 50th Wedding Anniversary –
Still Happy after all these years!

CPSIA information can be obtained
at www.ICGtesting.com
Printed in the USA
BVHW042305300422
635832BV00005B/90

9 781504 347945